SPSS

SPSS/PC+
Professional Statistics™
Version 5.0

Marija J. Norušis/SPSS Inc.

SPSS Inc.
444 N. Michigan Avenue
Chicago, Illinois 60611
Tel: (312) 329-2400
Fax: (312) 329-3668

SPSS Federal Systems (U.S.)
SPSS Latin America
SPSS Benelux BV
SPSS UK Ltd.
SPSS UK Ltd., New Delhi
SPSS GmbH Software
SPSS Scandinavia AB
SPSS Asia Pacific Pte. Ltd.
SPSS Japan Inc.
SPSS Australasia Pty. Ltd.

For more information about SPSS® software products, please write or call

Marketing Department
SPSS Inc.
444 North Michigan Avenue
Chicago, IL 60611
Tel: (312) 329-2400
Fax: (312) 329-3668

SPSS/PC+ Professional Statistics™, Version 5.0
Copyright © 1992
All rights reserved.
Printed in the United States of America.

1 2 3 4 5 6 7 8 9 0   95 94 93 92

ISBN 0-923967-67-2

Library of Congress Catalog Card Number: 92-085163

Preface

SPSS/PC+ Version 5 is a powerful software package for microcomputer data management and analysis. The Professional Statistics option is an add-on enhancement that provides additional statistical analysis techniques. The procedures in Professional Statistics must be used with the SPSS/PC+ Base System and are completely integrated into that system.

The Professional Statistics option includes procedures for discriminant, factor, cluster, and reliability analysis. The algorithms are identical to those used in SPSS software on mainframe computers, and the statistical results will be as precise as those computed on a mainframe.

SPSS/PC+ with the Professional Statistics option will enable you to perform many analyses on your PC that were once possible only on much larger machines. We hope that this statistical power will make SPSS/PC+ an even more useful tool in your work.

Compatibility

SPSS Inc. warrants that SPSS/PC+ and enhancements are designed for personal computers in the IBM PC and IBM PS/2™ lines with a hard disk and at least 640K of RAM. Versions of SPSS/PC+ that support extended memory require additional memory. See the installation instructions that came with your Base System for more information. These products also function on most IBM-compatible machines. Contact SPSS Inc. for details about specific IBM-compatible hardware.

Serial Numbers

Your serial number is your identification number with SPSS Inc. You will need this serial number when you call SPSS Inc. for information regarding support, payment, a defective diskette, or an upgraded system.

The serial number can be found on diskette 3 of your Base System. Before using the system, please copy this number to the **registration card.**

Registration Card

STOP! Before going on, *fill out and send us your registration card.* Until we receive your registration card, you have an unregistered system. Even if you have previously sent a card to us, please fill out and return the card enclosed in your Professional Statistics package. Registering your system entitles you to

- Technical support on our customer hotline.
- Favored customer status.
- New product announcements.

Of course, unregistered systems receive none of the above, so *don't put it off—send your registration card now!*

Replacement Policy

Call Customer Service at 1-800-521-1337 to report a defective diskette. You must provide us with the serial number of your system. (The normal installation procedure will detect any damaged diskettes.) SPSS will ship replacement diskettes the same day we receive notification from you.

Training Seminars

SPSS Inc. provides both public and onsite training seminars for SPSS/PC+. All seminars feature hands-on workshops. SPSS/PC+ seminars will be offered in major U.S. and European cities on a regular basis. For more information on these seminars, call the SPSS Inc. Training Department toll-free at 1-800-543-6607.

Technical Support

The services of SPSS Technical Support are available to registered customers of SPSS/PC+. Customers may call Technical Support for assistance in using SPSS products or for installation help for one of the warranted hardware environments.

To reach Technical Support, call 1-312-329-3410. Be prepared to identify yourself, your organization, and the serial number of your system.

If you are a Value Plus or Customer EXPress customer, use the priority 800 number you received with your materials. For information on subscribing to the Value Plus or Customer EXPress plan, call SPSS Software Sales at 1-800-543-2185 or 1-312-329-3300.

Additional Publications

Additional copies of all SPSS product manuals may be purchased separately. To order additional manuals, just fill out the Publications insert included with your system and send it to SPSS Publications Sales, 444 N. Michigan Avenue, Chicago, IL 60611.

Note: In Europe, additional copies of publications can be purchased by site-licensed customers only. For more information, please contact your local office at the address listed at the end of this preface.

Tell Us Your Thoughts

Your comments are important. So send us a letter and let us know about your experiences with SPSS products. We especially like to hear about new and interesting applications using the SPSS/PC+ system. Write to SPSS Inc. Marketing Department, Attn: Micro Software Products Manager, 444 N. Michigan Avenue, Chicago, IL 60611.

About This Manual

This manual is divided into three sections. The first section provides a guide to the various statistical techniques available with the Professional Statistics option and how to obtain the appropriate statistical analyses. The second section of this manual is a reference guide that provides complete command syntax for all the commands included in the Professional Statistics option. The last section provides annotated examples for each procedure included in the Professional Statistics option. The examples serve to illustrate how actual data are transformed and analyzed.

Contacting SPSS Inc.

If you would like to be on our mailing list, write to us at one of the addresses below. We will send you a copy of our newsletter and let you know about SPSS Inc. activities in your area.

SPSS Inc.
444 North Michigan Ave.
Chicago, IL 60611
Tel: (312) 329-2400
Fax: (312) 329-3668

SPSS Federal Systems
12030 Sunrise Valley Dr.
Suite 300
Reston, VA 22091
Tel: (703) 391-6020
Fax: (703) 391-6002

SPSS Latin America
444 North Michigan Ave.
Chicago, IL 60611
Tel: (312) 329-3556
Fax: (312) 329-3668

SPSS Benelux BV
P.O. Box 115
4200 AC Gorinchem
The Netherlands
Tel: +31.1830.36711
Fax: +31.1830.35839

SPSS UK Ltd.
SPSS House
5 London Street
Chertsey
Surrey KT16 8AP
United Kingdom
Tel: +44.932.566262
Fax: +44.932.567020

SPSS UK Ltd., New Delhi
c/o Ashok Business Centre
Ashok Hotel
50B Chanakyapuri
New Delhi 110 021
India
Tel: +91.11.600121 x1029
Fax: +91.11.6873216

SPSS GmbH Software
Steinsdorfstrasse 19
D-8000 Munich 22
Germany
Tel: +49.89.2283008
Fax: +49.89.2285413

SPSS Scandinavia AB
Sjöängsvägen 21
S-191 72 Sollentuna
Sweden
Tel: +46.8.7549450
Fax: +46.8.7548816

SPSS Asia Pacific Pte. Ltd.
10 Anson Road, #34-07
International Plaza
Singapore 0207
Singapore
Tel: +65.221.2577
Fax: +65.221.9920

SPSS Japan Inc.
Gyoen Sky Bldg.
2-1-11, Shinjuku
Shinjuku-ku
Tokyo 160
Japan
Tel: +81.3.33505261
Fax: +81.3.33505245

SPSS Australasia Pty. Ltd.
121 Walker Street
North Sydney, NSW 2060
Australia
Tel: +61.2.954.5660
Fax: +61.2.954.5616

Contents

2 Factor Analysis 53

Discriminant Analysis

Gazing into crystal balls is not the exclusive domain of soothsayers. Judges, college admissions counselors, bankers, and many other professionals must foretell outcomes such as parole violation, success in college, and creditworthiness.

An intuitive strategy is to compare the characteristics of a potential student or credit applicant to those of cases whose success or failure is already known. Based on similarities and differences, a prediction can be made. Often this is done subjectively, using only the experience and wisdom of the decision maker. However, as problems grow more complex and the consequences of bad decisions become more severe, a more objective procedure for predicting outcomes is often desirable.

Before considering statistical techniques, let's summarize the problem. Based on a collection of variables, such as yearly income, age, marital status, and total worth, we wish to distinguish among several mutually exclusive groups, such as good credit risks and bad credit risks. The available data are the values of the variables for cases whose group membership is known, that is, cases who have proven to be good or bad credit risks. We also wish to identify the variables that are important for distinguishing among the groups and to develop a procedure for predicting group membership for new cases whose group membership is undetermined.

Discriminant analysis, first introduced by Sir Ronald Fisher, is the statistical technique most commonly used to investigate this set of problems. The concept underlying discriminant analysis is fairly simple. Linear combinations of the **independent variables**, sometimes called **predictor variables**, are formed and serve as the basis for classifying cases into one of the groups.

For the linear discriminant function to be "optimal," that is, to provide a classification rule that minimizes the probability of misclassification, certain assumptions about the data must be met. Each group must be a sample from a multivariate normal population, and the population covariance matrices must all be equal. The section "When Assumptions Are Violated" on p. 40 discusses tests for violations of the assumptions and the performance of linear discriminant analysis when assumptions are violated.

The sections "Selecting Cases for the Analysis" on p. 3 through "Sum of Unexplained Variance" on p. 30 cover the basics of discriminant analysis and the SPSS/PC+ output using a two-group example. Extending this type of analysis to include more than two groups is discussed beginning in "Three-Group Discriminant Analysis" on p. 31.

Investigating Respiratory Distress Syndrome

Respiratory distress syndrome (RDS) is one of the leading causes of death in premature infants. Although intensive research has failed to uncover its causes, a variety of physiological disturbances, such as insufficient oxygen intake and high blood acidity, are characteristic of RDS. These are usually treated by administering oxygen and buffers to decrease acidity. However, a substantial proportion of RDS infants fail to survive.

P. K. J. Van Vliet and J. M. Gupta (1973) studied 50 infants with a diagnosis of RDS based on clinical signs and symptoms and confirmed by chest x-ray. For each case, they report the infant's outcome—whether the infant died or survived—as well as values for eight variables that might be predictors of outcome. Table 1.1 gives the SPSS/PC+ names and descriptions of these variables.

Table 1.1   Possible predictors of survival

Variable	Description
survival	Infant's outcome. Coded 1 if infant died, 2 if infant survived.
treatmnt	Type of buffer administered (buffer neutralizes acidity). Coded 1 for THAM, 0 for sodium carbonate.
time	Time that it took the infant to begin breathing spontaneously, measured in minutes.
weight	Birth weight measured in kilograms.
apgar	Score on the Apgar test, which measures infant's responsiveness. Scores range from 0 to 10.
sex	Infant's sex. Coded 0 for females, 1 for males.
age	The gestational age of the infant measured in weeks. Values of 36 to 38 are obtained for full-term infants.
ph	The acidity level of the blood, measured on a scale from 0 to 14.
resp	Indicates whether respiratory therapy was initiated. Coded 0 for no, 1 for yes.

Some dichotomous variables such as *sex* are included among the predictor variables. Although, as previously indicated, the linear discriminant function requires that the predictor variables have a multivariate normal distribution, the function has been shown to perform fairly well in a variety of other situations.

In this example, we will use discriminant analysis to determine whether the variables listed in Table 1.1 distinguish between infants who recover from RDS and those who do not. If high-risk infants can be identified early, special monitoring and treatment procedures may be instituted for them. It is also of interest to determine which variables contribute most to the separation of infants who survive from those who do not.

Selecting Cases for the Analysis

The first step in discriminant analysis is to select cases to be included in the computations. A case is excluded from the analysis if it contains missing information for the variable that defines the groups or for any of the predictor variables.

If many cases have missing values for at least one variable, the actual analysis will be based on a small subset of cases. This may be troublesome for two reasons. First, estimates based on small samples are usually quite variable. Second, if the cases with missing values differ from those without missing values, the resulting estimates may be too biased. For example, if highly educated people are more likely to provide information on the variables used in the analysis, selecting cases with complete data will result in a sample that is highly educated. Results obtained from such a sample might differ from those that would be obtained if people at all educational levels were included. Therefore, it is usually a good strategy to examine cases with missing values to see whether there is evidence that missing values are associated with some particular characteristics of the cases. If there are many missing values for some variables, you should consider eliminating those variables from the analysis.

Figure 1.1 shows the SPSS/PC+ output produced after all the data have been processed. The first line of the output indicates how many cases are eligible for inclusion. The second line indicates the number of cases excluded from analysis because of missing values for the predictor variables or the variable that defines the groups. In this example, two cases with missing values are excluded from the analysis. If cases are weighted, SPSS/PC+ displays the sum of the weights in each group and the actual number of cases.

Figure 1.1   Case summary

```
DSCRIMINANT GROUPS=SURVIVAL(1,2)
 /VARIABLES=TREATMNT TO RESP

On groups defined by SURVIVAL INFANT SURVIVAL

          50 (Unweighted) cases were processed.
           2 of these were excluded from the analysis.
              2 had at least one missing discriminating variable.
          48 (Unweighted) cases will be used in the analysis.


Number of cases by group

                Number of cases
      SURVIVAL  Unweighted    Weighted  Label
          1         26          26.0    DIE
          2         22          22.0    SURVIVE

      Total         48          48.0
```

Analyzing Group Differences

Although the variables are interrelated and we will need to employ statistical techniques that incorporate these dependencies, it is often helpful to begin analyzing the differences between groups by examining univariate statistics.

Figure 1.2 contains the means for the eight independent variables for infants who died (group 1) and who survived (group 2), along with the corresponding standard deviations. The last row of each table, labeled *Total*, contains the means and standard deviations calculated when all cases are combined into a single sample.

Figure 1.2   Group means and standard deviations

```
DSCRIMINANT GROUPS=SURVIVAL(1,2)
 /VARIABLES=TREATMNT TO RESP
 /STATISTICS=1 2.


Group means

  SURVIVAL       TREATMNT           TIME          WEIGHT           APGAR
        1          .38462        2.88462         1.70950         5.50000
        2          .59091        2.31818         2.36091         6.31818
    Total          .47917        2.62500         2.00806         5.87500

  SURVIVAL            SEX            AGE              PH            RESP
        1          .65385       32.38462         7.17962          .65385
        2          .68182       34.63636         7.34636          .27273
    Total          .66667       33.41667         7.25604          .47917


Group standard deviations

  SURVIVAL       TREATMNT           TIME          WEIGHT           APGAR
        1          .49614        3.48513          .51944         2.77489
        2          .50324        3.70503          .62760         2.69720
    Total          .50485        3.56027          .65353         2.74152

  SURVIVAL            SEX            AGE              PH            RESP
        1          .48516        3.11226          .08502          .48516
        2          .47673        2.71759          .60478          .45584
    Total          .47639        3.12051          .41751          .50485
```

From Figure 1.2, you can see that 38% of the infants who died were treated with THAM, 65% were male, and 65% received respiratory therapy. (When a variable is coded 0 or 1, the mean of the variable is the proportion of cases with a value of 1.) Infants who died took longer to breathe spontaneously, weighed less, and had lower Apgar scores than infants who survived.

Figure 1.3 shows significance tests for the equality of group means for each variable. The F values and their significance, shown in the third and fourth columns, are the same as those calculated from a one-way analysis of variance with survival as the grouping variable. For example, the F value in Figure 1.4, which is an analysis-of-variance table for *weight* from the SPSS/PC+ One-Way ANOVA procedure, is 15.49, as shown for weight in Figure 1.3. (When there are two groups, the F value is just the square of the t value from the two-sample t test.) The significance level for *weight* is 0.0003. If the observed significance level is small (less than 0.05), the hypothesis that all group means are equal is rejected.

Figure 1.3   Tests for univariate equality of group means

```
DSCRIMINANT GROUPS=SURVIVAL(1,2)
 /VARIABLES=TREATMNT TO RESP
 /STATISTICS=2 6.


Wilks' lambda (U-statistic) and univariate F-ratio
with 1 and          46 degrees of freedom

    Variable   Wilks' Lambda         F         Significance
    --------   -------------    -------------   ------------
    TREATMNT       .95766           2.034           .1606
    TIME           .99358           .2971           .5883
    WEIGHT         .74810          15.49            .0003
    APGAR          .97742          1.063            .3080
    SEX            .99913          .4024E-01        .8419
    AGE            .86798          6.997            .0111
    PH             .95956          1.939            .1705
    RESP           .85551          7.769            .0077
```

Figure 1.4   One-way analysis-of-variance table for weight

```
ONEWAY WEIGHT BY SURVIVAL(1,2)
  /OPTIONS=2.
```

| | Variable | WEIGHT | BIRTHWEIGHT IN KILOGRAMS | | |
| | By Variable | SURVIVAL | INFANT SURVIVAL | | |

Analysis of variance

Source	D.F.	Sum of Squares	Mean Squares	F Ratio	F Prob.
Between groups	1	5.0566	5.0566	15.4894	.0003
Within Groups	46	15.0171	.3265		
Total	47	20.0737			

Wilks' Lambda

Another statistic displayed in Figure 1.3 is **Wilks' lambda**, sometimes called the *U* **statistic** (see "Other Discriminant Function Statistics" on p. 17). When variables are considered individually, lambda is the ratio of the within-groups sum of squares to the total sum of squares. For example, Figure 1.4 shows the sums of squares for variable *weight*. The ratio of the within-groups sum of squares (15.02) to the total sum of squares (20.07) is 0.748, the value of Wilks' lambda for *weight* in Figure 1.3.

A lambda of 1 occurs when all observed group means are equal. Values close to 0 occur when within-groups variability is small compared to the total variability; that is, when most of the total variability is attributable to differences between the means of the groups. Thus, large values of lambda indicate that group means do not appear to be different, while small values indicate that group means do appear to be different.

From Figure 1.3, *weight*, *age*, and *resp* are the variables whose means are most different for survivors and nonsurvivors.

Correlations

Since interdependencies among the variables affect most multivariate analyses, it is worth examining the correlation matrix of the predictor variables. Figure 1.5 is the pooled within-groups correlation matrix. *Weight* and *age* have the largest correlation coefficient, 0.84. This is to be expected, since weight increases with gestational age. The section "Function-Variable Correlations" on p. 20 discusses some of the possible consequences of including highly correlated variables in the analysis.

A **pooled within-groups correlation matrix** is obtained by averaging the separate correlation matrices for all groups and then computing the correlation matrix. A **total correlation matrix** is obtained when all cases are treated as if they are from a single sample.

Figure 1.5   Pooled within-groups correlation matrix

```
DSCRIMINANT GROUPS=SURVIVAL(1,2)
  /VARIABLES=TREATMNT TO RESP
  /STATISTICS=4.
```

Pooled within-groups correlation matrix

	TREATMNT	TIME	WEIGHT	APGAR	SEX	AGE	PH	RESP
TREATMNT	1.00000							
TIME	.01841	1.00000						
WEIGHT	.09091	-.21244	1.00000					
APGAR	-.03394	-.50152	.22161	1.00000				
SEX	-.03637	-.12982	.19500	-.02098	1.00000			
AGE	.05749	-.20066	.84040	.36329	-.00129	1.00000		
PH	-.08307	.09102	.12436	-.07197	-.03156	.00205	1.00000	
RESP	-.00774	-.06994	-.02394	.16123	.26732	-.06828	.03770	1.00000

The total and pooled within-groups correlation matrices can be quite different. For example, Figure 1.6 shows a plot of two hypothetical variables for three groups. When each group is considered individually, the correlation coefficient is 0. Averaging, or pooling, these individual estimates also results in a coefficient of 0. However, the correlation coefficient computed for all cases combined (total) is 0.97, since groups with larger X values also have larger Y values.

Figure 1.6   Hypothetical variable plot for three groups

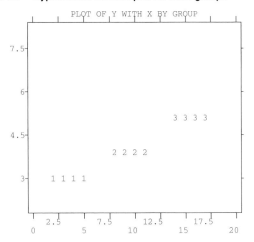

Estimating the Coefficients

Descriptive statistics and univariate tests of significance provide basic information about the distributions of the variables in the groups and help identify some differences among the groups. However, in discriminant analysis and other multivariate statistical procedures, the emphasis is on analyzing the variables together, not one at a time. By considering the variables simultaneously, we are able to incorporate important information about their relationships.

In discriminant analysis, a linear combination of the independent variables is formed and serves as the basis for assigning cases to groups. Thus, information contained in multiple independent variables is summarized in a single index. For example, by finding a weighted average of variables such as *age, weight,* and *apgar,* you can obtain a score that distinguishes infants who survive from those who do not. In discriminant analysis, the weights are estimated so that they result in the "best" separation between the groups.

The linear discriminant equation

$$D = B_0 + B_1X_1 + B_2X_2 + ... + B_pX_p$$

Equation 1.1

is similar to the multiple linear regression equation. The X's are the values of the independent variables and the B's are coefficients estimated from the data. If a linear discriminant function is to distinguish infants who die from those who survive, the two groups must differ in their D values.

Therefore, the B's are chosen so that the values of the discriminant function differ as much as possible between the groups, or that for the discriminant scores the ratio

$$\frac{\text{between-groups sum of squares}}{\text{within-groups sum of squares}}$$

Equation 1.2

is a maximum. Any other linear combination of the variables will have a smaller ratio. The actual mechanics of computing the coefficients, especially if there are more than two groups, is somewhat involved (see Morrison, 1967; Tatsuoka, 1971).

The coefficients for the eight variables listed in Table 1.1 are shown in Figure 1.7. Small and large values are sometimes displayed in scientific notation. For example, the number 0.0003678 might be displayed as 0.368E-03.

Figure 1.7   Unstandardized discriminant function coefficients

```
DSCRIMINANT GROUPS=SURVIVAL(1,2)
 /VARIABLES=TREATMNT TO RESP
 /STATISTICS=11.


Unstandardized canonical discriminant function coefficients

                    Func  1
TREATMNT           .4311545
TIME               .3671274E-01
WEIGHT            2.0440349
APGAR              .1264302
SEX                .6998343E-02
AGE               -.2180711
PH                 .4078705
RESP             -1.2445389
(Constant)        -.2309344
```

Calculating the Discriminant Score

Based on the coefficients in Figure 1.7, it is possible to calculate the discriminant score for each case. For example, Figure 1.8 contains the value of each variable for the first five cases in the data file.

Figure 1.8   Values of the variables for the first five cases

```
COMPUTE SCORE=.431*TREATMNT + .0367*TIME + 2.04*WEIGHT + .126*APGAR
           + .007*SEX - .218*AGE + .408*PH - 1.24*RESP - .231.
FORMAT SCORE(F6.3).
LIST CASES=5 /VARIABLES=TREATMNT TO RESP SURVIVAL SCORE
   /FORMAT=NUMBERED.


Case # TREATMNT TIME WEIGHT APGAR SEX AGE   PH RESP SURVIVAL   SCORE

      1       1  2.0  1.050     5   0  28 7.09    0        1   -.166
      2       1  2.0  1.175     4   0  28 7.11    1        1 -1.269
      3       1   .5  1.230     7   0  29 7.24    9        1      .
      4       1  4.0  1.310     4   1  29 7.13    1        1 -1.123
      5       1   .5  1.500     8   1  32 7.23    1        1  -.973
```

The discriminant score for case 1 is obtained by multiplying the unstandardized coefficients by the values of the variables, summing these products, and adding the constant. For case 1, the discriminant score is:

$$D_1 = 0.431\,(1) + 0.0367\,(2) + 2.044\,(1.05) + 0.126\,(5) + 0.007\,(0)$$
$$- 0.218\,(28) + 0.408\,(7.09) - 1.244\,(0) - 0.231 = -0.16$$

Equation 1.3

Figure 1.9 contains basic descriptive statistics for the discriminant scores (*discore1*) in the two groups. The mean score for all cases combined is 0 and the pooled within-groups variance is 1. This is always true for discriminant scores calculated by SPSS/PC+.

Figure 1.9   Descriptive statistics

```
DSCRIMINANT GROUPS=SURVIVAL(1,2)
  /VARIABLES=TREATMNT TO RESP
  /SAVE=SCORES=DISCORE.
VARIABLE LABELS DISCORE1 'DISCRIMINANT SCORE'.
MEANS TABLES=DISCORE1 BY SURVIVAL
  /STATISTICS=1.

Summaries of   DISCORE1   FUNCTION    1 FOR ANALYSIS      1
By levels of   SURVIVAL   INFANT SURVIVAL

      Value  Label                   Mean    Std Dev   Sum of Sq    Cases

          1  DIE                 -.7125152   .9055960 20.5026022       26
          2  SURVIVE              .8420634  1.1018901 25.4973978       22
                                -------------------------------------------
Within Groups Total              .0000000  1.0000000 46.0000000       48
```

Bayes' Rule

Using the discriminant score, it is possible to obtain a rule for classifying cases into one of the two groups. The technique used by SPSSPC+ is based on Bayes' rule. The probability that a case with a discriminant score of D belongs to group i is estimated by:

$$P(G_i|D) = \frac{P(D|G_i)\,P(G_i)}{\sum_{i=1}^{g} P(D|G_i)\,P(G_i)}$$

Equation 1.4

The next three sections describe the various components of this equation and their relationships.

Prior Probability

The **prior probability**, represented by $P(G_i)$, is an estimate of the likelihood that a case belongs to a particular group when no information about it is available. For example, if 30% of infants with RDS die, the probability that an infant with RDS will die is 0.3.

The prior probability can be estimated in several ways. If the sample is considered representative of the population, the observed proportions of cases in each group can serve as estimates of the prior probabilities. In this example, 26 out of 48 cases for whom all information is available, or 54%, belong to group 1 (nonsurvivors), and 22 (46%) belong to group 2 (survivors). The prior probability of belonging to group 1, then, is 0.54, and the prior probability of belonging to group 2 is 0.46.

Often, samples are chosen so that they include a fixed number of observations per group. For example, if deaths from RDS were rare, say occurring once per 100 RDS births, even reasonably large samples of RDS births would result in a small number of cases in the nonsurvivor group. Therefore, an investigator might include the same number of survivors and nonsurvivors in the study. In such situations, the prior probability of group membership can be estimated from other sources, such as hospital discharge records.

When all groups are equally likely, or when no information about the probability of group membership is known, equal prior probabilities for all groups may be selected. Since each case must belong to one of the groups, the prior probabilities must sum to 1.

Although prior probabilities convey some information about the likelihood of group membership, they ignore the attributes of the particular case. For example, an infant who is known to be very sick based on various criteria is assigned the same probability of dying as is an infant known to be healthier.

Conditional Probability

To take advantage of the additional information available for a case in developing a classification scheme, we need to assess the likelihood of the additional information under different circumstances. For example, if the discriminant function scores are normally distributed for each of two groups and the parameters of the distributions can be estimated, it is possible to calculate the probability of obtaining a particular discriminant function value of D if the case is a member of group 1 or group 2.

This probability is called the **conditional probability** of D given the group and is denoted by $P(D|G_i)$. To calculate this probability, the case is assumed to belong to a particular group and the probability of the observed score given membership in the group is estimated.

Posterior Probability

The conditional probability of D given the group gives an idea of how likely the score is for members of a particular group. However, when group membership is unknown, what is really needed is an estimate of how likely membership in the various groups is, given the available information. This is called the **posterior probability** and is denoted by $P(G_i|D)$. It can be estimated from $P(D|G_i)$ and $P(G_i)$ using Bayes' rule. A case is classified, based on its discriminant score D, in the group for which the posterior probability is the largest. That is, it is assigned to the most likely group based on its discriminant score. (See Tatsuoka, 1971, for further information.)

Classification Output

Figure 1.10 is an excerpt from the SPSS/PC+ output that lists classification information for each case for a group of cases whose membership is known. The first column, labeled *Case Number*, is the sequence number of the case in the file. The next column, *Mis Val*, contains the number of variables with missing values for that case. Cases with missing values are not used in estimating the coefficients and are not included in the output shown in Figure 1.10 (note the absence of cases 3 and 28). However, those two cases with missing values could have been classified and included in the table by substituting group means for missing values. The third column (*Sel*) indicates whether a case has been excluded from the computations using a selection variable.

Figure 1.10 Classification output

```
DSCRIMINANT GROUPS=SURVIVAL(1,2)
 /VARIABLES=TREATMNT TO RESP
 /STATISTICS=14.
```

Case Number	Mis Val	Sel	Actual Group	Highest Probability Group	P(D/G)	P(G/D)	2nd Highest Group	P(G/D)	Discriminant Scores...
1			1	1	.5821	.5873	2	.4127	-.1622
2			1	1	.5776	.8884	2	.1116	-1.2695
4			1	1	.6814	.8637	2	.1363	-1.1230
5			1	1	.7962	.8334	2	.1666	-.9708
6			1	1	.9080	.7367	2	.2633	-.5970
7		**	1	2	.4623	.5164	1	.4836	.1070
8			1	1	.8433	.7112	2	.2888	-.5149
9			1	1	.6581	.8695	2	.1305	-1.1551
10			1	1	.4577	.5134	2	.4866	.0302
11			1	1	.6087	.6017	2	.3983	-.2006
12			1	1	.1722	.9655	2	.0345	-2.0775
13			1	1	.1140	.9750	2	.0250	-2.2930
14			1	1	.3430	.9360	2	.0640	-1.6607
15			1	1	.7983	.6923	2	.3077	-.4569
16			1	1	.7008	.6482	2	.3518	-.3283
17			1	1	.2090	.9593	2	.0407	-1.9687
18			1	1	.1128	.9752	2	.0248	-2.2982
19			1	1	.4383	.9178	2	.0822	-1.4875
20		**	1	2	.9418	.7493	1	.2507	.7690
21			1	1	.7384	.6658	2	.3342	-.3786
22		**	1	2	.5161	.5495	1	.4505	.1927
23			1	1	.5399	.8967	2	.1033	-1.3255
24			1	1	.4409	.5026	2	.4974	.0582
25		**	1	2	.8126	.8288	1	.1712	1.0791
26			1	1	.7050	.6502	2	.3498	-.3339
27			1	1	.5804	.5864	2	.4136	-.1597
29		**	2	1	.4595	.5146	2	.4854	.0272
30			2	2	.8552	.7160	1	.2840	.6596
31			2	2	.6172	.6062	1	.3938	.3423
32			2	2	.6928	.6443	1	.3557	.4469
33			2	2	.8887	.8063	1	.1937	.9820
34			2	2	.6169	.8793	1	.1207	1.3423
35			2	2	.6823	.8635	1	.1365	1.2514
36			2	2	.7755	.6824	1	.3176	.5568
37			2	2	.6368	.8746	1	.1254	1.3143
38			2	2	.0874	.9795	1	.0205	2.5512
39			2	2	.1236	.9735	1	.0265	2.3821
40			2	2	.0181	.9925	1	.0075	3.2050
41			2	2	.9033	.7349	1	.2651	.7206
42		**	2	1	.5613	.8920	2	.1080	-1.2934
43		**	2	1	.5270	.5560	2	.4440	-.0799
44		**	2	1	.3851	.9281	2	.0719	-1.5810
45			2	2	.5574	.5735	1	.4265	.2553
46			2	2	.7718	.8401	1	.1599	1.1321
47			2	2	.6792	.6377	1	.3623	.4286
48			2	2	.9649	.7819	1	.2181	.8861
49			2	2	.5742	.8891	1	.1109	1.4040
50			2	2	.4533	.9148	1	.0852	1.5920

For cases included in the computation of the discriminant function, actual group membership is known and can be compared to that predicted using the discriminant function. The group to which a case actually belongs is listed in the column labeled *Actual Group*. The most likely group for a case based on the discriminant analysis (the group with the largest posterior probability) is listed in the column labeled *Highest Group*. Cases that are misclassified using the discriminant function are flagged with asterisks next to the actual group number.

The next value listed is the probability of a case's discriminant score, or one more extreme, if the case is a member of the most-likely group.

The larger posterior probabilities of membership in the two groups $P(G|D)$ follow in Figure 1.10. When there are only two groups, both probabilities are given, since one is the highest and the other the second highest. The probabilities 0.5873 and 0.4127 sum to 1, since a case must be a member of one of the two groups.

Classification Summary

You can obtain the number of misclassified cases by counting the number of cases with asterisks in Figure 1.10. In this example, 8 cases out of 48 are classified incorrectly.

More detailed information on the results of the classification phase is available from the output in Figure 1.11, sometimes called the **confusion matrix**. For each group, this output shows the numbers of correct and incorrect classifications. In this example, only the cases with complete information for all predictor variables are included in the classification results table. Correctly classified cases appear on the diagonal of the table, since the predicted and actual groups are the same. For example, of 26 cases in group 1, 22 were predicted correctly to be members of group 1 (84.6%), while 4 (15.4%) were assigned incorrectly to group 2. Similarly, 18 out of 22 (81.8%) of the group-2 cases were identified correctly, and 4 (18.2%) were misclassified. The overall percentage of cases classified correctly is 83.3% (40 out of 48).

Figure 1.11 Classification results

```
DSCRIMINANT GROUPS=SURVIVAL(1,2)
 /VARIABLES=TREATMNT TO RESP
 /STATISTICS=13.


Classification results -

                      No. of    Predicted Group Membership
       Actual Group    Cases        1            2
-------------------   ------    --------    --------

Group        1           26         22           4
DIE                                84.6%       15.4%

Group        2           22          4          18
SURVIVE                            18.2%       81.8%

Percent of "grouped" cases correctly classified:  83.33%
```

Histograms of Discriminant Scores

To see how much the two groups overlap and to examine the distribution of the discriminant scores, it is often useful to plot the discriminant function scores for the groups. Figure 1.12 shows histograms of the scores for each group separately. Four symbols (either 1's or 2's) represent one case. (The number of cases represented by a symbol depends on the number of cases used in an analysis.) The row of 1's and 2's underneath the plot denote the group to which scores are assigned.

Figure 1.12   Histograms of discriminant scores

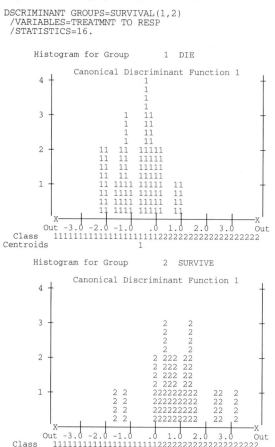

```
DSCRIMINANT GROUPS=SURVIVAL(1,2)
 /VARIABLES=TREATMNT TO RESP
 /STATISTICS=16.
```

The average score for a group is called the **group centroid** and is indicated on each plot as well as in Figure 1.13. These values are the same as the means in Figure 1.9. On the average, infants who died have smaller discriminant function scores than infants who survived. The average value for infants who died (group 1) is –0.71, whereas the average value for those who survived (group 2) is 0.84.

Figure 1.13 Discriminant functions evaluated at group means

```
DSCRIMINANT GROUPS=SURVIVAL(1,2)
 /VARIABLES=TREATMNT TO RESP.

Canonical discriminant functions evaluated at Group Means (Group Centroids)

   Group      FUNC   1

     1        -.71252
     2         .84206
```

In Figure 1.12, we note that three group-1 cases clearly fall into the group-2 classification region, whereas four group-1 cases are misclassified. Of the two cases that have values around 0.1, one (case 7) has a classification probability for group 1 of 0.48, while the other (case 24) has a value of 0.503. Thus, case 7 is misclassified, although on the plot it appears to be correctly classified because the boundary between the two territories falls within an interval attributed to group 1.

The combined distribution of the scores for the two groups is shown in Figure 1.14. Again, four symbols represent a case, and you can see the amount of overlap between the two groups. For example, the interval with midpoint −1.2 has four cases, three from group 1 and one from group 2.

Figure 1.14 All-groups stacked histogram: canonical discriminant function

```
DSCRIMINANT GROUPS=SURVIVAL(1,2)
 /VARIABLES=TREATMNT TO RESP
 /STATISTICS=15.

                  All-groups stacked Histogram

            Canonical Discriminant Function 1
    4 +                   2    1 2                              +
                          2    1 2
                          2    1 2
                          2    1 2
    3 +                   1    11222 2   2                      +
                          1    11222 2   2
                          1    11222 2   2
                          1    11222 2   2
    2 +             11 211 11111222222                          +
                    11 211 11111222222
                    11 211 11111222222
                    11 211 11111222222
    1 +             11 1111 111112211222     22  2              +
                    11 1111 111112211222     22  2
                    11 1111 111112211222     22  2
                    11 1111 111112211222     22  2
        X--+----+----+----+----+----+----+--X
       Out -3.0 -2.0 -1.0  .0  1.0  2.0  3.0  Out
   Class    1111111111111111111111122222222222222222222222
 Centroids                1         2
```

Estimating Misclassification Rates

A model usually fits the sample from which it is derived better than it will fit another sample from the same population. Thus, the percentage of cases classified correctly by the discriminant function is an inflated estimate of the true performance in the population, just as R^2 is an overly optimistic estimate of a model's fit in regression.

There are several ways to obtain a better estimate of the true misclassification rate. If the sample is large enough to be randomly split into two parts, you can use one to derive the discriminant function and the other to test it. Since the same cases are not used for both estimating the function and testing it, the observed error rate in the "test" sample should better reflect the function's effectiveness. However, this method requires large sample sizes and does not make good use of all of the available information.

Another technique for obtaining an improved estimate of the misclassification rate is the **jackknife method**, sometimes called the leaving-one-out method. It involves leaving out each of the cases in turn, calculating the function based on the remaining $n - 1$ cases, and then classifying the left-out case. Again, since the case that is being classified is not included in the calculation of the function, the observed (or apparent) misclassification rate is a less biased estimate of the true one.

When one of the groups is much smaller than the other, a highly correct classification rate can occur even when most of the "minority" group cases are misclassified. The smaller group, which can include adopters of a new product, diseased individuals, or parole violators, is, however, of particular interest, and its correct classification is of paramount importance. The desired result is not to minimize the overall misclassification rate but to identify most cases of the smaller group. For example, by judging everyone to be disease-free in a cancer-screening program, the error rate will be very small, since few people actually have the disease. However, the results are useless, since the goal is to identify the diseased individuals.

The result of different classification rules for identifying "minority" cases can be examined by ranking all cases on the value of their discriminant score and determining how many "minority" cases are in the various deciles. If most of the cases of interest are at the extremes of the distribution, a good rule for identifying them can be obtained at the expense of increasing the number of misclassified cases from the larger group. If the intent of the discriminant analysis is to identify persons to receive promotional materials for a new product, or undergo further screening procedures, this is a fairly reasonable tactic. Unequal costs for misclassification can also be incorporated into the classification rule by adjusting the prior probabilities to reflect them. For further discussion, see Lachenbruch (1975).

The Expected Misclassification Rate

The percentage of cases classified correctly is often taken as an index of the effectiveness of the discriminant function. When evaluating this measure it is important to compare the observed misclassification rate to that expected by chance alone. For example, if there are two groups with equal prior probabilities, assigning cases to groups based on the outcome of a flip of a coin—that is, heads allocated to group 1 and tails allocated to group 2—results in an expected misclassification rate of 50%. A discriminant function with an observed misclassification rate of 50% is performing no better than chance. In fact, if the rate is based on the sample used for deriving the function, it is probably doing worse.

As the number of groups with equal prior probabilities increases, the percentage of cases that can be classified correctly by chance alone decreases. If there are 10 groups, only 10% of the cases would be expected to be classified correctly by chance. Observed misclassification rates should always be viewed in light of results expected by chance.

Other Discriminant Function Statistics

The percentage of cases classified correctly is one indicator of the effectiveness of the discriminant function. Another indicator of effectiveness of the function is the actual discriminant scores in the groups. A "good" discriminant function is one that has much between-groups variability when compared to within-groups variability. In fact, the coefficients of the discriminant function are chosen so that the ratio of the between-groups sum of squares to the within-groups sum of squares is as large as possible. Any other linear combination of the predictor variables will have a smaller ratio.

Figure 1.15 is an analysis-of-variance table from the SPSS/PC+ Means procedure using the discriminant scores as the dependent variable and the group variable as the independent or classification variable. Figure 1.16 shows a variety of statistics based on the analysis-of-variance table. For example, the **eigenvalue** in Figure 1.16 is simply the ratio of the between-groups to within-groups sums of squares. Thus, from Figure 1.15, it is:

$$\text{eigenvalue} = \frac{\text{between-groups ss}}{\text{within-groups ss}} = \frac{28.8}{46.0} = 0.626 \qquad \textbf{Equation 1.5}$$

Large eigenvalues are associated with "good" functions. The next two entries in Figure 1.16, percentage of variance and cumulative percentage, are always 100 for the two-group situation. (See "Additional Statistics" on p. 35 for further explanation.)

Figure 1.15   Analysis-of-variance table for discriminant scores

```
DSCRIMINANT GROUPS=SURVIVAL(1,2)
  /VARIABLES=TREATMNT TO RESP
  /SAVE=SCORES=DISCORE.
VARIABLE LABELS DISCORE1 'DISCRIMINANT SCORE'.
MEANS TABLES=DISCORE1 BY SURVIVAL
  /STATISTICS=1.
```

```
                             Analysis of Variance

                      Sum of                    Mean
Source                Squares      D.F.         Square        F        Sig.

Between Groups        28.7992       1          28.7992     28.7992     .0000

Within Groups         46.0000      46           1.0000

                Eta =  .6205    Eta Squared =   .3850
```

Figure 1.16   Canonical discriminant functions

```
DSCRIMINANT GROUPS=SURVIVAL(1,2)
  /VARIABLES=TREATMNT TO RESP.
```

```
                   Canonical Discriminant Functions

            Pct of   Cum  Canonical  After  Wilks'
Fcn Eigenvalue Variance Pct    Corr     Fcn  Lambda  Chisquare  DF  Sig
                                    :     0   .6150    20.419     8  .0089
 1*     .6261  100.00 100.00   .6205  :

 * Marks the   1 canonical discriminant functions remaining in the analysis.
```

The **canonical correlation** is a measure of the degree of association between the discriminant scores and the groups. It is equivalent to eta from the one-way analysis of variance, in which the discriminant score is the dependent variable and group is the independent variable. Remember that eta^2 is the ratio of the between-groups sum of squares to the total sum of squares and represents the proportion of the total variance attributable to differences among the groups. Thus, from Figure 1.15, eta is:

$$eta = \sqrt{\frac{28.8}{74.8}} = 0.6205$$

Equation 1.6

In the two-group situation, the canonical correlation is simply the usual Pearson correlation coefficient between the discriminant score and the group variable, which is coded 0 and 1.

For the two-group case, Wilks' lambda is the ratio of the within-groups sum of squares to the total sum of squares. It is the proportion of the total variance in the discriminant scores not explained by differences among groups ($lambda + eta^2 = 1$). From Figure 1.15, lambda is:

$$\lambda = \frac{46}{74.8} = 0.615$$

Equation 1.7

As indicated in "Additional Statistics" on p. 35, small values of lambda are associated with functions that have much variability between groups and little variability within groups. A lambda of 1 occurs when the mean of the discriminant scores is the same in all groups and there is no between-groups variability.

A test of the null hypothesis that in the populations from which the samples are drawn there is no difference between the group means can be based on Wilks' lambda. Lambda is transformed to a variable that has approximately a chi-square distribution. Figure 1.16 shows that a lambda of 0.6150 is transformed to a chi-square value of 20.419 with eight degrees of freedom. The observed significance level is 0.0089. Thus, it appears unlikely that infants who die from RDS and those who survive have the same means on the discriminant function.

It is important to remember that even though Wilks' lambda may be statistically significant, it provides little information about the effectiveness of the discriminant function in classification. It only provides a test of the null hypothesis that the population means are equal. Small differences may be statistically significant but still not permit good discrimination among the groups. If the means and covariance matrices are equal, of course, discrimination is not possible.

Interpreting the Discriminant Function Coefficients

Table 1.2 contains the standardized and unstandardized discriminant function coefficients for the RDS example. The **unstandardized coefficients** are the multipliers of the variables when they are expressed in the original units. As in multiple regression, the **standardized coefficients** are used when the variables are standardized to a mean of 0 and a standard deviation of 1.

Table 1.2   Standardized and unstandardized discriminant function coefficients

Variable	Unstandardized	Standardized
treatmnt	0.43115	0.21531
time	0.03671	0.13170
weight	2.04404	1.16789
apgar	0.12643	0.34638
sex	0.00700	0.00337
age	−0.21807	−0.64084
ph	0.40787	0.16862
resp	−1.24454	−0.58743
(constant)	−0.23093	

The interpretation of the coefficients is also similar to that in multiple regression. Since the variables are correlated, it is not possible to assess the importance of an individual variable. The value of the coefficient for a particular variable depends on the other variables included in the function.

It is sometimes tempting to interpret the magnitudes of the coefficients as indicators of the relative importance of variables. Variables with large coefficients are thought to contribute more to the overall discriminant function. However, the magnitude of the unstandardized coefficients is not a good index of relative importance when the variables differ in the units in which they are measured. For example, the gestational age is measured in weeks and ranges from 28 to 39 weeks, while the pH level ranges from 6.85 to 7.37. When the absolute values of the unstandardized coefficients are ranked from largest to smallest, age (–0.22) has a rank of 5. However, when the coefficients are standardized to adjust for the unequal means and standard deviations of the independent variables, the coefficient for age (–0.64) is the second largest.

The actual signs of the coefficients are arbitrary. The negative coefficients for age and respiratory therapy could just as well be positive if the signs of the other coefficients were reversed.

By looking at the groups of variables that have coefficients of different signs, we can determine which variable values result in large and small function values. For example, since respiratory therapy is usually initiated for infants who are in considerable distress, it is a bad omen for survival. Values of 1 for the *resp* variable will decrease the function value. Infants who weigh more usually have better developed lungs and are more likely to survive. Thus, larger weights increase the function. Large function values are associated with survival, while small function values are associated with death.

Function-Variable Correlations

Another way to assess the contribution of a variable to the discriminant function is to examine the correlations between the values of the function and the values of the variables. The computation of the coefficients is straightforward. For each case the value of the discriminant function is computed, and the Pearson correlation coefficients between it and the original variables are obtained.

Separate correlation matrices can be calculated for each group and the results combined to obtain a pooled within-groups correlation matrix like that in Figure 1.17. Or all of the cases can be considered together and a total correlation matrix calculated. The total correlation coefficients are larger than the corresponding within-groups correlations. However, the relative magnitudes will be similar. Variables with high total correlations will also have high pooled within-groups correlations.

Figure 1.17   Pooled within-groups correlations

```
DSCRIMINANT GROUPS=SURVIVAL(1,2)
  /VARIABLES=TREATMNT TO RESP

Structure matrix:

Pooled within-groups correlations between discriminating variables
                                   and canonical discriminant functions
(Variables ordered by size of correlation within function)

              FUNC  1

WEIGHT          .73338
RESP           -.51940
AGE             .49290
TREATMNT        .26572
PH              .25946
APGAR           .19210
TIME           -.10157
SEX             .03738
```

Figure 1.17 indicates that variable *weight* has the highest correlation with the discriminant function. Variable *resp* has the second largest correlation in absolute value. The negative sign indicates that small function values are associated with the presence of respiratory therapy (coded 1) and larger values are associated with the absence of respiratory therapy. These results are similar to those obtained from the standardized coefficients.

However, if you compare Table 1.2 and Figure 1.17, you will notice that *age*, which has a negative standardized coefficient, is positively correlated with the discriminant function. Similarly, *time*, which has a positive standardized coefficient, has a negative correlation with the discriminant score. This occurs because *weight* and *age*, as expected, are highly correlated. The correlation coefficient is 0.84 from Figure 1.5. Thus, the contribution of *age* and *weight* is shared and the individual coefficients are not meaningful. You should exercise care when attempting to interpret the coefficients, since correlations between variables affect the magnitudes and signs of the coefficients.

Fisher's Classification Function Coefficients

In Table 1.2, the linear discriminant function coefficients are those that maximize the ratio of between-groups to within-groups sums of squares. These coefficients are sometimes called the **canonical discriminant function coefficients**, since they are identical to those obtained from canonical correlation analysis when maximally correlated linear combinations of the group membership variables and predictor variables are formed (see Tatsuoka, 1971).

Another set of coefficients, sometimes called **Fisher's linear discriminant function coefficients** or classification coefficients, can be used directly for classification. A set of coefficients is obtained for each group and a case is assigned to the group for which it has the largest discriminant score. The classification results are identical for both methods if all canonical discriminant functions are used (see Kshirsagar & Arseven, 1975; Green, 1979).

Relationship to Multiple Regression Analysis

Two-group linear discriminant analysis is closely related to multiple linear regression analysis. If the binary grouping variable is considered the dependent variable and the predictor variables are the independent variables, the multiple regression coefficients in Table 1.3 are obtained. A comparison of these coefficients to the discriminant function coefficients shows that the two sets of coefficients are proportional. The discriminant coefficients can be obtained by multiplying the regression coefficients by 4.04. The exact constant of proportionality varies from data set to data set, but the two sets of coefficients are always proportional. This is true only for two-group discriminant analysis.

Table 1.3   Regression and discriminant coefficients

Variable	B Regression	B Discriminant	Ratio
resp	−0.3082	−1.2445	4.04
time	0.0091	0.0367	4.04
ph	0.1010	0.4079	4.04
treatmnt	0.1068	0.4311	4.04
sex	0.0017	0.0070	4.04
age	−0.0540	−0.2180	4.04
apgar	0.0313	0.1264	4.04
weight	0.5062	2.0440	4.04

Variable Selection Methods

In many situations, discriminant analysis, like multiple regression analysis, is used as an exploratory tool. In order to arrive at a good model, a variety of potentially useful variables are included in the data set. It is not known in advance which of these variables are important for group separation and which are, more or less, extraneous. One of the desired end-products of the analysis is identification of the "good" predictor variables. All of the caveats for variable-selection procedures in multiple regression discussed in the *SPSS/PC+ Base System User's Guide* apply to discriminant analysis as well. If you have not read that chapter, you are advised to do so before continuing with this chapter.

A commonly used algorithm for variable selection, stepwise selection, is available in the SPSS/PC+ Discriminant procedure. The principles are the same as in multiple regression. What differs are the actual criteria for variable selection. In the following example, only minimization of Wilks' lambda will be considered. Other criteria are discussed in "Other Criteria for Variable Selection" on p. 29 through "Sum of Unexplained Variance" on p. 30.

A Stepwise Selection Example

Stepwise variable-selection algorithms combine the features of forward selection and backward elimination. Remember that in a **stepwise method**, the first variable included in the analysis has the largest acceptable value for the selection criterion. After the first variable is entered, the value of the criterion is reevaluated for all variables not in the model, and the variable with the largest acceptable criterion value is entered next. At this point, the variable entered first is reevaluated to determine whether it meets the removal criterion. If it does, it is removed from the model.

The next step is to examine the variables not in the equation for entry, followed by examination of the variables in the equation for removal. Variables are removed until no variables that meet the removal criterion remain. Variable selection terminates when no more variables meet entry or removal criteria.

Variable Selection Criteria

Figure 1.18 is output from the beginning of a stepwise variable-selection job, listing the criteria in effect. As mentioned previously, several criteria are available for variable selection. This example uses minimization of Wilks' lambda. Thus, at each step, the variable that results in the smallest Wilks' lambda for the discriminant function is selected for entry.

Figure 1.18   Stepwise variable selection

```
DSCRIMINANT GROUPS=SURVIVAL(1,2)
  /VARIABLES=TREATMNT TO RESP
  /METHOD=WILKS.

Stepwise variable selection

     Selection rule:  Minimize Wilks' lambda
     Maximum number of steps.................       16
     Minimum tolerance level.................   .00100
     Minimum F to enter......................    1.000
     Maximum F to remove.....................    1.000
```

Each entry or removal of a variable is considered a step. The maximum number of steps permitted in an analysis is twice the number of independent variables.

As in multiple regression, if there are independent variables that are linear combinations of other independent variables, a unique solution is not possible. To prevent computational difficulties, the tolerance of a variable is checked before it is entered into a model. The **tolerance** is a measure of the degree of linear association between the independent variables. For the ith independent variable, it is $1 - R_i^2$, where R_i^2 is the squared multiple correlation coefficient when the ith independent variable is considered the dependent variable and the regression equation between it and the other independent variables is calculated. Small values for the tolerance indicate that the ith independent variable is almost a linear combination of the other independent variables. Variables with small tolerances (less than 0.001) are not permitted to enter the analysis. Also, if entry of a variable would cause the tolerance of a variable already in the model to drop to an unacceptable level (less than 0.001), the variable is not entered. The smallest acceptable tolerance for a particular analysis is shown in Figure 1.18.

The significance of the change in Wilks' lambda when a variable is entered or removed from the model can be based on an F statistic. Either the actual value of F or its significance level can be used as the criterion for variable entry and removal. These two criteria are not necessarily equivalent, since a fixed F value has different significance levels depending on the number of variables in the model at any step. The actual significance levels associated with the F-to-enter and F-to-remove statistics are not those usually obtained from the F distribution, since many variables are examined and the largest and smallest F values selected. The true significance level is difficult to compute, since it depends on many factors, including the correlations between the independent variables.

The First Step

Before the stepwise selection algorithm begins, at step 0, basic information about the variables is displayed, as shown in Figure 1.19. The tolerance and minimum tolerance are 1, since there are no variables in the model. (The tolerance is based only on the independent variables in the model. The **minimum tolerance**, which is the smallest tolerance for any variable in the equation if the variable under consideration is entered, is also based only on the variables in the equation.) The F-to-enter in Figure 1.19 is equal to the F test for equality of group means in Figure 1.3. The univariate Wilks' lambda is also the same.

Figure 1.19 Output at step 0

```
DSCRIMINANT GROUPS=SURVIVAL(1,2)
  /VARIABLES=TREATMNT TO RESP
  /METHOD=WILKS.

---------------- Variables not in the analysis after step 0 ----------------

                        Minimum
Variable   Tolerance   Tolerance   F to Enter    Wilks' Lambda
TREATMNT   1.0000000   1.0000000      2.0335         .95766
TIME       1.0000000   1.0000000       .29713        .99358
WEIGHT     1.0000000   1.0000000     15.489          .74810
APGAR      1.0000000   1.0000000      1.0628         .97742
SEX        1.0000000   1.0000000       .40245E-01    .99913
AGE        1.0000000   1.0000000      6.9967         .86798
PH         1.0000000   1.0000000      1.9388         .95956
RESP       1.0000000   1.0000000      7.7693         .85551
```

The *weight* variable has the smallest Wilks' lambda and correspondingly the largest *F*-to-enter, so it is the first variable entered into the equation. When *weight* is entered, as shown in Figure 1.20, the Wilks' lambda and corresponding *F* are the same as in Figure 1.3 and Figure 1.19. The degrees of freedom for the Wilks' lambda displayed in Figure 1.20 are for its untransformed (not converted to an *F*) distribution.

After each step, SPSS/PC+ displays a table showing the variables in the model (see Figure 1.21). When only one variable is in the model, this table contains no new information. The *F*-to-remove corresponds to that in Figure 1.20, since it represents the change in Wilks' lambda if *weight* is removed. The last column usually contains the value of Wilks' lambda if the variable is removed. However, since removal of *weight* results in a model with no variables, no value is displayed at the first step.

Figure 1.20 Summary statistics for step 1

```
At step 1, WEIGHT   was included in the analysis.

                                 Degrees of Freedom  Signif.   Between Groups
Wilks' Lambda         .74810        1    1      46.0
Equivalent F        15.48938             1      46.0    .0003
```

Figure 1.21 Variables in the analysis after step 1

```
---------------- Variables in the analysis after step 1 ----------------

Variable   Tolerance   F to Remove   Wilks' Lambda
WEIGHT     1.0000000   15.489
```

Optionally, you can request a test of differences between pairs of groups after each step. When there are only two groups, the *F* value displayed is the same as that for Wilks' lambda for the overall model, as shown in Figure 1.21 and Figure 1.22.

Figure 1.22   F values and significance at step 1

```
DISCRIMINANT GROUPS=SURVIVAL(1,2)
  /VARIABLES=TREATMNT TO RESP
  /METHOD=WILKS
  /STATISTICS=5.

F statistics and significances between pairs of groups after step 1
Each F statistic has    1 and        46.0 degrees of freedom.

                          Group       1
                            DIE
        Group
            2  SURVIVE            15.489
                                   .0003
```

Statistics for Variables Not in the Model

Also displayed at each step is a set of summary statistics for variables not yet in the model. From Figure 1.23, *resp* is the variable that results in the smallest Wilks' lambda for the model if it is entered next. Note that the Wilks' lambda calculated is for the variables *weight* and *resp* jointly. Its *F* test is a multivariate significance test for group differences.

Figure 1.23   Variables not in the analysis after step 1

```
--------------- Variables not in the Analysis after Step 1 ---------------

                          Minimum
Variable   Tolerance   Tolerance   F to Enter    Wilks' Lambda
TREATMNT   .9917361    .9917361     .84207          .73435
TIME       .9548707    .9548707     .64894E-01      .74702
APGAR      .9508910    .9508        .19398E-01      .74777
SEX        .9619762    .9762        .24443          .74406
AGE        .2937327    .2937327    1.0931           .73035
PH         .9845349    .9845349     .60606          .73816
RESP       .9994270    .9994270    5.3111           .66912
```

The *F* value for the change in Wilks' lambda when a variable is added to a model that contains p independent variables is

$$F_{change} = \left(\frac{n - g - p}{g - 1} \right) \left(\frac{1 - \lambda_{p+1}/\lambda_p}{\lambda_{p+1}/\lambda_p} \right) \qquad \textbf{Equation 1.8}$$

where n is the total number of cases, g is the number of groups, λ_p is Wilks' lambda before adding the variable, and λ_{p+1} is Wilks' lambda after inclusion.

If variable *resp* is entered into the model containing variable *weight*, Wilks' lambda is 0.669. The lambda for *weight* alone is 0.748 (see Figure 1.20). The F value for the change, called F-to-enter, is from Equation 1.8:

$$F = \left(\frac{48 - 2 - 1}{2 - 1} \right) \left(\frac{1 - 0.669/0.748}{0.669/0.748} \right) = 5.31 \qquad \text{Equation 1.9}$$

This is the value for *resp* in Figure 1.23.

The Second Step

Figure 1.24 shows the output when *resp* is entered into the model. Wilks' lambda for the model is the same as Wilks' lambda for *resp* in Figure 1.23. If *weight* is removed from the current model, leaving only *resp*, the resulting Wilks' lambda is 0.855, the entry for *weight* in the second part of Figure 1.24. The F value associated with the change in lambda, F-to-remove, is 12.5, which is also displayed in Figure 1.24.

$$F\text{-to-remove} = \frac{(48 - 2 - 1)\ (1 - 0.669/0.855)}{(1)\ (0.669/0.855)} = 12.5 \qquad \text{Equation 1.10}$$

After *weight* and *resp* have both been included in the model, the next variable that would result in the smallest Wilks' lambda if entered is *age*. Its F-to-enter is 1.3783, and the resulting model lambda is 0.64880. Thus, *age* is entered in Step 3.

Figure 1.24   Variable for respiratory therapy included in analysis at step 2

```
At step 2, RESP       was included in the analysis.

                                 Degrees of Freedom  Signif.   Between Groups
Wilks' Lambda          .66912       2    1     46.0
Equivalent F          11.1260            2     45.0    .0001

--------------- Variables in the analysis after step 2 ---------------

Variable  Tolerance  F to Remove  Wilks' Lambda
WEIGHT    .9994270    12.535          .85551
RESP      .9994270     5.3111         .74810

--------------- Variables not in the analysis after step 2 ---------------

                      Minimum
Variable  Tolerance  Tolerance  F to Enter   Wilks' Lambda
TREATMNT  .9917051   .9911962    .71594          .65841
TIME      .9492383   .9492383    .53176E-02      .66904
APGAR     .9231403   .9231403    .25589          .66526
SEX       .8879566   .8879566    .19884E-01      .66882
AGE       .2914116   .2914116   1.3783           .64880
PH        .9828797   .9828797    .66764          .65912
```

The Last Step

After *age* is entered, all *F*-to-remove values are still greater than 1, so no variables are removed. All variables not in the model after step 3 have *F*-to-enter values less than 1, so they are not eligible for inclusion and variable selection stops (see Figure 1.25).

Figure 1.25   AGE included in analysis at step 3

```
At step    3, AGE       was included in the analysis.

                                Degrees of Freedom  Signif.   Between Groups
Wilks' Lambda          0.64880       3   1      46.0
Equivalent F           7.93913           3      44.0  0.0002


--------------- Variables in the analysis after step    3 ---------------

Variable  Tolerance  F to remove   Wilks' Lambda

WEIGHT    0.2926088    8.1466         0.76893
AGE       0.2914116    1.3783         0.66912
RESP      0.9915294    5.5307         0.73035


--------------- Variables not in the analysis after step   3 ---------------
                          Minimum
Variable  Tolerance  Tolerance  F to enter   Wilks' Lambda

TREATMNT  0.9904436  0.2907779   .61371         0.63967
TIME      0.9469645  0.2907135   .22714E-03     0.64880
APGAR     0.8055887  0.2543036   .92868         0.63509
SEX       0.8086141  0.2548962   .45854E-01     0.64811
PH        0.9482218  0.2778589   .34965         0.64357


F statistics and significances between pairs of groups after step    3
Each F statistic has   3 and       44.0 degrees of freedom.
```

Summary Tables

After the last step, SPSS/PC+ displays a summary table (see Figure 1.26). For each step, this table lists the action taken (entry or removal) and the resulting Wilks' lambda and its significance level.

Figure 1.26   Summary table

```
                              Summary Table

               Action    Vars  Wilks'
Step Entered Removed      in    Lambda   Sig.  Label
  1  WEIGHT               1    .74810   .0003  BIRTHWEIGHT IN KILOGRAMS
  2  RESP                 2    .66912   .0001  RESPIRATORY LEVEL
  3  AGE                  3    .64880   .0002  GESTATIONAL AGE
```

Table 1.4 shows the percentage of cases classified correctly at each step of the analysis. The model with variables *weight*, *resp*, and *age* classifies almost 80% of the cases correctly, while the complete model with eight variables classifies 83% of the cases correctly. Including additional variables does not always improve classification. In fact, sometimes the percentage of cases classified correctly actually decreases if poor predictors are included in the model.

Table 1.4   Cases correctly classified by step

Variables included	Percentage classified correctly
weight	68.00
weight, resp	75.00
weight, resp, age	79.17
All eight variables	83.33

Other Criteria for Variable Selection

In previous sections, variables were included in the model based on Wilks' lambda. At each step, the variable that resulted in the smallest Wilks' lambda was selected. Other criteria besides Wilks' lambda are sometimes used for variable selection.

Rao's V

Rao's V, also known as the **Lawley-Hotelling trace**, is defined as

$$V = (n - g) \sum_{i=1}^{p} \sum_{j=1}^{p} w_{ij}^{*} \sum_{k=1}^{g} (\bar{X}_{ik} - \bar{X}_i)(\bar{X}_{jk} - \bar{X}_j) \qquad \text{Equation 1.11}$$

where p is the number of variables in the model, g is the number of groups, n_k is the sample size in the kth group, $\bar{X}_{ik}$ is the mean of the ith variable for the kth group, $\bar{X}_i$ is the mean of the ith variable for all groups combined, and w_{ij}^{*} is an element of the inverse of the within-groups covariance matrix. The larger the differences between group means, the larger the Rao's V.

One way to evaluate the contribution of a variable is to see how much it increases Rao's V when it is added to the model. The sampling distribution of V is approximately a chi-square with $p(g - 1)$ degrees of freedom. A test of the significance of the change in Rao's V when a variable is included can also be based on the chi-square distribution. It is possible for a variable to actually decrease Rao's V when it is added to a model.

Mahalanobis Distance

Mahalanobis distance, D^2, is a generalized measure of the distance between two groups. The distance between groups a and b is defined as

$$D_{ab}^{2} = (n - g) \sum_{i=1}^{p} \sum_{j=1}^{p} w_{ij}^{*} (\bar{X}_{ia} - \bar{X}_{ib})(\bar{X}_{ja} - \bar{X}_{jb}) \qquad \text{Equation 1.12}$$

where p is the number of variables in the model, $\overline{X}_{ia}$ is the mean for the ith variable in group a, and w_{ij}^{*} is an element from the inverse of the within-groups covariance matrix.

When Mahalanobis distance is the criterion for variable selection, the Mahalanobis distances between all pairs of groups are calculated first. The variable that has the largest D^2 for the two groups that are closest (have the smallest D^2 initially) is selected for inclusion.

Between-Groups F

A test of the null hypothesis that the two sets of population means are equal can be based on Mahalanobis distance. The corresponding F statistic is:

$$F = \frac{(n-1-p)\,n_1 n_2}{p\,(n-2)\,(n_1+n_2)} D_{ab}^2 \qquad \text{Equation 1.13}$$

This F value can also be used for variable selection. At each step, the variable chosen for inclusion is the one with the largest F value. Since the Mahalanobis distance is weighted by the sample sizes when the between-groups F is used as the criterion for stepwise selection, the results from the two methods may differ.

Sum of Unexplained Variance

As mentioned previously, two-group discriminant analysis is analogous to multiple regression in which the dependent variable is either 0 or 1, depending on the group to which a case belongs. In fact, the Mahalanobis distance and R^2 are proportional. Thus:

$$R^2 = cD^2 \qquad \text{Equation 1.14}$$

For each pair of groups, a and b, the unexplained variation from the regression is $1 - R_{ab}^2$, where R_{ab}^2 is the square of the multiple correlation coefficient when a variable coded as 0 or 1 (depending on whether the case is a member of a or b) is considered the dependent variable.

The sum of the unexplained variation for all pairs of groups can also be used as a criterion for variable selection. The variable chosen for inclusion is the one that minimizes the sum of the unexplained variation.

Three-Group Discriminant Analysis

The previous example used discriminant analysis to distinguish between members of two groups. This section presents a three-group discriminant example. The basics are the same as in two-group discriminant analysis, although there are several additional considerations.

One of the early applications of discriminant analysis in business was for credit-granting decisions. Many different models for extending credit based on a variety of predictor variables have been proposed. Churchill (1979) describes the case of the Consumer Finance Company, which must screen credit applicants. It has available for analysis 30 cases known to be poor, equivocal, and good credit risks. For each case, the annual income (in thousands of dollars), the number of credit cards, the number of children, and the age of the head of household are known. The task is to use discriminant analysis to derive a classification scheme for new cases based on the available data.

The Number of Functions

With two groups, it is possible to derive one discriminant function that maximizes the ratio of between- to within-groups sums of squares. When there are three groups, two discriminant functions can be calculated (assuming there are two or more predictors). The first function, as in the two-group case, has the largest ratio of between-groups to within-groups sums of squares. The second function is uncorrelated with the first and has the next largest ratio. In general, if there are k groups, $k-1$ discriminant functions can be computed. They are all uncorrelated with each other and maximize the ratio of between-groups to within-groups sums of squares, subject to the constraint of being uncorrelated.

Figure 1.27 contains the two sets of unstandardized discriminant function coefficients for the credit risk example. Based on these coefficients, it is possible to compute two scores for each case, one for each function. Consider, for example, the first case in

Figure 1.27   Unstandardized canonical discriminant function coefficients

```
DSCRIMINANT GROUPS=RISK(1,3)
  /VARIABLES=INCOME TO CHILDREN
  /STATISTICS=11.
Unstandardized Canonical Discriminant Function Coefficients

                  FUNC   1         FUNC   2

   INCOME          .3257077        -.2251991
   CREDIT          .1344126        -.5564818E-02
   AGEHEAD         .2444825         .1497008
   CHILDREN        .1497964         .1778159
   (Constant)    -14.46811        -2.540298
```

the file with an annual income of $9,200, two credit cards, three children, and a 27-year-old head of household. For function 1, the discriminant score is:

$$D_{11} = -14.47 + 0.33\,(9.2) + 0.13\,(2) + 0.24\,(27) + 0.15\,(3) \; = \; -4.2 \qquad \textbf{Equation 1.15}$$

The discriminant score for function 2 is obtained the same way, using the coefficients for the second function. Figure 1.28 shows the discriminant scores and other classification information for the first 15 cases. The score for function 1 is shown on the first row for a case; the second discriminant score is shown on the second row.

Figure 1.28 Classification output

```
DSCRIMINANT GROUPS=RISK(1,3)
   /VARIABLES=INCOME TO CHILDREN
   /STATISTICS=14.
```

Case Number	Mis Val	Sel	Actual Group	Highest Probability Group	P(D/G)	P(G/D)	2nd Highest Group	P(G/D)	Discrim Scores
1			1	1	.8229	.9993	2	.0007	-4.1524
									-.0479
2			1	1	.2100	.9999	2	.0001	-4.7122
									-1.3738
3			1	1	.7864	.9885	2	.0115	-3.3119
									.5959
4			1	1	.8673	.9718	2	.0282	-2.9966
									-.0155
5			1	1	.7610	.9646	2	.0354	-2.9464
									.3933
6			1	1	.8797	.9865	2	.0135	-3.2056
									-.4530
7			1	1	.7589	.9995	2	.0005	-4.2685
									-.1243
8			1	1	.5684	.9812	2	.0188	-3.1762
									.9402
9			1	1	.8191	.9980	2	.0020	-3.7851
									-.6398
10			1	1	.7160	.9336	2	.0664	-2.7267
									.0973
11			2	2	.9923	.9938	1	.0060	-.3287
									-.0043
12			2	2	.7764	.9922	1	.0076	-.3718
									-.5939
13			2	2	.6003	.9938	3	.0059	.5383
									.6958
14			2	2	.2482	.6334	1	.3666	-1.7833
									.8513
15			2	2	.5867	.9856	3	.0143	.7262
									-.0908

Classification

When there is one discriminant function, classification of cases into groups is based on the values for the single function. When there are several groups, a case's values on all functions must be considered simultaneously.

Figure 1.29 contains group means for the two functions. Group 1 has negative means for both functions, group 2 has a negative mean for function 1 and a positive mean for function 2, while group 3 has a positive mean for function 1 and a slightly negative mean for function 2.

Figure 1.29 Canonical discriminant function—group means

```
DSCRIMINANT GROUPS=RISK(1,3)
  /VARIABLES=INCOME TO CHILDREN


Canonical Discriminant Functions evaluated at Group Means (Group Centroids)

    Group      Func  1     Func  2
      1       -3.52816     -.06276
      2        -.28634      .11238
      3        3.81449     -.04962
```

Figure 1.30 shows the **territorial map** for the three groups on the two functions. The mean for each group is indicated by an asterisk (*). The numbered boundaries mark off the combination of function values that result in the classification of the cases into the three groups. All cases with values that fall into the region bordered by the 3's are classified into the third group, those that fall into the region bordered by 2's are assigned to the second group, and so on.

Figure 1.30 Territorial map

```
DSCRIMINANT GROUPS=RISK(1,3)
  /VARIABLES=INCOME TO CHILDREN
  /STATISTICS=10.

Symbols used in territorial map

Symbol  Group  Label
------  -----  --------------------
  1       1    POOR RISK
  2       2    EQUIVOCAL RISK
  3       3    GOOD RISK
  *            Group Centroids
```

```
         +--+--+--+--+--+--+--+--+
    8.0 +             12    23            +
                      12    23
                      12    23
                      122   23
                      112   23
    4.0 +    +    +    12 +  23    +    +  +
                      12    23
                      12    23
                      12    23
                      12    223
     .0 +    +    +* 12 *+  233   *    +  +
                      12    23
                      122   23
                      112   23
                      12    23
   -4.0 +    +    + +12 +  23     +    +  +
                      12    23
                      12    23
                      12    23
                      12    23
   -8.0 +            12    23            +
         +--+--+--+--+--+--+--+--+
       -8.0 -6.0 -4.0 -2.0  .0  2.0 4.0 6.0 8.0
```

Territorial Map

* indicates a
  group centroid

Across: Function 1
Down: Function 2

Figure 1.31 is a plot of the values of the two discriminant scores for each case. From Figure 1.30 and Figure 1.31 you can see approximately how many cases are misclassified. For example, the case at the (1.6,1.6) coordinates is a good credit risk but falls into the equivocal risk region.

Figure 1.31   All-groups scatterplot

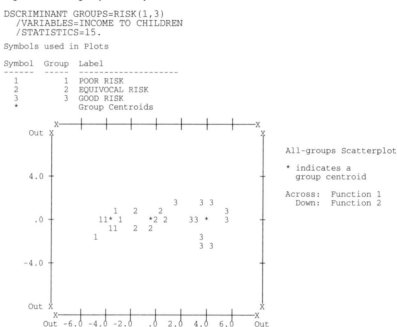

Figure 1.32 is the summary of the classification results. The diagonal elements are the number of cases classified correctly into the groups. For example, all poor and equivocal risks are classified correctly (10 out of 10 in each group). One of the good risks is misclassified as an equivocal risk. The overall percentage of cases classified correctly is the sum of the number of cases classified correctly in each group divided by the total number of cases. In this example, 29 out of 30 cases (96.67%) are classified correctly.

Figure 1.32 Classification table

```
DSCRIMINANT GROUPS=RISK(1,3)
  /VARIABLES=INCOME TO CHILDREN
  /STATISTICS=13.


Classification Results -

                       No. of   Predicted Group Membership
      Actual Group     Cases        1         2         3
--------------------   ------   --------  --------  --------

Group        1           10        10         0         0
POOR RISK                       100.0%      .0%       .0%

Group        2           10         0        10         0
EQUIVOCAL RISK                     .0%    100.0%       .0%

Group        3           10         0         1         9
GOOD RISK                          .0%     10.0%     90.0%

Percent of "grouped" cases correctly classified:  96.67%

Classification processing summary
        30 cases were processed.
         0 cases were excluded for missing or out-of-range group codes.
         0 cases had at least one missing discriminating variable.
        30 cases were used for printed output.
```

Additional Statistics

When more than one discriminant function is derived, several statistics other than those discussed in "Other Discriminant Function Statistics" on p. 17 are of interest. Consider Figure 1.33. For each function, the **eigenvalue** is the ratio of between-groups to within-groups sums of squares. From Figure 1.34 (the analysis-of-variance tables for the two functions), the eigenvalue for function 1 is 10.03 ($270.8/27$). For function 2, it is 0.007 ($0.19/27$).

Figure 1.33 Additional statistics

```
DSCRIMINANT GROUPS=RISK(1,3)
  /VARIABLES=INCOME TO CHILDREN.


                    Canonical Discriminant Functions


                 Pct of   Cum  Canonical  After  Wilks'
    Fcn Eigenvalue Variance Pct    Corr     Fcn  Lambda  Chisquare  df  Sig
                                          :   0   .0900    61.394     8  .0000
    1*    10.0297   99.93  99.93   .9536  :   1   .9930      .179     3  .9809
    2*      .0070     .07 100.00   .0837  :

    * marks the   2 canonical discriminant functions remaining in the analysis.
```

Figure 1.34   One-way analysis of variance for the two functions

```
DSCRIMINANT GROUPS=RISK(1,3)
  /VARIABLES=INCOME TO CHILDREN
  /SAVE=SCORES=DISCORE.
ONEWAY DISCORE1 TO DISCORE2 BY RISK(1,3).
```

```
- - - - - - - - - - - - - - - - - O N E W A Y - - - - - - - - - - - - - - - - - -

        Variable  DISCORE1     FUNCTION 1 FOR ANALYSIS 1

    By Variable  RISK


                            Analysis of Variance

                            Sum of         Mean          F      F
        Source         D.F.  Squares      Squares       Ratio  Prob.

Between Groups          2    270.8023     135.4011     135.4011  .0000

Within Groups          27     27.0000       1.0000

Total                  29    297.8023

- - - - - - - - - - - - - - - - - O N E W A Y - - - - - - - - - - - - - - - - - -

        Variable  DISCORE2     FUNCTION 2 FOR ANALYSIS 1

    By Variable  RISK


                            Analysis of Variance

                            Sum of         Mean          F      F
        Source         D.F.  Squares      Squares       Ratio  Prob.

Between Groups          2      .1903        .0951        .0951  .9095

Within Groups          27     27.0000       1.0000

Total                  29     27.1903
```

The canonical correlation for a function is the square root of the between-groups to total sums of squares. When squared, it is the proportion of total variability explained by differences between groups. For example, for function 1 the canonical correlation is:

$$\sqrt{\frac{270.8}{297.8}} = 0.954 \qquad \qquad \textbf{Equation 1.16}$$

When two or more functions are derived, it may be of interest to compare their merits. One frequently encountered criterion is the percentage of the total between-groups variability attributable to each function. Remember from the two-group example that the canonical discriminant functions are derived so that the pooled within-groups variance is 1. (This is seen in Figure 1.34 by the value of 1 for the within-groups mean square.) Thus, each function differs only in the between-groups sum of squares.

The first function always has the largest between-groups variability. The remaining functions have successively less between-groups variability. From Figure 1.33, function 1 accounts for 99.93% of the total between-groups variability:

$$\frac{\text{between-groups SS for function 1}}{\text{between-groups SS for function 1 + between-groups SS for function 2}} = 0.9993$$

Equation 1.17

Function 2 accounts for the remaining 0.07% of the between-groups variability. These values are listed in the column labeled *Pct of Variance* in Figure 1.33. The next column, *Cum Pct*, is simply the sum of the percentage of variance of that function and the preceding ones.

Testing the Significance of the Discriminant Functions

When there are no differences among the populations from which the samples are selected, the discriminant functions reflect only sampling variability. A test of the null hypothesis that the means of all discriminant functions in all groups in the population are really equal and 0 can be based on Wilks' lambda. Since several functions must be considered simultaneously, Wilks' lambda is not just the ratio of the between-groups to within-groups sums of squares but is the product of the univariate Wilks' lambda for each function. For example, the Wilks' lambda for both functions considered simultaneously is, from Figure 1.34:

$$\Lambda = \left(\frac{27}{297.8}\right)\left(\frac{27}{27.19}\right) = 0.09$$
Equation 1.18

The significance level of the observed Wilks' lambda can be based on a chi-square transformation of the statistic. The value of lambda and its associated chi-square value, the degrees of freedom, and the significance level are shown in the right half of Figure 1.33, in the first row. Since the observed significance level is less than 0.00005, the null hypothesis that the means of both functions are equal in the three populations can be rejected.

When more than one function is derived, you can successively test the means of the functions by first testing all means simultaneously and then excluding one function at a time, testing the means of the remaining functions at each step. Using such successive tests, it is possible to find that a subset of discriminant functions accounts for all differences and that additional functions do not reflect true population differences, only random variation.

As shown in Figure 1.33, SPSS/PC+ displays Wilks' lambda and the associated statistics as functions are removed successively. The column labeled *After Fcn* contains the number of the last function removed. The 0 indicates that no functions are removed, while a value of 2 indicates that the first two functions have been removed. For this example, the Wilks' lambda associated with function 2 after function 1 has been removed is 0.993. Since it is the last remaining function, the Wilks' lambda obtained is just the univariate value from Figure 1.34. The significance level associated with the second function is 0.981, indicating that it does not contribute substantially to group differences. This can also be seen in Figure 1.31, since only the first function determines the classification boundaries. All three groups have similar values for function 2.

Figure 1.35 is a classification map that illustrates the situation in which both functions contribute to group separation. In other words, a case's values on both functions are important for classification. For example, a case with a value of –2 for the first discriminant function will be classified into group 2 if the second function is negative and into group 1 if the second function is positive.

Figure 1.35   Territorial map

```
DISCRIMINANT GROUPS=SURVIVAL(1,3)
  /VARIABLES=TREATMNT TO RESP
  /STATISTICS=10.


Symbol  Group  Label
------  -----  --------------------
  1       1    POOR RISK
  2       2    EQUIVOCAL RISK
  3       3    GOOD RISK
```

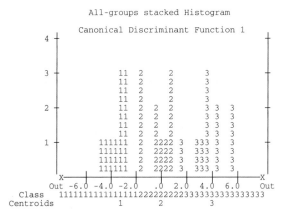

```
                 All-groups stacked Histogram

              Canonical Discriminant Function 1
       4 +                                            +



       3 +         11  2     2        3
                   11  2     2        3
                   11  2     2        3
                   11  2     2        3
       2 +         11  2  2  2        3  3  3
                   11  2  2  2        3  3  3
                   11  2  2  2        3  3  3
                   11  2  2  2        3  3  3
       1 +     111111  2  2222 3   333 3  3
               111111  2  2222 3   333 3  3
               111111  2  2222 3   333 3  3
               111111  2  2222 3   333 3  3
            X-+--+--+--+--+--+--+--+--X
           Out -6.0 -4.0 -2.0  .0  2.0  4.0  6.0  Out
     Class    1111111111111111122222222223333333333333333
   Centroids        1         2         3
```

Classification with One Function

Instead of using all available functions to classify cases into groups, you can restrict the functions to the subset that has substantial between-groups variability. Eliminating weak functions should result in a more stable classification rule, since some of the sampling variability is removed.

When only one discriminant function is used to classify the credit risk cases, 96.67% of the cases are still classified correctly, as shown in Figure 1.36.

Figure 1.36   Classification with one table

```
DSCRIMINANT GROUPS=RISK(1,3)
   /VARIABLES=INCOME TO CHILDREN
   /FUNCTIONS= 1
   /STATISTICS=13.


Classification Results -

                          No. of    Predicted Group Membership
      Actual Group        Cases        1          2          3
 --------------------     ------    --------   --------   --------
 Group        1            10          10          0          0
 POOR RISK                           100.0%        .0%        .0%

 Group        2            10           0         10          0
 EQUIVOCAL RISK                         .0%      100.0%        .0%

 Group        3            10           0          1          9
 GOOD RISK                              .0%       10.0%      90.0%

 Percent of "grouped" cases correctly classified:  96.67%
```

Figure 1.37 shows the all-groups histogram for the single discriminant function. Large negative values are associated with poor risks, large positive values with good risks, and small positive and negative values with equivocal risks.

Figure 1.37   All-groups histogram

```
DSCRIMINANT GROUPS=RISK(1,3)
   /VARIABLES=INCOME TO CHILDREN
   /FUNCTIONS=1
   /STATISTICS=15.
                     All-groups stacked Histogram

               Canonical Discriminant Function 1
        4 +                                                  +
          |                                                  |
          |                                                  |
          |                                                  |
        3 +          11  2      2       3                    +
          |          11  2      2       3                    |
          |          11  2      2       3                    |
          |          11  2      2       3                    |
        2 +          11  2  2   2       3  3  3              +
          |          11  2  2   2       3  3  3              |
          |          11  2  2   2       3  3  3              |
          |          11  2  2   2       3  3  3              |
        1 +        111111  2  2222 3  333 3   3              +
          |        111111  2  2222 3  333 3   3              |
          |        111111  2  2222 3  333 3   3              |
          |        111111  2  2222 3  333 3   3              |
          X----+----+----+----+----+----+----+----X
         Out -6.0 -4.0 -2.0  0.0  2.0  4.0  6.0   Out
   Class 111111111111111111222222222233333333333333333
 Centroids         1         2            3
```

The Variables

To assess the contribution of each variable to the discriminant functions, you can compute standardized coefficients. From Figure 1.38, income and age of the head of household appear to be the variables with the largest standardized coefficients.

Figure 1.38   Standardized canonical discriminant functions

```
DSCRIMINANT GROUPS=RISK(1,3)
  /VARIABLES=INCOME TO CHILDREN.

Standardized Canonical Discriminant Function Coefficients

            FUNC  1     FUNC  2

INCOME       .89487     -.61872
CREDIT       .31363     -.01298
AGEHEAD      .84508      .51746
CHILDREN     .22936      .27226
```

Another way to examine the contributions of the variables is to examine the correlation coefficients between the variables and the functions, as shown in Figure 1.39. To help you interpret the functions, variables with large coefficients for a particular function are grouped together. These groupings are indicated with asterisks.

Figure 1.39   Correlations between variables and functions

```
DSCRIMINANT GROUPS=RISK(1,3)
  /VARIABLES=INCOME TO CHILDREN
  /STATISTICS=4.

Structure Matrix:

Pooled-within-groups correlations between discriminating variables
                          and canonical discriminant functions
(Variables ordered by size of correlation within function)

            FUNC  1     FUNC  2
CREDIT       .22728*     .19774
INCOME       .48482     -.84832*
AGEHEAD      .58577      .72023*
CHILDREN    -.00069      .38568*
```

When Assumptions Are Violated

As previously indicated, the linear discriminant function minimizes the probability of misclassification if in each group the variables are from multivariate normal distributions and the covariance matrices for all groups are equal. A variety of tests for multivariate normality are available (see Andrews et al., 1973). A simple tactic is to examine first the distributions of each of the variables individually. If the variables are jointly distributed as a multivariate normal, it follows that each is individually distributed normally. Therefore, if any of the variables have markedly non-normal distributions, there is reason to suspect that the multivariate normality assumption is violated. However, if all variables are normally distributed, the joint distribution is not necessarily multivariate normal.

There are several ways to test equality of the group covariance matrices. SPSS/PC+ displays **Box's *M* test**, which is based on the determinants of the group covariance matrices. As shown in Figure 1.40, the significance probability is based on an *F* transformation. A small probability might lead us to reject the null hypothesis that the covariance matrices are equal. However, when sample sizes in the groups are large, the significance probability may be small even if the group covariance matrices are not too dissimilar. The test is also sensitive to departures from multivariate normality. That is, it tends to call matrices unequal if the normality assumption is violated.

Figure 1.40   Test of equality of group covariance matrices

```
DSCRIMINANT GROUPS=SURVIVAL(1,2)
  /VARIABLES=TREATMNT TO RESP
  /METHOD=WILKS
  /STATISTICS=7.

Test of equality of group covariance matrices using Box's M

  The ranks and natural logarithms of determinants printed are those
  of the group covariance matrices.

      Group Label                    Rank   Log Determinant
          1 DIE                        3        -1.722152
          2 SURVIVE                    3        -1.902866
      Pooled Within-Groups
      Covariance Matrix                3        -1.698666

    Box's M        Approximate F   Degrees of freedom  Significance
    4.8753            .75422         6,      14168.3       .6058
```

If the covariance matrices are unequal but the joint distribution of the variables is multivariate normal, the optimum classification rule is the quadratic discriminant function. However, if the covariance matrices are not too dissimilar, the linear discriminant function performs quite well, especially if the sample sizes are small (Wahl & Kronmal, 1977). Simulation studies suggest that with small sample sizes the quadratic rule can perform quite poorly. Since SPSS/PC+ uses the discriminant function values to classify cases, not the original variables, it is not possible to obtain the optimum quadratic rule. (When covariance matrices are assumed identical, classification based on the original variables and all canonical functions are equivalent.) However, results obtained using the functions and their covariance matrices might not be too different from those obtained using covariance matrices for the original variables (Tatsuoka, 1971). For two groups, SPSS/PC+ Logistic Regression (available in the Advanced Statistics option), which does not require multivariate normality, can also be considered.

In situations where the independent variables are all binary (yes–no, male–female) or a mixture of continuous and discrete variables, the linear discriminant function is not optimal. A variety of nonparametric procedures as well as special procedures for binary variables are available (see Hand, 1981; Goldstein & Dillon, 1978). In the case of dichotomous variables, most evidence suggests that the linear discriminant function often performs reasonably well (Gilbert, 1968; Moore, 1973). The SPSS/PC+ Logistic Regression procedure can also be used to classify cases into one of two groups. It requires much more limited assumptions about the distributions of the data. (See the Logistic Regression chapter in *SPSS/PC+ Advanced Statistics*.)

Running the Discriminant Procedure

The Discriminant procedure provides six methods for obtaining discriminant functions: forced entry and five stepwise procedures. You can use the discriminant functions to classify cases, and you can assess the accuracy of these classifications by examining classification results tables, plots of classified cases, and other statistical output provided by DSCRIMINANT.

Only two subcommands are required to obtain discriminant functions using the forced-entry method: the GROUPS subcommand, which specifies the grouping variable; and the VARIABLES subcommand, which specifies the predictor variables. These subcommands produce the eigenvalue and Wilks' lambda for each function, the standardized discriminant-function coefficients, the pooled within-groups correlations between the discriminant scores and the predictor variables, and the group centroids. To obtain unstandardized discriminant function coefficients, you must use the STATISTICS subcommand (see "Specifying Optional Statistics" on p. 50).

Specifying the Groups

Use the GROUPS subcommand to specify the grouping variable and its range of values. For example, the subcommand `/GROUPS=RISK(1,3)` indicates that *risk* is the grouping variable, with integer values from 1 to 3. This subcommand produces a three-group analysis. If there were no cases for one of the specified *risk* values, DSCRIMINANT would perform a two-group analysis.

Cases with values outside the range specified for the grouping variable are not used to obtain the discriminant functions. However, such cases are classified into one of the existing groups if classification is requested.

You can specify only one GROUPS subcommand per DSCRIMINANT command.

Specifying the Variables

List all variables to be used as predictor variables on the VARIABLES subcommand. You can specify only numeric variables, and you can use only one VARIABLES subcommand per DSCRIMINANT command.

Example

```
DSCRIMINANT GROUPS=SURVIVAL(1,2)
  /VARIABLES=TREATMENT TO RESP
```

• This command produces the output in Figure 1.1, Figure 1.13, Figure 1.16, and Figure 1.17.

Specifying the Analyses

Use the ANALYSIS subcommand to specify several discriminant analyses, each with the same grouping variable but different predictor variables. Name all variables to be used in your analysis on the VARIABLES subcommand, and then use the ANALYSIS subcommand to specify subsets of these variables for particular analyses. In this way, you can specify several analyses on a single DSCRIMINANT command.

The variable list on ANALYSIS follows the usual SPSS/PC+ conventions for variable lists with one exception: the TO keyword refers to the order of variables on the VARIABLES subcommand, not their order in the active file. You can use the keyword ALL to refer to all variables listed on the VARIABLES subcommand. A maximum of ten ANALYSIS subcommands are allowed in any one execution of DSCRIMINANT.

Example

```
DSCRIMINANT GROUPS=RISK(1,3)
  /VARIABLES=INCOME CREDIT AGEHEAD CHILDREN
  /ANALYSIS=INCOME CREDIT
  /ANALYSIS=INCOME TO CHILDREN.
```

- This command produces two discriminant analyses, both with *risk* as the grouping variable.

- The first analysis uses *income* and *credit* as the predictor variables. The second analysis uses *income, credit, agehead,* and *children* as the predictor variables.

Specifying the Selection Method

Use the METHOD subcommand to specify the method for selecting variables for inclusion in the discriminant analysis. The METHOD subcommand must follow the ANALYSIS subcommand (or after the VARIABLES subcommand if ANALYSIS is not used). Each METHOD subcommand applies only to the previous ANALYSIS subcommand or to the default analysis if ANALYSIS is omitted.

DIRECT   *Forced entry.* All variables named on the VARIABLES or ANALYSIS subcommand are entered simultaneously (if they satisfy tolerance criteria). This is the default. (See "Investigating Respiratory Distress Syndrome" on p. 2 through "Relationship to Multiple Regression Analysis" on p. 22.)

WILKS   *Stepwise analysis based on minimizing the overall Wilks' lambda.* (See "Variable Selection Criteria" on p. 23 through "Summary Tables" on p. 28.)

RAO   *Stepwise analysis based on maximizing the increase in Rao's V.* (See "Rao's V" on p. 29.)

MAHAL   *Stepwise analysis based on maximizing Mahalanobis distance between the two closest groups.* (See "Mahalanobis Distance" on p. 29.)

MAXMINF   *Stepwise analysis based on maximizing the smallest F ratio for pairs of groups.* (See "Between-Groups F" on p. 30.)

MINRESID   *Stepwise analysis based on minimizing the sum of unexplained variation between groups.* (See "Sum of Unexplained Variance" on p. 30.)

To obtain forced entry, omit the METHOD subcommand or use keyword DIRECT.

Example

```
DSCRIMINANT GROUPS=RISK(1,3)
  /VARIABLES=INCOME CREDIT AGEHEAD CHILDREN
  /METHOD=WILKS.
```

- This command produces a stepwise analysis based on Wilks' lambda.

Inclusion Levels

When you specify a stepwise method, you can use the ANALYSIS subcommand to control the order in which variables are considered for entry. By default, variables are examined for entry or removal on the basis of their partial F values. To control the order in which sets of variables are examined, specify an inclusion level in parentheses following the sets of variables on the ANALYSIS subcommand. The inclusion level can be any integer between 0 and 99.

- The inclusion level controls the order in which variables are entered, the way in which they are entered, and whether or not they should be considered for removal according to the rules outlined below. All variables must still pass the tolerance criterion to be entered.

- Variables with higher inclusion levels are considered for entry before variables with lower levels. Variables do not have to be ordered by their inclusion level on the subcommand itself.

- Variables with even inclusion levels are entered together.

- Variables with odd inclusion levels are entered one variable at a time according to the stepwise method specified on the METHOD subcommand.

- Only variables with an inclusion level of 1 may be considered for removal. To make a variable with a higher inclusion level eligible for removal, name it twice on the ANALYSIS subcommand, first specifying the desired inclusion level and then an inclusion level of 1.

- An inclusion level of 0 prevents a variable from being entered, although an entry criterion is computed and displayed.

- The default inclusion level is 1.

Example

```
DSCRIMINANT GROUPS=SURVIVAL(1,2)
  /VARIABLES=SEX TO RESP
  /ANALYSIS SEX TO RESP(2)
             SEX TO RESP(1)
  /METHOD=WILKS.
```

- This command enters all variables meeting the tolerance criteria and then removes those meeting removal criteria..

Specifying the Number of Steps

By default, the maximum number of steps in a stepwise analysis is twice the number of variables with inclusion level of 1 (the default), plus the number of variables with inclusion level greater than 1. Use the MAXSTEPS subcommand to decrease the maximum. Specify MAXSTEPS after the METHOD subcommand. Supply the desired maximum number of steps (*n*), for example, /MAXSTEPS=3 . The specification applies only to the previous ANALYSIS subcommand.

Setting Statistical Criteria

Several subcommands are available to override the default statistical criteria for discriminant analysis. Specify these subcommands, in any order, *after* the METHOD subcommand. These subcommands apply only to the previous ANALYSIS subcommand. For further discussion of the criteria, see "Variable Selection Criteria" on p. 23 unless otherwise referenced.

TOLERANCE=n *Tolerance level.* The default tolerance level is 0.001. You can reset it to any decimal number between 0 and 1. This sets the minimum tolerance as well as the tolerance for individual variables.

FIN=n *F-to-enter.* The default *F*-to-enter is 1.0. You may reset it to any non-negative number.

FOUT=n *F-to-remove.* The default *F*-to-remove is 1.0. You may reset it to any non-negative number.

PIN=n *Probability of* F-*to-enter.* Use PIN to maintain a fixed significance level as the entry criterion. You can specify any number between 0 and 1. There is no default value. When PIN is not specified, FIN is used.

POUT=n *Probability of* F-*to-remove.* Use POUT to maintain a fixed significance level as the removal criterion. You can specify any number between 0 and 1. There is no default value. When POUT is not specified, FOUT is used.

VIN=n *Rao's* V-*to-enter.* The default value is 0. (See "Rao's V" on p. 29.)

Example

```
DSCRIMINANT GROUPS=RISK(1,3)
  /VARIABLES=INCOME CREDIT AGEHEAD CHILDREN
  /ANALYSIS=INCOME CREDIT
  /TOLERANCE=.01
  /ANALYSIS=INCOME TO CHILDREN
  /METHOD=RAO
  /VIN=.01.
```

- This command requests two discriminant analyses. The first requests a forced entry with the tolerance criterion reset to 0.01, and the second requests a stepwise analysis based on Rao's *V*, with the increase in Rao's *V* required to be at least 0.01 for entry.

Specifying the Number of Functions

By default, DSCRIMINANT calculates all discriminant functions available. To reduce the number of functions obtained, specify the number of functions desired on the FUNCTIONS subcommand, for example, /FUNCTIONS=1. FUNCTIONS applies only to the previous ANALYSIS subcommand.

Selecting Cases

Use the SELECT subcommand to select a subset of cases for computing basic statistics and coefficients. You can then use these coefficients to classify either all the cases or only the unselected cases. The SELECT subcommand must precede the first ANALYSIS subcommand. It remains in effect for all analyses.

The specification for the SELECT subcommand is a variable name followed by a value in parentheses. Only cases with the specified value on the selection variable are used during the analysis phase. The value must be an integer.

Example

```
DSCRIMINANT GROUPS=TYPE(1,5) /VARIABLES=A TO H
  /SELECT=LASTYEAR(81).
```

- This command limits the analysis phase to cases containing the value 81 for variable *lastyear*.

- By default, DSCRIMINANT reports classification statistics separately for selected and unselected cases. To limit classification to unselected cases, use the options described in "Specifying Options" on p. 48.

Specifying the Prior Probabilities

By default, DSCRIMINANT assumes the prior probabilities of group membership to be equal. You can specify other prior probabilities with the PRIORS subcommand. It follows the ANALYSIS subcommand and applies only to the previous ANALYSIS subcommand. You can specify any of the following:

EQUAL   *Equal prior probabilities.* This is the default specification.

SIZE   *Sample proportion of cases actually falling into each group.*

value list *User-specified list of probabilities.* These must sum to 1, and there must be as many probabilities as there are groups.

Example

```
DSCRIMINANT GROUPS=RISK(1,3)
  /VARIABLES=INCOME CREDIT AGEHEAD CHILDREN
  /PRIORS=.2 .4 .4.
```

• This command specifies a prior probability of 0.2 for the first *risk* group and 0.4 for the second and third groups.

Saving Discriminant Statistics

Much of the casewise information produced by Statistic 14 (see "Discriminant Scores and Membership Probabilities" on p. 51) can be added to the active file. Use the SAVE subcommand to specify the type of information to be saved and assign variable names to each piece of information. Three different types of variables can be saved using the following keywords:

CLASS   *Save a variable containing the predicted group value.*

PROBS   *Save posterior probabilities of group membership for each case.* For example, if you have three groups, the first probability is the probability of the case being in group 1 given its discriminant scores, the second probability is its probability of being in group 2, and the third probability is its probability of being in group 3. Since DSCRIMINANT produces more than one probability, you need to supply a rootname up to seven characters long. DSCRIMINANT creates a set of variables by adding a sequential number to the rootname.

SCORES *Save the discriminant scores.* The number of scores equals the number of functions derived. As with the PROBS parameter, specify a rootname up to seven characters long.

Example

```
DSCRIMINANT GROUPS=RISK(1,3)
  /VARIABLES=INCOME CREDIT AGEHEAD CHILDREN
  /SAVE=CLASS=PRDCLAS SCORES=SCORE PROBS=PRB.
```

• Since the number of groups is three, DSCRIMINANT adds the six variables illustrated in Table 1.5 to the active file.

Table 1.5   Saved casewise results

Name	Description
prdclas	Predicted Group
score1	Discriminant score for Function 1
score2	Discriminant score for Function 2
prb1	Probability of being in Risk Group 1
prb2	Probability of being in Risk Group 2
prb3	Probability of being in Risk Group 3

Only the types of variables specified are saved. You can specify the keywords in any order, but the order in which the variables are added to the file is fixed. The group variable (CLASS) is always written first, followed by discriminant scores (SCORES) and probabilities (PROBS). Variable labels are provided automatically for the newly saved variables. Any value labels defined for the group variable are also saved for the predicted-group variable.

The SAVE subcommand applies only to the previous ANALYSIS subcommand. If there are multiple analyses and you want to save casewise materials from each, use multiple SAVE subcommands. Be sure to use different rootnames.

Specifying Options

You can request the following options by using the OPTIONS subcommand with the DSCRIMINANT command:

Missing Values

By default, cases missing on any of the variables named on the VARIABLES subcommand and cases out of range or missing on the GROUPS subcommand are not used during the analysis phase. Cases missing or out of range for the variable specified on the GROUPS subcommand are used during the classification phase.

Option 1   *Include user-missing values.* User-missing values are treated as valid values. Only the system-missing value is treated as missing.

Option 8   *Substitute means for missing values during classification.* Cases with missing values are not used during analysis. During classification, means are substituted for missing values and cases containing missing values are classified.

Display Options

Two options are available to reduce the amount of output produced during stepwise analysis.

Option 4   *Suppress display of step-by-step output.*

Option 5   *Suppress display of the summary table.*

These two options only affect display, not the computation of intermediate results.

Rotation Options

The pattern and structure matrices displayed during the analysis phase can be rotated to facilitate interpretation of results.

Option 6   *Rotate pattern matrix.*

Option 7   *Rotate structure matrix.*

Neither Option 6 nor Option 7 affects the classification of cases since the rotation is orthogonal.

Classification Options

Three options related to the classification phase are available via the associated OPTIONS subcommand.

Option 9   *Classify only unselected cases.* If you use the SELECT subcommand, by default DSCRIMINANT classifies all nonmissing cases. Two sets of classification results are produced, one for the selected cases and one for the nonselected cases. Option 9 suppresses the classification phase for cases selected via the SELECT subcommand.

Option 10   *Classify only unclassified cases.* Cases whose values on the grouping variable fall outside the range specified on the GROUPS subcommand are considered initially unclassified. During classification, these ungrouped cases are classified as a separate entry in the classification results table. Option 10 suppresses classification of cases that fall into the range specified on the GROUPS subcommand and classifies only cases falling outside the range.

Option 11   *Use separate-group covariance matrices of the discriminant functions for classification.* By default, DSCRIMINANT uses the pooled within-groups covariance matrix to classify cases. Option 11 uses the separate-group covariance matrices for classification. However, since classification is based on the discriminant functions and not the original variables, this option is not equivalent to quadratic discrimination (Tatsuoka, 1971).

Specifying Optional Statistics

You can request the following optional statistics by using the STATISTICS subcommand with the DSCRIMINANT command:

Statistic 1   *Means.* Total and group means for all variables named on the ANALYSIS subcommand. (See "Analyzing Group Differences" on p. 4.)

Statistic 2   *Standard deviations.* Total and group standard deviations for all variables named on the ANALYSIS subcommand. (See "Analyzing Group Differences" on p. 4.)

Statistic 3   *Pooled within-groups covariance matrix.*

Statistic 4   *Pooled within-groups correlation matrix.* (See "Correlations" on p. 6 and "The Variables" on p. 40.)

Statistic 5   *Matrix of pairwise* F *ratios.* The *F* ratio for each pair of groups. The *F*'s are for significance tests for the Mahalanobis distances between groups. This statistic is available only with stepwise methods. (See "The First Step" on p. 24.)

Statistic 6   *Univariate* F *ratios.* *F* for each variable. This is a one-way analysis-of-variance test for equality of group means for a single predictor variable. (See "Analyzing Group Differences" on p. 4.)

Statistic 7   *Box's* M *test.* Test the equality of group covariance matrices. (See "When Assumptions Are Violated" on p. 40.)

Statistic 8   *Group covariance matrices.*

Statistic 9   *Total covariance matrix.*

Statistic 11   *Unstandardized discriminant functions and coefficients.* (See "Estimating the Coefficients" on p. 7 and "The Number of Functions" on p. 31.)

Statistic 12   *Classification function coefficients.*

Classification Tables and Plots

You can request classification tables and plots using the STATISTICS subcommand:

Statistic 10   *Territorial map.* A territorial map is available when there is more than one discriminant function. (See "Classification" on p. 32 and "Testing the Significance of the Discriminant Functions" on p. 37.)

Statistic 13   *Classification results table.* (See "Classification Summary" on p. 13.)

Statistic 15   *All-groups scatterplot or histogram.*

Statistic 16   *Separate-groups scatterplot or histogram.*

For Statistics 15 and 16, if you have at least two functions, you can obtain scatterplots with the axes defined by the first two functions (see "Classification" on p. 32). If you have only one function, you can obtain histograms. (See "Histograms of Discriminant Scores" on p. 13 and "Classification with One Function" on p. 38.)

Discriminant Scores and Membership Probabilities

You can request casewise information that includes the observed group, the classified group, group membership probabilities, and discriminant scores using the STATISTICS subcommand.

Statistic 14   *Discriminant scores and classification information.* (See "Classification Output" on p. 11 and "The Number of Functions" on p. 31.)

Annotated Example

The following commands produce the output in Figure 1.18 through Figure 1.26:

```
DATA LIST  /CASEID 1-2 SURVIVAL 4 TREATMNT 6 TIME 8-10(1)
   WEIGHT 12-15(3) APGAR 17-18 SEX 20 AGE 22-23 PH 33-
35(2) RESP 37.
VARIABLE LABELS  SURVIVAL 'INFANT SURVIVAL'
   TREATMNT 'TREATMENT ADMINISTERED'
   TIME 'TIME TO SPONTANEOUS RESPIRATION'
   WEIGHT 'BIRTHWEIGHT IN KILOGRAMS'
   APGAR 'APGAR SCORE'
   SEX 'SEX OF RESPONDENT'
   AGE 'GESTATION AGE'
   PH 'PH LEVEL'
   RESP 'RESPIRATORY LEVEL'.
VALUE LABELS SURVIVAL 1'DIE' 2'SURVIVE'/
   TREATMNT 1'THAM' 0'SODIUM BICARBONATE'/
   SEX 1'MALE' 0'FEMALE'/
```

```
     RESP 1'YES' 0'NO' 9'NO ANSWER'.
RECODE SURVIVAL (0=1)(1=2).
MISSING VALUES  RESP(9).
BEGIN DATA.
data records
END DATA.
DSCRIMINANT GROUPS=SURVIVAL(1,2)
  /VARIABLES=TREATMNT TO RESP
  /METHOD=WILKS
  /STATISTICS=5
  /OPTIONS=6 7.
```

- The DATA LIST command gives the variable names and column locations for the variables in the analysis.

- The VARIABLE LABELS and VALUE LABELS commands provide descriptive labels to be used in the output.

- The RECODE command recodes the values of *survival*.

- The MISSING VALUES command assigns the value 9 as a user-missing value for *resp*.

- The DSCRIMINANT command requests the Wilks' method for entering the variables into the analysis phase. It also requests a matrix of pairwise *F* ratios (Statistic 5) and a varimax rotation of both the function matrix and structure matrix (Options 6 and 7).

2 Factor Analysis

What are creativity, love, and altruism? Unlike variables such as weight, blood pressure, and temperature, they cannot be measured on a scale, sphygmomanometer, or thermometer, in units of pounds, millimeters of mercury, or degrees Fahrenheit. Instead, they can be thought of as unifying constructs or labels that characterize responses to related groups of variables. For example, answers of "strongly agree" to items such as "sends me flowers," "listens to my problems," "reads my manuscripts," "laughs at my jokes," and "gazes deeply into my soul" may lead you to conclude that love is present. Thus, love is not a single measurable entity but a construct that is derived from measurement of other, directly observable variables. Identification of such underlying dimensions—factors—greatly simplifies the description and understanding of complex phenomena like social interaction. For example, postulating the existence of something called "love" explains the observed correlations between the responses to numerous and varied situations.

Factor analysis is a statistical technique used to identify a relatively small number of factors that can be used to represent relationships among sets of many interrelated variables. For example, variables such as scores on a battery of aptitude tests may be expressed as a linear combination of factors that represent verbal skills, mathematical aptitude, and perceptual speed. Variables such as consumer ratings of products in a survey can be expressed as a function of factors such as product quality and utility. Factor analysis helps identify these underlying constructs that are not directly observable.

A huge number of variables can be used to describe a community—degree of industrialization, commercial activity, population, mobility, average family income, extent of home ownership, birth rate, and so forth. However, descriptions of what is meant by the term *community* might be greatly simplified if it were possible to identify underlying dimensions, or factors, of communities. This was attempted by Jonassen and Peres (1960), who examined 82 community variables from 88 counties in Ohio. This chapter uses a subset of their variables (shown in Table 2.1) to illustrate the basics of factor analysis.

Table 2.1   Community variables

popstabl	Population stability.
newscirc	Weekly per capita local newspaper circulation.
femempld	Percentage of females 14 years or older in labor force.
farmers	Percentage of farmers and farm managers in labor force.
retailng	Per capita retail sales in dollars.
commercl	Total per capita commercial activity in dollars.
industzn	Industrialization index.
health	Health index.
chldnegl	Total per capita expenditures on county Aid to Dependent Children.
commeffc	Index of the extent to which a community fosters a high standard of living.
dwelgnew	Percentage of dwelling units built recently.
migrnpop	Index of the extent of migration into and out of the community.
unemploy	Unemployment index.
mentalil	Extent of mental illness.

The Factor Analysis Model

The basic assumption of factor analysis is that underlying dimensions, or factors, can be used to explain complex phenomena. Observed correlations between variables result from their sharing these factors. For example, correlations between test scores might be attributable to such shared factors as general intelligence, abstract reasoning skill, and reading comprehension. The correlations between the community variables might be due to factors such as amount of urbanization, the socioeconomic level or welfare of the community, and the population stability. The goal of factor analysis is to identify, based on a set of observable variables, the factors that are not directly observable.

The mathematical model for factor analysis appears somewhat similar to a multiple regression equation. Each variable is expressed as a linear combination of factors that are not actually observed. For example, the industrialization index might be expressed as:

$$\text{industzn} = a\,(\text{urbanism}) + b\,(\text{welfare}) + c\,(\text{influx}) + U_{\text{industzn}} \qquad \textbf{Equation 2.1}$$

This equation differs from the usual multiple regression equation in that *urbanism*, *welfare*, and *influx* are not single independent variables. Instead, they are labels for groups of variables that characterize these concepts. These groups of variables constitute the factors. Usually, the factors useful for characterizing a set of variables are not known in advance but are determined by factor analysis.

Urbanism, *welfare*, and *influx* are called **common factors**, since all variables are expressed as functions of them. The *U* in Equation 2.1 is called a **unique factor**, since it represents that part of the industrialization index that cannot be explained by the common factors. It is unique to the industrialization index variable.

In general, the model for the *i*th standardized variable is written as

$$X_i = A_{i1}F_1 + A_{i2}F_2 + \ldots + A_{ik}F_k + U_i$$ **Equation 2.2**

where the F's are the common factors, the U is the unique factor, and the A's are the coefficients used to combine the k factors. The unique factors are assumed to be uncorrelated with each other and with the common factors.

The factors are inferred from the observed variables and can be estimated as linear combinations of the variables. For example, the estimated urbanism factor is expressed as

$$\text{urbanism} = C_1 (\text{popstabl}) + C_2 (\text{newscirc}) + \ldots + C_{14} (\text{mentalil})$$ **Equation 2.3**

where the C's are coefficients. While it is possible that all of the variables contribute to the urbanism factor, we hope that only a subset of variables characterizes urbanism, as indicated by their large coefficients. The general expression for the estimate of the *j*th factor, F_j, is:

$$F_j = \sum_{i=1}^{p} W_{ji}X_i = W_{j1}X_1 + W_{j2}X_2 + \ldots + W_{jp}X_p$$ **Equation 2.4**

The W_i's are known as factor score coefficients, and p is the number of variables.

Ingredients of a Good Factor Analysis Solution

Before examining the mechanics of a factor analysis solution, let's consider the characteristics of a successful factor analysis. One goal is to represent relationships among sets of variables parsimoniously. That is, we would like to explain the observed correlations using as few factors as possible. If many factors are needed, little simplification or summarization occurs. We would also like the factors to be meaningful. A good factor solution is both simple and interpretable. When factors can be interpreted, new insights are possible. For example, if liquor preferences can be explained by such factors as sweetness and regional tastes (Stoetzel, 1960), marketing strategies can reflect this.

Steps in a Factor Analysis

Factor analysis usually proceeds in four steps.

1. In the first step, the correlation matrix for all variables is computed, as shown in Figure 2.1. Variables that do not appear to be related to other variables can be identified from the matrix and associated statistics. The appropriateness of the factor model can

also be evaluated. At this step, you should also decide what to do with cases that have missing values for some of the variables.

2. In the second step, factor extraction—the number of factors necessary to represent the data and the method for calculating them—must be determined. At this step, you also ascertain how well the chosen model fits the data.

3. The third step, rotation, focuses on transforming the factors to make them more interpretable.

4. At the fourth step, scores for each factor can be computed for each case. These scores can then be used in a variety of other analyses.

Examining the Correlation Matrix

The correlation matrix for the 14 community variables is shown in Figure 2.1. Since one of the goals of factor analysis is to obtain factors that help explain these correlations, the variables must be related to each other for the factor model to be appropriate. If the correlations between variables are small, it is unlikely that they share common factors. Figure 2.1 shows that almost half the coefficients are greater than 0.3 in absolute value. All variables, except the extent of mental illness, have a large correlation with at least one of the other variables in the set.

Bartlett's test of sphericity can be used to test the hypothesis that the correlation matrix is an **identity matrix**; that is, all diagonal terms are 1 and all off-diagonal terms are 0. The test requires that the data be a sample from a multivariate normal population. From Figure 2.2, the value of the test statistic for sphericity (based on a chi-square transformation of the determinant of the correlation matrix) is large and the associated significance level is small, so it appears unlikely that the population correlation matrix is an identity. If the hypothesis that the population correlation matrix is an identity cannot be rejected because the observed significance level is large, you should reconsider the use of the factor model.

Figure 2.1   Correlation matrix of 14 community variables

```
DATA LIST MATRIX FREE
 /POPSTABL NEWSCIRC FEMEMPLD FARMERS RETAILNG COMMERCL INDUSTZN
   HEALTH CHLDNEGL COMMEFFC DWELGNEW MIGRNPOP UNEMPLOY MENTALIL.
N 88.
BEGIN DATA.
1.000
-.175 1.000
rest of matrix
END DATA.
FACTOR READ=COR TRIANGLE
 /VARIABLES=POPSTABL TO MENTALIL
 /PRINT=CORRELATION.
```

Correlation Matrix:

	POPSTABL	NEWSCIRC	FEMEMPLD	FARMERS	RETAILNG	COMMERCL	INDUSTZN
POPSTABL	1.00000						
NEWSCIRC	-.17500	1.00000					
FEMEMPLD	-.27600	.61600	1.00000				
FARMERS	.36900	-.62500	-.63700	1.00000			
RETAILNG	-.12700	.62400	.73600	-.51900	1.00000		
COMMERCL	-.06900	.65200	.58900	-.30600	.72700	1.00000	
INDUSTZN	-.10600	.71200	.74200	-.54500	.78500	.91100	1.00000
HEALTH	-.14900	-.03000	.24100	-.06800	.10000	.12300	.12900
CHLDNEGL	-.03900	-.17100	-.58900	.25700	-.55700	-.35700	-.42400
COMMEFFC	-.00500	.10000	.47100	-.21300	.45200	.28700	.35700
DWELGNEW	-.67000	.18800	.41300	-.57900	.16500	.03000	.20300
MIGRNPOP	-.47600	-.08600	.06400	-.19800	.00700	-.06800	-.02400
UNEMPLOY	.13700	-.37300	-.68900	.45000	-.65000	-.42400	-.52800
MENTALIL	.23700	.04600	-.23700	.12100	-.19000	-.05500	-.09500

	HEALTH	CHLDNEGL	COMMEFFC	DWELGNEW	MIGRNPOP	UNEMPLOY	MENTALIL
HEALTH	1.00000						
CHLDNEGL	-.40700	1.00000					
COMMEFFC	.73200	-.66000	1.00000				
DWELGNEW	.29000	-.13800	.31100	1.00000			
MIGRNPOP	.08300	.14800	.06700	.50500	1.00000		
UNEMPLOY	-.34800	.73300	-.60100	-.26600	.18100	1.00000	
MENTALIL	-.27900	.24700	-.32400	-.26600	-.30700	.21700	1.00000

Figure 2.2   Test statistic for sphericity

```
FACTOR READ=CORRELATION TRIANGLE
 /VARIABLES=POPSTABL TO MENTALIL
 /PRINT=KMO.
```

```
KAISER-MEYER-OLKIN MEASURE OF SAMPLING ADEQUACY =  .76968

BARTLETT TEST OF SPHERICITY = 946.15313, SIGNIFICANCE =    .00000
```

Another indicator of the strength of the relationship among variables is the partial correlation coefficient. If variables share common factors, the partial correlation coefficients between pairs of variables should be small when the linear effects of the other variables are eliminated. The partial correlations are then estimates of the correlations between the unique factors and should be close to 0 when the factor analysis assumptions are met. (Recall that the unique factors are assumed to be uncorrelated with each other.)

The negative of the partial correlation coefficient is called the **anti-image correla-tion**. The matrix of anti-image correlations is shown in Figure 2.3. If the proportion of large coefficients is high, you should reconsider the use of the factor model.

Figure 2.3   Anti-image correlation matrix

```
FACTOR READ=CORRELATION TRIANGLE
 /VARIABLES=POPSTABL TO MENTALIL
 /PRINT=AIC.
```

```
Anti-Image Correlation Matrix:

              POPSTABL  NEWSCIRC  FEMEMPLD   FARMERS  RETAILNG  COMMERCL  INDUSTZN

POPSTABL       .58174
NEWSCIRC       .01578    .82801
FEMEMPLD       .10076   -.24223    .90896
FARMERS        .03198    .43797   -.00260    .73927
RETAILNG       .14998   -.14295   -.12037    .16426    .86110
COMMERCL       .20138   -.27622    .20714   -.49344   -.19535    .68094


              POPSTABL  NEWSCIRC  FEMEMPLD   FARMERS  RETAILNG  COMMERCL  INDUSTZN

INDUSTZN      -.23815    .08231   -.32790    .41648   -.04602   -.85499    .75581
HEALTH         .26114   -.02839   -.02332    .05845    .38421   -.16150    .08627
CHLDNEGL       .10875   -.24685    .27281   -.03446    .13062    .07043   -.07979
COMMEFFC      -.39878    .05772    .03017   -.16386   -.33700    .09427   -.06742
DWELGNEW       .55010    .04505   -.09493    .33479    .26678    .13831   -.13726
MIGRNPOP       .20693    .22883   -.06689    .11784   -.15886   -.07421    .06501
UNEMPLOY      -.17774   -.05946    .18631   -.12699    .19591   -.01262   -.02503
MENTALIL      -.08437   -.10058    .07770    .03053    .07842   -.02921   -.00056


               HEALTH  CHLDNEGL  COMMEFFC  DWELGNEW  MIGRNPOP  UNEMPLOY  MENTALIL

HEALTH         .59124
CHLDNEGL       .02899    .87023
COMMEFFC      -.70853    .19554    .68836
DWELGNEW       .07480   -.04008   -.30434    .70473
MIGRNPOP       .07460   -.10809   -.14292   -.24074    .61759
UNEMPLOY      -.02904   -.33523    .19240    .02181   -.38208    .87230
MENTALIL       .06821   -.04163    .04728   -.02505    .20487   -.02708    .88390
```

MEASURES OF SAMPLING ADEQUACY (MSA) ARE PRINTED ON THE DIAGONAL.

The **Kaiser-Meyer-Olkin measure** of sampling adequacy is an index for comparing the magnitudes of the observed correlation coefficients to the magnitudes of the partial cor-relation coefficients. It is computed as

$$KMO = \frac{\sum\sum_{i \neq j} r_{ij}^2}{\sum\sum_{i \neq j} r_{ij}^2 + \sum\sum_{i \neq j} a_{ij}^2}$$

Equation 2.5

where r_{ij} is the simple correlation coefficient between variables i and j, and a_{ij} is the partial correlation coefficient between variables i and j. If the sum of the squared partial correlation coefficients between all pairs of variables is small when compared to the sum of the squared correlation coefficients, the KMO measure is close to 1. Small values for the KMO measure indicate that a factor analysis of the variables may not be a good idea, since correlations between pairs of variables cannot be explained by the other variables. Kaiser (1974) characterizes measures in the 0.90's as *marvelous*, in the 0.80's as *meritorious*, in the 0.70's as *middling*, in the 0.60's as *mediocre*, in the 0.50's as *miserable*, and below 0.5 as *unacceptable*. The value of the overall KMO statistic for this example is shown in Figure 2.2. Since the KMO measure is close to 0.8, we can comfortably proceed with the factor analysis.

A measure of sampling adequacy can be computed for each individual variable in a similar manner. Instead of including all pairs of variables in the summations, only coefficients involving that variable are included. For the ith variable, the measure of sampling adequacy is:

$$MSA_i = \frac{\sum_{j \neq i} r_{ij}^2}{\sum_{j \neq i} r_{ij}^2 + \sum_{j \neq i} a_{ij}^2}$$

Equation 2.6

These measures of sampling adequacy are displayed on the diagonals of Figure 2.3. Again, reasonably large values are needed for a good factor analysis. Thus, you might consider eliminating variables with small values for the measure of sampling adequacy.

The squared multiple correlation coefficient between a variable and all other variables is another indication of the strength of the linear association among the variables. These values are shown in the column labeled *Communality* in Figure 2.4. The variable for extent of mental illness has a small multiple R^2, suggesting that it should be eliminated from the set of variables being analyzed. However, it will be kept in the analysis for illustrative purposes.

Factor Extraction

The goal of **factor extraction** is to determine the factors. In this example, we will obtain estimates of the initial factors from principal components analysis. Other methods for factor extraction are described in "Methods for Factor Extraction" on p. 68. In **principal components analysis**, linear combinations of the observed variables are formed. The first principal component is the combination that accounts for the largest amount of variance in the sample. The second principal component accounts for the next largest amount of variance and is uncorrelated with the first. Successive components explain progressively smaller portions of the total sample variance, and all are uncorrelated with each other.

It is possible to compute as many principal components as there are variables. If all principal components are used, each variable can be exactly represented by them, but nothing has been gained, since there are as many factors (principal components) as variables. When all factors are included in the solution, all of the variance of each variable is accounted for, and there is no need for a unique factor in the model. The proportion of variance accounted for by the common factors, or the **communality** of a variable, is 1 for all the variables, as shown in Figure 2.4. In general, principal components analysis is a separate technique from factor analysis. That is, it can be used whenever uncorrelated linear combinations of the observed variables are desired. All it does is transform a set of correlated variables to a set of uncorrelated variables (principal components).

Figure 2.4   Initial statistics

```
FACTOR READ=CORRELATION TRIANGLE
  /VARIABLES=POPSTABL TO MENTALIL.

EXTRACTION  1  FOR ANALYSIS  1, PRINCIPAL-COMPONENTS ANALYSIS (PC)


INITIAL STATISTICS:


VARIABLE      COMMUNALITY  *  FACTOR   EIGENVALUE   PCT OF VAR   CUM PCT
                           *
POPSTABL        1.00000    *    1       5.70658       40.8        40.8
NEWSCIRC        1.00000    *    2       2.35543       16.8        57.6
FEMEMPLD        1.00000    *    3       2.00926       14.4        71.9
FARMERS         1.00000    *    4        .89745        6.4        78.3
RETAILNG        1.00000    *    5        .75847        5.4        83.8
COMMERCL        1.00000    *    6        .53520        3.8        87.6
INDUSTZN        1.00000    *    7        .50886        3.6        91.2
HEALTH          1.00000    *    8        .27607        2.0        93.2
CHLDNEGL        1.00000    *    9        .24511        1.8        94.9
COMMEFFC        1.00000    *   10        .20505        1.5        96.4
DWELGNEW        1.00000    *   11        .19123        1.4        97.8
MIGRNPOP        1.00000    *   12        .16982        1.2        99.0
UNEMPLOY        1.00000    *   13        .10202         .7        99.7
MENTALIL        1.00000    *   14        .03946         .3       100.0
```

To help us decide how many factors we need to represent the data, it is helpful to examine the percentage of total variance explained by each. The total variance is the sum of the variance of each variable. For simplicity, all variables and factors are expressed in standardized form, with a mean of 0 and a standard deviation of 1. Since there are 14 variables and each is standardized to have a variance of 1, the total variance is 14 in this example.

Figure 2.4 contains the initial statistics for each factor. The total variance explained by each factor is listed in the column labeled *Eigenvalue*. The next column contains the percentage of the total variance attributable to each factor. For example, the linear combination formed by factor 2 has a variance of 2.35, which is 16.8% of the total variance of 14. The last column, the cumulative percentage, indicates the percentage of variance attributable to that factor and those that precede it in the table. Note that the factors are arranged in descending order of variance explained. Note also that although variable names and factors are displayed on the same line, there is no correspondence between the lines in the two halves of the table. The first two columns provide information about the individual variables, while the last four columns describe the factors.

Figure 2.4 shows that almost 72% of the total variance is attributable to the first three factors. The remaining eleven factors together account for only 28.1% of the variance. Thus, a model with three factors may be adequate to represent the data.

Several procedures have been proposed for determining the number of factors to use in a model. One criterion suggests that only factors that account for variances greater than 1 (eigenvalue greater than 1) should be included. Factors with a variance less than 1 are no better than a single variable, since each variable has a variance of 1. Although this is the default criterion in the SPSS/PC+ Factor procedure, it is not always a good solution (see Tucker, Koopman, & Linn, 1969).

Figure 2.5 is a plot of the total variance associated with each factor. The plot shows a distinct break between the steep slope of the large factors and the gradual trailing off of the rest of the factors. This gradual trailing off is called the **scree** (Cattell, 1966) because it resembles the rubble that forms at the foot of a mountain. Experimental evidence indicates that the scree begins at the kth factor, where k is the true number of factors. From the scree plot, it again appears that a three-factor model should be sufficient for the community example.

Figure 2.5   Scree plot

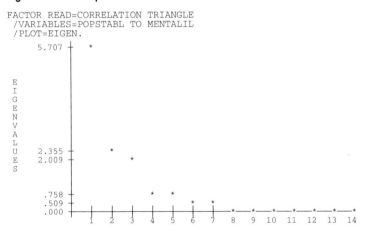

The Three Factors

Figure 2.6 displays the coefficients that relate the variables to the three factors. The figure shows that the industrialization index can be expressed as:

$$industzn = 0.844F_1 + 0.300F_2 + 0.238F_3 \qquad \text{Equation 2.7}$$

Similarly, the health index is:

$$health = 0.383F_1 - 0.327F_2 - 0.635F_3 \qquad \text{Equation 2.8}$$

Each row of Figure 2.6 contains the coefficients used to express a standardized variable in terms of the factors. These coefficients are called **factor loadings**, since they indicate how much weight is assigned to each factor. Factors with large coefficients (in absolute value) for a variable are closely related to the variable. For example, factor 1 is the factor with the largest loading for the industrialization index. The matrix of factor loadings is called the **factor pattern matrix**.

Figure 2.6   Factor matrix

```
FACTOR READ=CORRELATION TRIANGLE
  /VARIABLES=POPSTABL TO MENTALIL.

FACTOR MATRIX:

                 FACTOR  1      FACTOR  2      FACTOR  3

POPSTABL          -.30247         .68597        -.36451
NEWSCIRC           .67238         .28096         .49779
FEMEMPLD           .89461         .01131         .08063
FARMERS           -.68659         .20002        -.40450
RETAILNG           .85141         .24264         .09351
COMMERCL           .72503         .39394         .19896
INDUSTZN           .84436         .29956         .23775
HEALTH             .38347        -.32718        -.63474
CHLDNEGL          -.67430        -.12139         .52896
COMMEFFC           .63205        -.15540        -.64221
DWELGNEW           .45886        -.73940         .18706
MIGRNPOP           .07894        -.74371         .24335
UNEMPLOY          -.78714        -.09777         .30110
MENTALIL          -.30025         .45463         .27134
```

When the estimated factors are uncorrelated with each other (orthogonal), the factor loadings are also the correlations between the factors and the variables. Thus, the correlation between the health index and factor 1 is 0.383. Similarly, there is a slightly smaller correlation between the health index and factor 2 (-0.327). The matrix of correlations between variables and factors is called the **factor structure matrix**. When the factors are orthogonal, the factor structure matrix and the factor pattern matrix are equivalent. As shown in Figure 2.6, such a matrix is called the *Factor Matrix* in SPSS/PC+ output.

More on the Factor Matrix

There is yet another interpretation of the factor matrix in Figure 2.6. Whether the factors are orthogonal or not, the factor loadings are the standardized regression coefficients in the multiple regression equation, with the original variable as the dependent variable and the factors as the independent variables. If the factors are uncorrelated, the values of the coefficients are not dependent on each other. They represent the unique contribution of each factor and are the correlations between the factors and the variable.

To judge how well the three-factor model describes the original variables, we can compute the proportion of the variance of each variable explained by the three-factor model. Since the factors are uncorrelated, the total proportion of variance explained is simply the sum of the variance proportions explained by each factor.

Consider, for example, the health index. Factor 1 accounts for 14.7% of the variance for this variable. This is obtained by squaring the correlation coefficient for factor 1 and *health* (0.383). Similarly, factor 3 explains 40.3% ($(-0.635)^2$) of the variance. The total percentage of variance in the health index accounted for by this three-factor model is therefore 65.7% (14.7% + 10.7% + 40.3%). The proportion of variance explained by the common factors is called the communality of the variable.

The communalities for the variables are shown in Figure 2.7, together with the percentage of variance accounted for by each of the retained factors. This table is called *Final Statistics,* since it shows the communalities and factor statistics after the desired number of factors has been extracted. When factors are estimated using the method of principal components, the factor statistics are the same in the tables for initial statistics and final statistics. However, the communalities are different, since all of the variances of the variables are not explained when only a subset of factors is retained.

Figure 2.7   Communality of variables

```
FACTOR READ=CORRELATION TRIANGLE
  /VARIABLES=POPSTABL TO MENTALIL.


FINAL STATISTICS:

VARIABLE    COMMUNALITY  *  FACTOR   EIGENVALUE   PCT OF VAR   CUM PCT
                         *
POPSTABL       .69491    *     1       5.70658       40.8        40.8
NEWSCIRC       .77882    *     2       2.35543       16.8        57.6
FEMEMPLD       .80696    *     3       2.00926       14.4        71.9
FARMERS        .67503    *
RETAILNG       .79253    *
COMMERCL       .72044    *
INDUSTZN       .85921    *
HEALTH         .65699    *
CHLDNEGL       .74921    *
COMMEFFC       .83607    *
DWELGNEW       .79226    *
MIGRNPOP       .61855    *
UNEMPLOY       .71981    *
MENTALIL       .37047    *
```

Communalities can range from 0 to 1, with 0 indicating that the common factors explain none of the variance and 1 indicating that all the variance is explained by the common factors. The variance that is not explained by the common factors is attributed to the unique factor and is called the **uniqueness** of the variable.

The Reproduced Correlation Matrix

One of the basic assumptions of factor analysis is that the observed correlation between variables is due to the sharing of common factors. Therefore, the estimated correlations between the factors and the variables can be used to estimate the correlations between the variables. In general, if factors are orthogonal, the estimated correlation coefficient for variables i and j is

$$r_{ij} = \sum_{f=1}^{k} r_{fi} r_{fj} = r_{1i} r_{1j} + r_{2i} r_{2j} + \ldots + r_{ki} r_{kj}$$ Equation 2.9

where k is the number of common factors and r_{fi} is the correlation between the fth factor and the ith variable.

From Figure 2.6 and Equation 2.9, the estimated correlation coefficient for *health* and *commeffc*, based on the three-factor model, is:

$$r_{8, 10} = (0.38)\,(0.63) + (-0.33)\,(-0.16) + (-0.63)\,(-0.64) = 0.70$$ Equation 2.10

Figure 2.1 shows that the observed correlation coefficient between *health* and *commeffc* is 0.73, so the difference between the observed correlation coefficient and that estimated from the model is about -0.03. This difference is called a **residual**. The estimated correlation coefficients and the residuals are shown in Figure 2.8.

The residuals are listed above the diagonal and the estimated correlation coefficients are below the diagonal. The values with asterisks (on the diagonal) are reproduced communalities.

Below the matrix is a message indicating how many residuals are greater than 0.05 in absolute value. In the community data example, less than half (46%) are greater than 0.05 in absolute value. The magnitudes of the residuals indicate how well the fitted model reproduces the observed correlations. If the residuals are large, the model does not fit the data well and should probably be reconsidered.

Figure 2.8   Estimated correlations and residuals

```
FACTOR READ=CORRELATION TRIANGLE
  /VARIABLES=POPSTABL TO MENTALIL
  /PRINT=REPR.
```

Reproduced Correlation Matrix:

	POPSTABL	NEWSCIRC	FEMEMPLD	FARMERS	RETAILNG
POPSTABL	.69491*	.01709	.01623	-.12332	-.00183
NEWSCIRC	-.19209	.77882*	-.02883	-.01820	-.06320
FEMEMPLD	-.29223	.64483	.80696*	.00758	-.03597
FARMERS	.49232	-.60680	-.64458	.67503*	.05486
RETAILNG	-.12517	.68720	.77197	-.57386	.79253*
COMMERCL	-.02159	.69721	.66912	-.49948	.73149
INDUSTZN	-.13656	.77024	.77793	-.61598	.81382
HEALTH	-.10906	-.15005	.28818	-.07198	.18775
CHLDNEGL	-.07212	-.22418	-.56196	.22473	-.55410
COMMEFFC	-.06368	.06163	.51190	-.20527	.44037
DWELGNEW	-.71418	.19390	.41722	-.53861	.22876
MIGRNPOP	-.62274	-.03474	.08183	-.30139	-.09049
UNEMPLOY	.06126	-.40684	-.68101	.39909	-.66575
MENTALIL	.30378	.06093	-.24158	.18733	-.11995

	COMMERCL	INDUSTZN	HEALTH	CHLDNEGL	COMMEFFC
POPSTABL	-.04741	.03056	-.03994	.03312	.05868
NEWSCIRC	-.04521	-.05824	.12005	.05318	.03837
FEMEMPLD	-.08012	-.03593	-.04718	-.02704	-.04090
FARMERS	.19348	.07098	.00398	.03227	-.00773
RETAILNG	-.00449	-.02882	-.08775	-.00290	.01163
COMMERCL	.72044*	.13350	.10014	.07447	.01773
INDUSTZN	.77750	.85921*	.05413	.05596	.02256
HEALTH	.02286	.07487	.65699*	.14761	.03114
CHLDNEGL	-.43147	-.47996	-.55461	.74921*	.08703
COMMEFFC	.26927	.33444	.70086	-.74703	.83607*
DWELGNEW	.07863	.21042	.29914	-.12070	.28479
MIGRNPOP	-.18732	-.09828	.11913	.16577	.00918
UNEMPLOY	-.54931	-.62233	-.46098	.70191	-.67569
MENTALIL	.01539	-.05282	-.43612	.29080	-.43468

	DWELGNEW	MIGRNPOP	UNEMPLOY	MENTALIL
POPSTABL	.04418	.14674	.07574	-.06678
NEWSCIRC	-.00590	-.05126	.03384	-.01493
FEMEMPLD	-.00422	-.01783	-.00799	.00458
FARMERS	-.04039	.10339	.05091	-.06633
RETAILNG	-.06376	.09749	.01575	-.07005
COMMERCL	-.04863	.11932	.12531	-.07039
INDUSTZN	-.00742	.07428	.09433	-.04218
HEALTH	-.00914	-.03613	.11298	.15712
CHLDNEGL	-.01730	-.01777	.03109	-.04380
COMMEFFC	.02621	.05782	.07469	.11068
DWELGNEW	.79226*	-.12664	-.03343	.15717
MIGRNPOP	.63164	.61855*	.09715	-.01121
UNEMPLOY	-.23257	.08385	.71981*	-.05659
MENTALIL	-.42317	-.29579	.27359	.37047*

The lower left triangle contains the reproduced correlation matrix; the
diagonal, reproduced communalities; and the upper right triangle residuals
between the observed correlations and the reproduced correlations.

There are   42 (46.0%) residuals (above diagonal) that are > 0.05.

Some Additional Considerations

If a method other than principal components analysis is used to extract the initial factors, there are differences in parts of the factor output. For example, consider Figure 2.9, which contains the initial statistics obtained when the maximum-likelihood algorithm is used.

Figure 2.9   Maximum-likelihood extractions

```
FACTOR READ=CORRELATION TRIANGLE
 /VARIABLES=POPSTABL TO MENTALIL
 /EXTRACTION=ML.

INITIAL STATISTICS:


VARIABLE      COMMUNALITY  *  FACTOR   EIGENVALUE   PCT OF VAR   CUM PCT
                           *
POPSTABL         .62385    *    1       5.70658       40.8        40.8
NEWSCIRC         .71096    *    2       2.35543       16.8        57.6
FEMEMPLD         .77447    *    3       2.00926       14.4        71.9
FARMERS          .74519    *    4        .89745        6.4        78.3
RETAILNG         .79259    *    5        .75847        5.4        83.8
COMMERCL         .90987    *    6        .53520        3.8        87.6
INDUSTZN         .92914    *    7        .50886        3.6        91.2
HEALTH           .66536    *    8        .27607        2.0        93.2
CHLDNEGL         .67987    *    9        .24511        1.8        94.9
COMMEFFC         .79852    *   10        .20505        1.5        96.4
DWELGNEW         .72576    *   11        .19123        1.4        97.8
MIGRNPOP         .50560    *   12        .16982        1.2        99.0
UNEMPLOY         .72549    *   13        .10202         .7        99.7
MENTALIL         .23825    *   14        .03946         .3       100.0
```

Regardless of the algorithm used, by default the number of factors to be retained is determined by the principal components solution because it is easily obtainable. Thus, most of the output in Figure 2.9 is identical to that displayed in Figure 2.4. The only exception is the communalities column. In the principal components solution, all initial communalities are listed as 1's. In all other solutions, the initial estimate of the communality of a variable is the multiple R^2 from the regression equation that predicts that variable from all other variables. These initial communalities are used in the estimation algorithm.

When a method other than principal components analysis is used to estimate the final factor matrix, the percentage of variance explained by each final factor is usually different. Figure 2.10 contains the final statistics from a maximum-likelihood solution. The final three factors extracted explain only 63% of the total variance, as compared to 72% for the first three principal components. The first factor accounts for 35.5% of the total variance, as compared to 40.8% for the first principal component.

Figure 2.10 Maximum-likelihood final statistics

```
FACTOR READ=CORRELATION TRIANGLE
 /VARIABLES=POPSTABL TO MENTALIL
 /EXTRACTION=ML.

Final Statistics:

Variable     Communality  *  Factor   SS Loadings  Pct of Var   Cum Pct
                          *
POPSTABL       .52806     *    1        4.96465       35.5        35.5
NEWSCIRC       .57439     *    2        2.17833       15.6        51.0
FEMEMPLD       .75057     *    3        1.67661       12.0        63.0
FARMERS        .56808     *
RETAILNG       .72089     *
COMMERCL       .87128     *
INDUSTZN       .96817     *
HEALTH         .33382     *
CHLDNEGL       .78341     *
COMMEFFC       .62762     *
DWELGNEW       .87445     *
MIGRNPOP       .35074     *
UNEMPLOY       .70833     *
MENTALIL       .15977     *
```

The proportion of the total variance explained by each factor can be calculated from the factor matrix. The proportion of the total variance explained by factor 1 is calculated by summing the proportions of variance of each variable attributable to factor 1. Figure 2.11, the factor matrix for the maximum-likelihood solution, shows that factor 1 accounts for $(-0.16)^2$ of the *popstabl* variance, 0.72^2 of the *newscirc* variance, 0.81^2 of the *femempld* variance, and so on for the other variables. The total variance attributable to factor 1 is therefore:

$$\text{Total variance for factor } 1 = (-0.16)^2 + 0.72^2 + 0.81^2 + (-0.59)^2$$
$$+ 0.83^2 + 0.89^2 + 0.97^2 + 0.20^2$$
$$+ (-0.52)^2 + 0.44^2 + 0.27^2 + (-0.00)^2$$
$$+ (-0.62)^2 + (-0.15)^2 = 4.96$$

Equation 2.11

This is the value displayed in the column labeled *SS Loadings* for factor 1 in Figure 2.10.

Figure 2.11 Maximum-likelihood factor matrix

```
FACTOR READ=CORRELATION TRIANGLE
 /VARIABLES=POPSTABL TO MENTALIL
 /EXTRACTION=ML.
```

```
FACTOR MATRIX:
```

	FACTOR 1	FACTOR 2	FACTOR 3
POPSTABL	-.16474	-.62235	-.33705
NEWSCIRC	.71934	-.04703	.23394
FEMEMPLD	.80703	.27934	-.14573
FARMERS	-.58607	-.43787	-.18130
RETAILNG	.83267	.00538	-.16588
COMMERCL	.88945	-.27142	.08063
INDUSTZN	.97436	-.10452	.08869
HEALTH	.19912	.35743	-.40795
CHLDNEGL	-.51856	-.17816	.69481
COMMEFFC	.44351	.33795	-.56277
DWELGNEW	.27494	.86373	.22983
MIGRNPOP	-.00353	.49141	.33052
UNEMPLOY	-.62354	-.25283	.50558
MENTALIL	-.14756	-.33056	.16948

Methods for Factor Extraction

Several different methods can be used to obtain estimates of the common factors. These methods differ in the criterion used to define "good fit." **Principal-axis factoring** proceeds much the same as principal components analysis, except that the diagonals of the correlation matrix are replaced by estimates of the communalities. At the first step, squared multiple correlation coefficients can be used as initial estimates of the communalities. Based on these, the requisite number of factors is extracted. The communalities are reestimated from the factor loadings, and factors are again extracted with the new communality estimates replacing the old. This continues until negligible change occurs in the communality estimates.

The **unweighted least-squares method** produces, for a fixed number of factors, a factor pattern matrix that minimizes the sum of the squared differences between the observed and reproduced correlation matrices (ignoring the diagonals). The **generalized least-squares method** minimizes the same criterion; however, correlations are weighted inversely by the uniqueness of the variables. That is, correlations involving variables with high uniqueness are given less weight than correlations involving variables with low uniqueness.

The **maximum-likelihood method** produces parameter estimates that are the most likely to have produced the observed correlation matrix if the sample is from a multivariate normal distribution. Again, the correlations are weighted by the inverse of the uniqueness of the variables, and an iterative algorithm is employed.

The **alpha method** considers the variables in a particular analysis to be a sample from the universe of potential variables. It maximizes the alpha reliability of the factors. This differs from the previously described methods, which consider the cases to be a sample from some population and the variables to be fixed. With alpha factor extraction, the eigenvalues can no longer be obtained as the sum of the squared factor loadings, and the communalities for each variable are not the sum of the squared loadings on the individual factors.

In **image factoring**, the common part of a variable is defined as its linear regression on remaining variables, rather than a function of hypothetical factors. This common part is called a **partial image**. The residual about the regression, which represents the unique part of a variable, is called a **partial anti-image**. See Harman (1967) and Kim and Mueller (1978) for discussions of the different factor estimation algorithms.

Goodness of Fit of the Factor Model

When factors are extracted using generalized least squares or maximum-likelihood estimation, and it is assumed that the sample is from a multivariate normal population, it is possible to obtain goodness-of-fit tests for the adequacy of a k-factor model. For large sample sizes, the goodness-of-fit statistic tends to be distributed as a chi-square variate. In most applications, the number of common factors is not known, and the number of factors is increased until a reasonably good fit is obtained—that is, until the observed significance level is no longer small. The statistics obtained in this fashion are not independent, and the true significance level is not the same as the observed significance level at each step.

The value of the chi-square goodness-of-fit statistic is directly proportional to the sample size. The degrees of freedom are a function of only the number of common factors and the number of variables. (For the chi-square statistic to have positive degrees of freedom, the number of common factors cannot exceed the largest integer satisfying $m < 0.5\,(2p + 1 - \sqrt{8p + 1})$, where m is the number of common factors to be extracted and p is the number of variables). For large sample sizes, the goodness-of-fit test may cause rather small discrepancies in fit to be deemed statistically significant, resulting in a larger number of factors being extracted than is really necessary.

Table 2.2 contains the goodness-of-fit statistics for maximum-likelihood extraction for different numbers of common factors. Using this criterion, at least six common factors are needed to represent the community data adequately.

Table 2.2   Goodness-of-fit statistics

Number of factors	Chi-square statistic	Iterations required	Significance
3	184.8846	13	0.0000
4	94.1803	8	0.0000
5	61.0836	11	0.0010
6	27.3431	15	0.1985

Summary of the Extraction Phase

In the factor extraction phase, the number of common factors needed to adequately describe the data is determined. This decision is based on eigenvalues and the percentage of the total variance accounted for by different numbers of factors. A plot of the eigenvalues (the scree plot) is also helpful in determining the number of factors.

The Rotation Phase

Although the factor matrix obtained in the extraction phase indicates the relationship between the factors and the individual variables, it is usually difficult to identify meaningful factors based on this matrix. Often the variables and factors do not appear correlated in any interpretable pattern. Most factors are correlated with many variables. Since one of the goals of factor analysis is to identify factors that are substantively meaningful (in the sense that they summarize sets of closely related variables), the **rotation** phase of factor analysis attempts to transform the initial matrix into one that is easier to interpret.

Consider Figure 2.12, which is a factor matrix for four hypothetical variables. From the factor loadings, it is difficult to interpret any of the factors, since the variables and factors are intertwined. That is, all factor loadings are quite high, and both factors explain all of the variables.

Figure 2.12   Hypothetical factor matrix

```
FACTOR VARIABLES=X1 X2 X3 X4
  /READ=FACTOR(2).

Factor Matrix:

                  FACTOR  1       FACTOR  2

X1                  .50000          .50000
X2                  .50000         -.40000
X3                  .70000          .70000
X4                 -.60000          .60000
```

In the factor matrix in Figure 2.13, variables $x1$ and $x3$ are highly related to factor 1, while $x2$ and $x4$ load highly on factor 2. By looking at what variables $x2$ and $x4$ have in common (such as a measurement of job satisfaction, or a characterization of personality), we may be able to identify factor 2. Similar steps can be taken to identify factor 1. The goal of rotation is to transform complicated matrices like the one in Figure 2.12 into simpler matrices like the one in Figure 2.13.

Figure 2.13   Rotated hypothetical factor matrix

```
Rotated Factor Matrix:

                  FACTOR  1       FACTOR  2

X1                  .70684         -.01938
X2                  .05324         -.63809
X3                  .98958         -.02713
X4                  .02325          .84821
```

Consider Figure 2.14, which is a plot of variables *x1* to *x4* using the factor loadings in Figure 2.12 as the coordinates, and Figure 2.15, which is the corresponding plot for factor loadings in Figure 2.13. Note that Figure 2.14 would look exactly like Figure 2.15 if the dotted lines were rotated to be the reference axes. When the axes are maintained at right angles, the rotation is called **orthogonal**. If the axes are not maintained at right angles, the rotation is called **oblique**. Oblique rotation is discussed on p. 77.

Figure 2.14   Prior to rotation

```
FACTOR VARIABLES=X1 X2 X3 X4
 /READ=FACTOR(2)
 /ROTATION=NOROTATE
 /PLOT=ROTATION(1,2).
```

Horizontal Factor   1   Vertical Factor   2

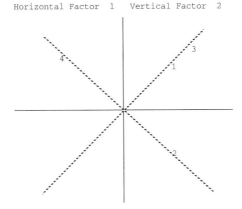

Symbol	Variable	Coordinates	
1	X1	.500	.500
2	X2	.500	-.400
3	X3	.700	.700
4	X4	-.600	.600

Figure 2.15   Orthogonal rotation

```
FACTOR VARIABLES=X1 X2 X3 X4
 /READ=FACTOR(2)
 /ROTATION=VARIMAX
 /PLOT=ROTATION(1,2).
```

Horizontal Factor   1   Vertical Factor   2

Symbol	Variable	Coordinates	
1	X1	.707	-.019
2	X2	.053	-.638
3	X3	.990	-.027
4	X4	.023	.848

The purpose of rotation is to achieve a **simple structure**. This means that we would like each factor to have nonzero loadings for only some of the variables. This helps us interpret the factors. We would also like each variable to have nonzero loadings for only a few factors, preferably one. This permits the factors to be differentiated from each other. If several factors have high loadings on the same variables, it is difficult to ascertain how the factors differ.

Rotation does not affect the goodness of fit of a factor solution. That is, although the factor matrix changes, the communalities and the percentage of total variance explained do not change. The percentage of variance accounted for by each of the factors *does* change, however. Rotation redistributes the explained variance for the individual factors. Different rotation methods may actually result in the identification of somewhat different factors.

A variety of algorithms is used for orthogonal rotation to a simple structure. The most commonly used method is the **varimax method,** which attempts to minimize the number of variables that have high loadings on a factor. This should enhance the interpretability of the factors.

The **quartimax method** emphasizes simple interpretation of variables, since the solution minimizes the number of factors needed to explain a variable. A quartimax rotation often results in a general factor with high-to-moderate loadings on most variables. This is one of the main shortcomings of the quartimax method.

The **equamax method** is a combination of the varimax method, which simplifies the factors, and the quartimax method, which simplifies variables.

Consider Figure 2.16 through Figure 2.19, which show the factor matrices for the community data before rotation and again after a varimax, quartimax, and equamax orthogonal rotation procedure.

Figure 2.16   Unrotated factor matrix

```
FACTOR READ=CORRELATION TRIANGLE
 /VARIABLES=POPSTABL TO MENTALIL
 /EXTRACTION=PC.


Factor Matrix:



                 FACTOR   1      FACTOR   2      FACTOR   3

POPSTABL          -.30247         .68597         -.36451
NEWSCIRC           .67238         .28096          .49779
FEMEMPLD           .89461         .01131          .08063
FARMERS           -.68659         .20002         -.40450
RETAILNG           .85141         .24264          .09351
COMMERCL           .72503         .39394          .19896
INDUSTZN           .84436         .29956          .23775
HEALTH             .38347        -.32718         -.63474
CHLDNEGL          -.67430        -.12139          .52896
COMMEFFC           .63205        -.15540         -.64221
DWELGNEW           .45886        -.73940          .18706
MIGRNPOP           .07894        -.74371          .24335
UNEMPLOY          -.78714        -.09777          .30110
MENTALIL          -.30025         .45463          .27134
```

Figure 2.17   Varimax-rotated factor matrix

```
FACTOR READ=CORRELATION TRIANGLE
 /VARIABLES=POPSTABL TO MENTALIL
 /EXTRACTION=PC
 /ROTATION=VARIMAX.

Varimax converged in    6 iterations.

rotated factor matrix:
```

	FACTOR 1	FACTOR 2	FACTOR 3
POPSTABL	-.13553	.00916	-.82247
NEWSCIRC	.86634	-.14256	.08920
FEMEMPLD	.78248	.37620	.23055
FARMERS	-.65736	-.04537	-.49077
RETAILNG	.83993	.29454	.01705
COMMERCL	.83432	.11068	-.11000
INDUSTZN	.91325	.15773	.01730
HEALTH	-.05806	.79424	.15101
CHLDNEGL	-.39791	-.75492	.14486
COMMEFFC	.21186	.88794	.05241
DWELGNEW	.17484	.22931	.84208
MIGRNPOP	-.12119	-.00660	.77706
UNEMPLOY	-.57378	-.62483	.01311
MENTALIL	.03133	-.47460	-.37979

Figure 2.18   Equamax-rotated factor matrix

```
FACTOR READ=CORRELATION TRIANGLE
 /VARIABLES=POPSTABL TO MENTALIL
 /EXTRACTION=PC
 /ROTATION=EQUAMAX.

Equamax converged in    6 iterations.

Rotated Factor Matrix:
```

	FACTOR 1	FACTOR 2	FACTOR 3
POPSTABL	-.12961	.01218	-.82338
NEWSCIRC	.86917	-.12003	.09470
FEMEMPLD	.77037	.39514	.23949
FARMERS	-.65223	-.05898	-.49613
RETAILNG	.83157	.31678	.02580
COMMERCL	.83185	.13387	-.10273
INDUSTZN	.90854	.18199	.02554
HEALTH	-.08047	.79116	.15682
CHLDNEGL	-.37857	-.76645	.13585
COMMEFFC	.18756	.89284	.06103
DWELGNEW	.16236	.22710	.84518
MIGRNPOP	-.12675	-.01613	.77603
UNEMPLOY	-.55688	-.64006	.00379
MENTALIL	.04688	-.47050	-.38327

Figure 2.19   Quartimax-rotated factor matrix

```
FACTOR READ=CORRELATION TRIANGLE
 /VARIABLES=POPSTABL TO MENTALIL
 /EXTRACTION=PC
 /ROTATION=QUARTIMAX.
```

Quartimax converged in   5 iterations.

Rotated Factor Matrix:

	FACTOR 1	FACTOR 2	FACTOR 3
POPSTABL	-.14884	.00769	-.82018
NEWSCIRC	.85549	-.20254	.07706
FEMEMPLD	.81105	.32272	.21214
FARMERS	-.66736	-.00515	-.47920
RETAILNG	.85885	.23432	-.00105
COMMERCL	.83802	.04963	-.12529
INDUSTZN	.92229	.09267	.00000
HEALTH	.00097	.79832	.14028
CHLDNEGL	-.44778	-.72272	.16242
COMMEFFC	.27508	.87127	.03590
DWELGNEW	.20527	.22763	.83565
MIGRNPOP	-.10781	.01249	.77896
UNEMPLOY	-.61627	-.58226	.03168
MENTALIL	-.00897	-.48069	-.37326

The unrotated factor matrix is difficult to interpret. Many variables have moderate-size correlations with several factors. After rotation, the number of large and small factor loadings increases. Variables are more highly correlated with single factors. Interpretation of the factors also appears possible. For example, the first factor shows positive correlation with newspaper circulation, percentage of females in the labor force, sales, commercial activity, and the industrialization index. It also shows a strong negative correlation with the number of farmers. Thus, factor 1 might be interpreted as measuring something like "urbanism." The second factor is positively correlated with health and a high standard of living and negatively correlated with Aid to Dependent Children, unemployment, and mental illness. This factor describes the affluence or welfare of a community. The last factor is associated with the instability or influx of a community. Thus, communities may be fairly well characterized by three factors—urbanism, welfare, and influx.

Factor Loading Plots

A convenient means of examining the success of an orthogonal rotation is to plot the variables using the factor loadings as coordinates. Let's look at the effect of the rotation on factors 1 and 2. In Figure 2.20, the variables are plotted using factors 1 and 2 after varimax rotation of the two factors.

Figure 2.20   Varimax-rotated solution for factors 1 and 2

```
FACTOR READ=CORRELATION TRIANGLE
 /VARIABLES=POPSTABL TO MENTALIL
 /EXTRACTION=PC
 /ROTATION=VARIMAX
 /PLOT=ROTATION (1,2).
```

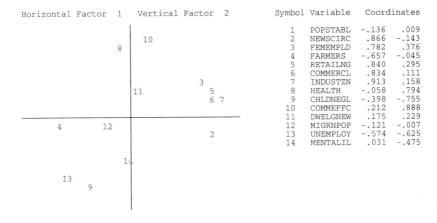

Horizontal Factor 1 Vertical Factor 2	Symbol	Variable	Coordinates	
	1	POPSTABL	-.136	.009
	2	NEWSCIRC	.866	-.143
	3	FEMEMPLD	.782	.376
	4	FARMERS	-.657	-.045
	5	RETAILNG	.840	.295
	6	COMMERCL	.834	.111
	7	INDUSTZN	.913	.158
	8	HEALTH	-.058	.794
	9	CHLDNEGL	-.398	-.755
	10	COMMEFFC	.212	.888
	11	DWELGNEW	.175	.229
	12	MIGRNPOP	-.121	-.007
	13	UNEMPLOY	-.574	-.625
	14	MENTALIL	.031	-.475

In Figure 2.21, the variables are plotted using factors 1 and 2 before rotation.

Figure 2.21   Unrotated solution for factors 1 and 2

```
FACTOR READ=CORRELATION TRIANGLE
 /VARIABLES=POPSTABL TO MENTALIL
 /EXTRACTION=PC
 /ROTATION=NOROTATE
 /PLOT=ROTATION (1,2).
```

Horizontal Factor 1 Vertical Factor 2	Symbol	Variable	Coordinates	
	1	POPSTABL	-.302	.686
	2	NEWSCIRC	.672	.281
	3	FEMEMPLD	.895	.011
	4	FARMERS	-.687	.200
	5	RETAILNG	.851	.243
	6	COMMERCL	.725	.394
	7	INDUSTZN	.844	.300
	8	HEALTH	.383	-.327
	9	CHLDNEGL	-.674	-.121
	10	COMMEFFC	.632	-.155
	11	DWELGNEW	.459	-.739
	12	MIGRNPOP	.079	-.744
	13	UNEMPLOY	-.787	-.098
	14	MENTALIL	-.300	.455

If a rotation has achieved a simple structure, clusters of variables should occur near the ends of the axes and at their intersection. Variables at the end of an axis are those that have high loadings on only that factor. Variables near the origin of the plot (0,0) have small loadings on both factors. Variables that are not near the axes are explained by both factors. If a simple structure has been achieved, there should be few if any variables with large loadings on more than one factor.

Interpreting the Factors

To identify the factors, it is necessary to group the variables that have large loadings for the same factors. Plots of the loadings are one way of determining the clusters of variables. Another convenient strategy is to sort the factor pattern matrix so that variables with high loadings on the same factor appear together, as shown in Figure 2.22. Small factor loadings can be omitted from such a table. In Figure 2.23, no loadings less than 0.5 in absolute value are displayed. Note that the mental illness variable, as expected, does not correlate highly with any of the factors.

Figure 2.22   Sorted loadings

```
FACTOR READ=CORRELATION TRIANGLE
  /VARIABLES=POPSTABL TO MENTALIL
  /FORMAT=SORT
  /ROTATION=VARIMAX.
```

Rotated Factor Matrix:

	FACTOR 1	FACTOR 2	FACTOR 3
INDUSTZN	.91325	.15773	.01730
NEWSCIRC	.86634	-.14256	.08920
RETAILNG	.83993	.29454	.01705
COMMERCL	.83432	.11068	-.11000
FEMEMPLD	.78248	.37620	.23055
FARMERS	-.65736	-.04537	-.49077
COMMEFFC	.21186	.88794	.05241
HEALTH	-.05806	.79424	.15101
CHLDNEGL	-.39791	-.75492	.14486
UNEMPLOY	-.57378	-.62483	.01311
MENTALIL	.03133	-.47460	-.37979
DWELGNEW	.17484	.22931	.84208
POPSTABL	-.13553	.00916	-.82247
MIGRNPOP	-.12119	-.00660	.77706

Figure 2.23 Sorted and blanked loadings

```
FACTOR READ=CORRELATION TRIANGLE
  /VARIABLES=POPSTABL TO MENTALIL
  /FORMAT=SORT BLANK(.5)
  /ROTATION=VARIMAX.
Rotated Factor Matrix:

              FACTOR  1      FACTOR  2      FACTOR  3

INDUSTZN       .91325
NEWSCIRC       .86634
RETAILNG       .83993
COMMERCL       .83432
FEMEMPLD       .78248
FARMERS       -.65736

COMMEFFC                      .88794
HEALTH                        .79424
CHLDNEGL                     -.75492
UNEMPLOY      -.57378        -.62483
MENTALIL

DWELGNEW                                     .84208
POPSTABL                                    -.82247
MIGRNPOP                                     .77706
```

Oblique Rotation

Orthogonal rotation results in factors that are uncorrelated. Although this is an appealing property, sometimes allowing for correlations among factors simplifies the factor pattern matrix. Consider Figure 2.24, which is a plot of the factor loadings for six variables. Note that if the axes (the dotted lines) went through the points, a simpler factor pattern matrix would result than with an orthogonal rotation. Factor pattern matrices for both rotations are shown in Figure 2.25.

Figure 2.24 Plot of factor loadings

```
FACTOR VAR=X1 TO X6
  /READ=FAC(2)
  /ROTATION=NOROTATE
  /PLOT=ROTATION(1,2).
```

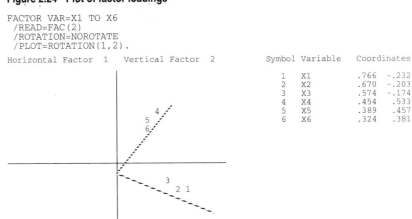

Horizontal Factor 1 Vertical Factor 2	Symbol	Variable	Coordinates
	1	X1	.766 -.232
	2	X2	.670 -.203
	3	X3	.574 -.174
	4	X4	.454 .533
	5	X5	.389 .457
	6	X6	.324 .381

Figure 2.25   Rotated varimax and oblique factor loadings

```
FACTOR VAR=X1 TO X6
 /READ=FAC(2)
 /ROTATION=VARIMAX
 /ROTATION=OBLIMIN.

 Varimax converged in    3 iterations.

Rotated Factor Matrix:

               FACTOR  1      FACTOR  2

X1                .78312         .16345
X2                .68524         .14301
X3                .58734         .12259
X4                .14301         .68523
X5                .12258         .58735
X6                .10216         .48945


 Oblimin converged in    4 iterations.

Pattern Matrix:

               FACTOR  1      FACTOR  2

X1                .80000         .00000
X2                .70001         .00000
X3                .60000         .00000
X4                .00000         .70000
X5                .00000         .60000
X6                .00000         .50000
```

There are several reasons why oblique rotation is useful. It is unlikely that influences in nature are uncorrelated. And even if they are uncorrelated in the population, they need not be so in the sample. Thus, oblique rotations have often been found to yield substantively meaningful factors.

Factor Pattern and Structure Matrices

Oblique rotation preserves the communalities of the variables, as does orthogonal rotation. When oblique rotation is used, however, the factor loadings and factor variable correlations are no longer identical. The factor loadings are still partial regression coefficients, but since the factors are correlated, they are no longer equal to the simple factor variable correlations. (Remember that the regression coefficients depend on the interrelationships of the independent variables when these are correlated.) Therefore, separate factor loading and factor structure matrices are displayed as part of the output.

Algorithm for Oblique Rotation

The method for oblique rotation available in the SPSS/PC+ Factor procedure is called **oblimin**. A parameter called **delta** (δ) controls the extent of obliqueness. When δ is 0, the factors are most oblique. For negative values of δ, the factors become less oblique as δ becomes more negative. Harman (1967) recommends that δ be either 0 or negative.

The factor loadings for the community data after an oblique rotation are shown in the factor pattern matrix in Figure 2.26. The loadings are no longer constrained to a range of -1 to $+1$. The correlations between the factors and variables are shown in Figure 2.27, the factor structure matrix.

Figure 2.26   Factor pattern matrix

```
FACTOR READ=CORRELATION TRIANGLE
 /VARIABLES=POPSTABL TO MENTALIL
 /FORMAT=SORT
 /ROTATION=OBLIMIN.
```

Pattern Matrix:

	FACTOR 1	FACTOR 2	FACTOR 3
INDUSTZN	.91577	.02882	-.04731
NEWSCIRC	.90594	-.06987	.26053
COMMERCL	.84325	.15024	-.01504
RETAILNG	.82253	.03760	-.19782
FEMEMPLD	.74906	-.17274	-.27862
FARMERS	-.65969	.46636	-.06041
POPSTABL	-.12570	.82380	-.06787
DWELGNEW	.13426	-.82258	-.17248
MIGRNPOP	-.13720	-.78724	.03070
COMMEFFC	.09940	.02770	-.88775
HEALTH	-.16689	-.08909	-.81993
CHLDNEGL	-.31128	-.22218	.73693
UNEMPLOY	-.50651	-.08531	.57387
MENTALIL	.10140	.34462	.47495

Figure 2.27   Factor structure matrix

Structure Matrix:

	FACTOR 1	FACTOR 2	FACTOR 3
INDUSTZN	.92553	-.04717	-.27457
RETAILNG	.86963	-.05222	-.40031
NEWSCIRC	.84545	-.10235	.02205
COMMERCL	.83566	.08423	-.20712
FEMEMPLD	.83252	-.26822	-.49178
FARMERS	-.67979	.50798	.17096
DWELGNEW	.24017	-.85671	-.32064
POPSTABL	-.17101	.82390	.07829
MIGRNPOP	-.08527	-.77258	-.04400
COMMEFFC	.32149	-.10314	-.90901
HEALTH	.04692	-.19032	-.79016
CHLDNEGL	-.48053	-.09623	.78468
UNEMPLOY	-.64496	.03280	.68993
MENTALIL	-.04466	.40290	.49721

The correlation matrix for the factors is shown in Figure 2.28. Note that there are small correlations between all three factors. In the case of an orthogonal rotation, the factor correlation matrix is an identity matrix. That is, there are 1's on the diagonal and 0's elsewhere.

Figure 2.28   Factor correlation matrix

```
Factor Correlation Matrix:

                  FACTOR  1     FACTOR  2     FACTOR  3

FACTOR   1        1.00000
FACTOR   2        -.07580       1.00000
FACTOR   3        -.25253        .13890       1.00000
```

The oblique rotation resulted in the same grouping of variables as did the orthogonal rotation. The interpretation of the factors does not change based on oblique rotation.

Factor Scores

Since one of the goals of factor analysis is to reduce a large number of variables to a smaller number of factors, it is often desirable to estimate factor scores for each case. The factor scores can be used in subsequent analyses to represent the values of the factors. Plots of factor scores for pairs of factors are useful for detecting unusual observations.

Recall from "The Factor Analysis Model" on p. 54 that a factor can be estimated as a linear combination of the original variables. That is, for case k, the score for the jth factor is estimated as

$$\hat{F}_{jk} = \sum_{i=1}^{p} W_{ji} X_{ik}$$

Equation 2.12

where X_{ik} is the standardized value of the ith variable for case k and W_{ji} is the factor score coefficient for the jth factor and the ith variable. Except for principal components analysis, exact factor scores cannot be obtained. Estimates are obtained instead.

There are several methods for estimating factor score coefficients. Each has different properties and results in different scores (Tucker, 1971; Harman, 1967). The three methods available in the SPSS/PC+ Factor procedure (Anderson-Rubin, regression, and Bartlett) all result in scores with a mean of 0. The Anderson-Rubin method always produces uncorrelated scores with a standard deviation of 1, even when the original factors are estimated to be correlated. The regression factor scores (the default) have a variance equal to the squared multiple correlation between the estimated factor scores and the true factor values. (These are shown on the diagonal in Figure 2.30.) Regression-method factor scores can be correlated even when factors are assumed to be orthogonal. If principal components extraction is used, all three methods result in the same factor scores, which are no longer estimated but are exact.

Figure 2.29 contains the factor score coefficients used to calculate regression-method factor scores for the community data. The covariance matrix for the estimated scores is shown in Figure 2.30.

Figure 2.29   Factor coefficient matrix

```
FACTOR READ=CORRELATION TRIANGLE
 /VARIABLES=POPSTABL TO MENTALIL
 /PRINT=FSCORES
 /EXTRACTION=ML
 /ROTATION=VARIMAX.

Factor Score Coefficient Matrix:

                  FACTOR  1      FACTOR  2      FACTOR  3

POPSTABL          -.00150         .03191        -.15843
NEWSCIRC           .05487        -.06095         .03524
FEMEMPLD           .01729         .14014         .05328
FARMERS           -.01797         .00113        -.11462
RETAILNG           .03728         .09460        -.03577
COMMERCL           .20579        -.11667        -.10723
INDUSTZN           .77285        -.27024         .00882
HEALTH            -.02786         .09971        -.00161
CHLDNEGL           .08404        -.44657         .16521
COMMEFFC          -.05030         .23211        -.03623
DWELGNEW          -.05117         .07034         .68792
MIGRNPOP           .00029        -.03198         .09778
UNEMPLOY           .03856        -.26435         .05378
MENTALIL           .01264        -.04224        -.01691
```

Figure 2.30   Covariance matrix for estimated regression factor scores

```
Covariance Matrix for Estimated Regression Factor Scores:

                  FACTOR  1      FACTOR  2      FACTOR  3

FACTOR  1          .96763
FACTOR  2          .03294         .87641
FACTOR  3          .00042         .02544         .89452
```

To see how factor scores are calculated, consider Table 2.3, which contains standardized values for the original 14 variables for five counties, and factor score values for the three factors. For each factor, the factor scores are obtained by multiplying the standardized

Table 2.3   Standardized values and factor scores

| Variable | County | | | | |
	Adams	Butler	Crawford	Cuyahoga	Hamilton
popstabl	−0.36	−1.49	2.44	−0.13	−0.30
newscirc	−0.93	0.39	−0.26	2.04	1.17
femempld	−1.06	0.41	0.24	1.30	1.03
farmers	2.20	−0.67	0.01	−0.93	−0.90
retailng	−1.41	0.49	0.58	1.15	1.07
commercl	−0.89	−0.30	−0.07	1.58	2.02
industzn	−1.14	−0.11	0.03	1.53	1.85
health	−0.25	−0.56	−1.32	−0.36	−1.17
chldnegl	−1.26	0.79	−0.61	0.63	0.99
commeffc	−0.20	0.78	−0.87	−0.78	−1.66
dwelgnew	−0.52	0.52	−1.09	−0.01	−0.22
migrnpop	−0.98	0.16	−0.60	0.63	1.13
unemploy	−0.75	−0.36	−0.44	1.56	0.76
mentalil	−0.76	−0.77	−0.46	−0.14	0.61

Factor	Scores				
Factor 1	−1.328	−0.089	0.083	1.862	2.233
Factor 2	0.897	0.027	0.197	−1.362	−1.79
Factor 3	−0.830	0.831	−1.290	0.342	0.226

values by the corresponding factor score coefficients. Thus, for Adams county the value for factor 1 is:

$$\text{Value for factor } 1 = (-0.00150)\,(-0.36) + (0.05487)\,(-0.93)$$
$$+ (0.01729)\,(-1.06) + \ldots + (0.01264)\,(-0.76) \qquad \textbf{Equation 2.13}$$
$$= -1.328$$

Running the Factor Procedure

A variety of extraction and rotation techniques is available in the SPSS/PC+ Factor procedure. The extraction methods available include principal components analysis (see "Factor Extraction" on p. 59) and the maximum-likelihood factor method (see "Some Additional Considerations" on p. 66). The factor rotation methods are varimax, equamax, quartimax, and oblimin.

You can also request scree plots and factor loading plots to help in selecting and interpreting factors. FACTOR accepts a correlation matrix or a factor loading matrix as input, as well as the original cases.

Global and Analysis Block Subcommands

There are two main types of FACTOR subcommands: global and analysis block. **Global subcommands** are specified once and are in effect for the entire Factor procedure. **Analysis block subcommands** apply only to the ANALYSIS subcommand that precedes them.

The global subcommands are VARIABLES, MISSING, and WIDTH. The VARIABLES subcommand identifies the variables to be used in the Factor procedure. The MISSING subcommand specifies missing-value treatment. The WIDTH subcommand controls the width of the display.

An analysis block begins with an ANALYSIS subcommand, which names a subset of variables from the list specified on the VARIABLES subcommand. If you omit the ANALYSIS subcommand, which is permitted only for the first analysis block, all variables named on the VARIABLES subcommand are used. An analysis block contains one or more extraction phases, and an extraction phase contains one or more rotation phases (see the Syntax Reference section in this manual).

The extraction phase is initiated by the EXTRACTION subcommand, which specifies the factor extraction method. A default principal components analysis is performed if no EXTRACTION subcommand is specified. The rotation phase is initiated by the ROTATION subcommand, which specifies the rotation method. A default varimax rotation is obtained if you omit both EXTRACTION and ROTATION. No rotation occurs if EXTRACTION is specified without ROTATION. The CRITERIA subcommand controls subsequent rotation as well as extraction criteria.

You can also tailor the statistics displayed for an analysis block by specifying the PRINT subcommand to request optional statistics, the FORMAT subcommand to reformat factor loading and structure matrices, the PLOT subcommand to obtain scree plots and factor loading plots, and the SAVE subcommand to save factor scores from any rotated or unrotated extraction.

Optional subcommands are available to write and read matrices for FACTOR (see Figure 2.1 for an example of matrix input).

Subcommand Order

The global subcommands VARIABLES and MISSING must be the first specifications. The remaining subcommands can appear in any logical order.

Within an analysis block, the placement of CRITERIA is important, as it affects all extractions and rotations that follow. Once specified, a CRITERIA subcommand is in effect for the remainder of the Factor procedure unless superseded by another CRITERIA subcommand.

Specifying the Variables

The VARIABLES subcommand lists the variables to analyze.

- VARIABLES is the only required subcommand and must be placed before all other subcommands except MISSING and WIDTH.

- Only variables named on the VARIABLES subcommand can be referred to in subsequent subcommands.

- You can specify only one VARIABLES subcommand on a FACTOR command.

- If you do not specify a subsequent ANALYSIS, EXTRACTION, or ROTATION subcommand, the default principal components analysis with varimax rotation is produced for all variables named on VARIABLES.

Example

```
FACTOR VARIABLES=POPSTABL NEWSCIRC FEMEMPLD FARMERS
   RETAILNG COMMERCL INDUSTZN HEALTH CHLDNEGL COMMEFFC
   DWELGNEW MIGRNPOP UNEMPLOY MENTALIL.
```

- This command produces the output shown in Figure 2.4, Figure 2.6, and Figure 2.7.

- If the variables exist in that order in the active file, the following command produces the same output:

```
FACTOR VARIABLES=POPSTABL TO MENTALIL.
```

Missing Values

FACTOR results are based on the correlation matrix for the variables listed on the VARIABLES subcommand. Use the MISSING subcommand to specify the missing-value treatment for this matrix. If you omit the MISSING subcommand, or include it with no specifications, missing values are deleted listwise.

You can specify only one MISSING subcommand per FACTOR command. The MISSING subcommand must be placed before all other subcommands except VARIABLES and WIDTH. MISSING is ignored with matrix input.

LISTWISE   *Delete missing values listwise.* Only cases with valid values on all variables named on the VARIABLES subcommand are used. This is the default.

PAIRWISE   *Delete missing values pairwise.* Cases with complete data on each pair of variables correlated are used.

MEANSUB   *Replace missing values with the variable mean.*

INCLUDE   *Include user-missing values.* Cases with user-missing values are treated as valid observations. Only system-missing values are excluded or substituted.

DEFAULT   *Same as LISTWISE.*

Example

```
FACTOR VARIABLES=IQ GPA TESTSCOR STRESS SAT PSYCHTST
 /MISSING=PAIRWISE.
```

- This command requests a default analysis that uses pairwise missing-value treatment in calculating the correlation matrix.

Specifying Output Width

The WIDTH subcommand controls the display width for factor output. For example, the subcommand `/WIDTH=80` requests output that is 80 characters wide. The value on WIDTH must be an integer. This value overrides the one specified on the SET command. You can specify only one WIDTH subcommand per FACTOR command. The WIDTH subcommand can be placed anywhere.

Specifying Analyses

The ANALYSIS subcommand allows you to perform analyses on subsets of variables named on the VARIABLES subcommand.

- The TO keyword in a variable list on the ANALYSIS subcommand refers to the order of variables named on the VARIABLES subcommand, not to their order in the file. Otherwise, the usual SPSS/PC+ conventions for variable lists are followed.

- You can use the keyword ALL to refer to all of the variables listed on the VARIABLES subcommand.

- If you do not include the ANALYSIS subcommand, FACTOR uses all of the variables listed on the VARIABLES subcommand for the analysis. This is allowed only for the first analysis block.

- If you specify any analysis block subcommand before the first ANALYSIS subcommand, FACTOR performs a default analysis using all variables before the explicitly specified analysis.

Example

```
FACTOR VARIABLES=POPSTABL TO MENTALIL
 /ANALYSIS=FEMEMPLD FARMERS INDUSTZN HEALTH CHLDNEGL DWELGNEW
 /ANALYSIS=POPSTABL NEWSCIRC FEMEMPLD COMMERCL UNEMPLOY
MENTALIL.
```

- This command requests two default principal components analyses.

- The first analysis uses variables *femempld, farmers, industzn, health, chldnegl,* and *dwelgnew.*

- The second uses variables *popstabl, newscirc, femempld, commercl, unemploy,* and *mentalil.*

Example

```
FACTOR VARIABLES=POPSTABL TO MENTALIL
 /PRINT=DEFAULTS CORRELATIONS
 /ANALYSIS=FEMEMPLD FARMERS INDUSTZN HEALTH CHLDNEGL DWELGNEW
 /ANALYSIS=POPSTABL NEWSCIRC FEMEMPLD COMMERCL UNEMPLOY
MENTALIL.
```

- This command implicitly requests a default analysis for all variables with the PRINT subcommand. The correlation matrix along with the defaults are printed for this analysis.
- The second and third analyses use different subsets of the variable list and print only the defaults.

Specifying the Extraction Method

Use the EXTRACTION subcommand to specify the extraction method.

- You can use multiple EXTRACTION subcommands within an analysis block to produce output using different extraction methods for the same subset of variables.
- If you use the EXTRACTION subcommand without a subsequent ROTATION subcommand, the factor pattern matrix is not rotated (see "The Rotation Phase" on p. 70). The following extraction methods are available in the Factor procedure:.

PC   *Principal components analysis.* This is the default.

PAF   *Principal axis factoring.*

ML   *Maximum likelihood.*

ALPHA   *Alpha factoring.*

IMAGE   *Image factoring.*

ULS   *Unweighted least squares.*

GLS   *Generalized least squares.*

PA1   *Same as PC.*

PA2   *Same as PAF.*

DEFAULT   *Same as PC.*

Example

```
FACTOR VARIABLES=IQ GPA TESTSCOR STRESS SAT PSYCHTST
 /EXTRACTION=ML
 /EXTRACTION=PC.
```

- This example produces output based on two extraction methods—maximum likelihood and principal components. All variables named on the VARIABLES subcommand are used in the analysis.

Specifying Diagonal Values

Use the DIAGONAL subcommand to specify initial diagonal values in conjunction with principal axis factoring (PAF). The default for the method is the communality estimates on the diagonal. You can specify a value list on DIAGONAL to be used as initial diagonal values.

- User-supplied diagonal values are used only for principal axis factoring.

- You can use keyword DEFAULT to request default values explicitly.

- When a value list is specified, the number of the values in the list must be the same as the number of the variables in the analysis.

- You can use the prefix n and an asterisk to indicate replicated values. For example, $5*0.80$ is the same as specifying 0.80 five times.

Example

```
FACTOR VARIABLES=IQ GPA TESTSCOR SAT EDYEARS
 /DIAGONAL=.55 .45 .35 .40 .50
 /EXTRACTION=PAF.
```

- This command assigns five diagonal values for the specified principal axis factoring.

Specifying Extraction and Rotation Criteria

Use CRITERIA to control criteria for subsequent extractions and rotations.

FACTORS(n)   *Number of factors extracted.* The default is the number of eigenvalues greater than MINEIGEN (see below).

MINEIGEN(n)   *Minimum eigenvalue for the factor to be retained.* The default value is 1.

ITERATE(n)   *Number of iterations for the factor solution.* The default value is 25.

ECONVERGE(n) *Convergence criterion for extraction.* The default value is 0.001.

RCONVERGE(n) *Convergence criterion for rotation.* The default value is 0.0001.

KAISER   *Kaiser normalization in rotation.* This is the default.

NOKAISER   *No Kaiser normalization.*

DELTA(d)	*Value of delta for direct oblimin rotation.* The default value is 0.
DEFAULT	*Use default values for all criteria.*

Once specified, criteria stay in effect for the procedure until explicitly overridden.

Example

```
FACTOR VARIABLES=IQ GPA TESTSCOR STRESS SAT PSYCHTST
 /CRITERIA=FACTORS(2)
 /ANALYSIS=ALL
 /CRITERIA=DEFAULT.
```

- This command produces two factor analyses for the same set of variables.
- The first analysis limits the number of factors extracted to 2. The ANALYSIS subcommand for this analysis block is omitted.
- The second analysis extracts all factors whose eigenvalue is greater than 1.

Rotating Factors

Four rotation methods are available in FACTOR: varimax, equamax, quartimax, and oblimin (see "The Rotation Phase" on p. 70). When both the EXTRACTION and ROTATION subcommands are omitted, the factors are rotated using the varimax method. However, if EXTRACTION is specified but ROTATION is not, the factors are not rotated.

To specify a rotation method other than these defaults, use the ROTATION subcommand. You can specify more than one rotation for a given extraction by using multiple ROTATION subcommands.

The following keywords are available on ROTATION:

VARIMAX	*Varimax rotation.* This is the default if both EXTRACTION and ROTATION are omitted.
EQUAMAX	*Equamax rotation.*
QUARTIMAX	*Quartimax rotation.*
OBLIMIN	*Direct oblimin rotation.*
NOROTATE	*No rotation.* This is the default if EXTRACTION is specified but ROTATION is not.
DEFAULT	*Same as VARIMAX.*

OBLIMIN uses a default delta value of 0. Use the CRITERIA subcommand to change this default (see "Specifying Extraction and Rotation Criteria" on p. 87).

To obtain a factor loading plot based on unrotated factors, use the PLOT subcommand (see "Obtaining Plots" on p. 90) and specify NOROTATE on the ROTATION subcommand.

Example

```
FACTOR VARIABLES=IQ GPA TESTSCOR STRESS SAT PSYCHTST
 /PLOT=EIGEN ROTATION(1,2)
 /ROTATION=NOROTATE.
```

Optional Statistics

By default, the statistics for INITIAL, EXTRACTION, and ROTATION are printed. If you specify PRINT, only those statistics explicitly named are displayed. You can use only one PRINT subcommand for each analysis block.

INITIAL	*Initial communalities, eigenvalues, and percentage of variance explained.* (See "Factor Extraction" on p. 59 and "More on the Factor Matrix" on p. 62.)
EXTRACTION	*Communalities, eigenvalues, and rotated factor loadings.* (See "Factor Extraction" on p. 59 through "Methods for Factor Extraction" on p. 68.)
ROTATION	*Rotated factor pattern and structure matrices, factor transformation matrix, and factor correlation matrix.* (See "The Rotation Phase" on p. 70.)
UNIVARIATE	*Numbers of valid observations, means, and standard deviations for the variables named on the ANALYSIS subcommand.*
CORRELATION	*Correlation matrix for the variables named on the ANALYSIS subcommand.*
SIG	*Significance levels of correlations.* These are one-tailed probabilities.
DET	*The determinant of the correlation matrix.*
INV	*The inverse of the correlation matrix.*
AIC	*The anti-image covariance and correlation matrices.*
KMO	*The Kaiser-Meyer-Olkin measure of sampling adequacy and Bartlett's test of sphericity.* (See "Examining the Correlation Matrix" on p. 56.)
REPR	*Reproduced correlations and their residuals.* (See "The Reproduced Correlation Matrix" on p. 63.)
FSCORE	*The factor score coefficient matrix.* By default, this is based on a regression solution. (See "Factor Scores" on p. 80.)
DEFAULT	*INITIAL, EXTRACTION, and ROTATION statistics.* If you use the EXTRACTION subcommand without a subsequent ROTATION subcommand, only the statistics specified by INITIAL and EXTRACTION are displayed since a rotation is not done.
ALL	*All available statistics.*

Example

```
FACTOR VARIABLES=POPSTABL TO MENTALIL
 /PRINT=REPR.
```

- This command produces the output in Figure 2.8.

Sorting the Factor Pattern Matrix

Use the FORMAT subcommand to reformat the display of the factor loading and structure matrices to help you interpret the factors (see "Interpreting the Factors" on p. 76). You can use only one FORMAT subcommand per analysis block. The following keywords may be specified on FORMAT:

SORT   *Order the factor loadings by magnitude.*

BLANK(n)   *Suppress coefficients lower in absolute value than* n.

DEFAULT   *Turn off blanking and sorting.*

Example

```
FACTOR VARIABLES=POPSTABL TO MENTALIL
 /FORMAT=SORT BLANK(.5).
```

- This command produces the output in Figure 2.23.

Obtaining Plots

To obtain a scree plot (see "Factor Extraction" on p. 59) or a factor loading plot (see "Factor Loading Plots" on p. 74), use the PLOT subcommand with the following keywords:

EIGEN   *Scree plot.* Plot the eigenvalues in descending order.

ROTATION(n1 n2) *Factor loading plot.* The specifications $n1$ and $n2$ refer to the factors used as the axes. Several pairs of factors in parentheses can be specified on one ROTATION keyword. A plot is displayed for each pair of factor numbers enclosed in parentheses.

You can specify only one PLOT subcommand per analysis block. Plots are based on rotated factors. To get an unrotated factor plot, you must explicitly specify NOROTATE on the ROTATION subcommand (see "Rotating Factors" on p. 88).

The plots in Figure 2.5 and Figure 2.20 can be augmented with two additional factor plots if you specify the following:

```
FACTOR VARIABLES=POPSTABL TO MENTALIL
 /PLOT=EIGEN ROTATION(1 2)(1 3)(2 3).
```

Saving Factor Scores

Use the SAVE subcommand to compute and save factor scores in the active file.

- Factor scores cannot be produced from matrix input.
- Specify one of the method keywords listed below, followed by the number of factor scores to calculate, and a rootname to be used in naming the factor scores. The number and the rootname must be enclosed in parentheses.
- The maximum number of scores is equal to the number of factors retained. You can use keyword ALL to calculate factor scores for all retained factors.
- The rootname can be up to seven characters long. FACTOR uses the rootname to name the factor scores sequentially; for example, *root1*, *root2*, and *root3*. If you are calculating factor scores for a many-factor solution, make sure that the rootname is short enough to accommodate the number added for the variable holding the highest order factor score.
- When FACTOR saves the variables on the active file, it automatically supplies a variable label indicating the method used to calculate it, its positional order, and the analysis number.
- You can use multiple SAVE subcommands for an extraction.

The following keywords are available on SAVE:

REG   *The regression method.* This is the default.

BART   *The Bartlett method.*

AR   *The Anderson-Rubin method.*

DEFAULT   *Same as REG.*

Example
```
FACTOR VARIABLES=ABDEFECT TO ABSINGLE
 /MISSING=MEANSUB
 /CRITERIA=FACTORS(2)
 /EXTRACTION=ULS
 /ROTATION=VARIMAX
 /SAVE=AR (ALL FSULS).
```

- This command saves factor scores for a study of abortion items.
- FACTOR calculates two factor scores named *fsuls1* and *fsuls2* using the Anderson-Rubin method and saves them in the active file.

Example

```
FACTOR VARIABLES=ABDEFECT TO ABSINGLE
 /MISSING=MEANSUB
 /EXTRACTION=ULS
 /ROTATION=VARIMAX
 /SAVE=AR (ALL FSULS)
 /SAVE=BART (ALL BFAC).
```

- This command saves two sets of factor scores. The first set is computed using the Anderson-Rubin method and the second is computed using the Bartlett method.

Reading and Writing Matrices

You can read either the correlation matrix or factor loadings into FACTOR by specifying *one* of the following keywords on the READ subcommand.

CORRELATION *Read the correlation matrix.* This is the default.

FACTOR(n) *Read the factor matrix.* In the parentheses following the keyword, specify the number of factors in the analysis.

DEFAULT *Same as CORRELATION.*

You can specify keyword TRIANGLE after keyword CORRELATION on the READ subcommand, as in `/READ=CORRELATION  TRIANGLE` if the correlation matrix is in lower-triangular form and contains a diagonal of 1's.

When you read a correlation or factor loading matrix with FACTOR, you must first specify a DATA LIST MATRIX command that points to the file containing the matrix materials and names the variables that will be read. If you supply an N command, FACTOR is able to calculate significance levels for the extraction techniques that use chi-square as a test statistic for the adequacy of the model and Bartlett's test of sphericity, which is available with the KMO keyword on the PRINT subcommand.

When FACTOR reads correlation matrices written by other procedures such as CORRELATION, it skips the record or matrix of N's and prints a message for each line of the matrix of N's.

Example

```
DATA LIST MATRIX FILE='FACT.MAT' / SUICIDE1 TO SUICIDE5.
FACTOR VARIABLES=SUICIDE1 TO SUICIDE5
 /READ.
```

- These two commands read a correlation matrix from an external file and use it for a factor analysis.

You can use the WRITE subcommand with one of the following keywords to write the correlation matrix or the factor loadings to a specified file:

CORRELATION *Write the correlation matrix.* This is the default.

FACTOR *Write the factor matrix.*

DEFAULT *Same as CORRELATION.*

The matrix is written to the results file specified on the SET command. By default, the file is named *spss.prc*.

Annotated Example

Part of the output produced by the following commands is shown in Figure 2.1, Figure 2.3, Figure 2.4, Figure 2.6, Figure 2.7, Figure 2.8, Figure 2.22, and Figure 2.26.

```
DATA LIST MATRIX FREE
 /POPSTABL NEWSCIRC FEMEMPLD FARMERS RETAILNG COMMERCL
 INDUSTZN  HEALTH CHLDNEGL COMMEFFC DWELGNEW MIGRNPOP
 UNEMPLOY MENTALIL.

N 88.

BEGIN DATA.
1.000
-.175 1.000
-.276  .616 1.000
 .369 -.625 -.637 1.000
-.127  .624  .736 -.519 1.000
-.069  .652  .589 -.306  .727 1.000
-.106  .712  .742 -.545  .785  .911 1.000
-.149 -.030  .241 -.068  .100  .123  .129 1.000
-.039 -.171 -.589  .257 -.557 -.357 -.424 -.407 1.000
-.005  .100  .471 -.213  .452  .287  .357  .732 -.660 1.000
-.670  .188  .413 -.579  .165  .030  .203  .290 -.138  .311
  1.000
-.476 -.086  .064 -.198  .007 -.068 -.024  .083  .148  .067
  505 1.000
 .137 -.373 -.689  .450 -.650 -.424 -.528 -.348  .733 -.601
-.266 181 1.000
 .237  .046 -.237  .121 -.190 -.055 -.095 -.279  .247 -.324
-.266 -.307  .217  1.000
END DATA.

FACTOR READ=COR TRIANGLE
 /VARIABLES=POPSTABL TO MENTALIL
 /PRINT=ALL
 /FORMAT=SORT
 /ROTATION=VARIMAX/
 /ROTATION=OBLIMIN.
```

- The DATA LIST command specifies the variable names used in the analysis and tells SPSS/PC+ that the data are input as a matrix.
- The N command tells SPSS/PC+ upon how many cases the matrix is based.
- The READ subcommand on the FACTOR command reads a correlation matrix in lower-triangular form.
- The VARIABLES subcommand specifies the variables available to the procedure.
- The PRINT subcommand specifies all possible factor results.
- The FORMAT subcommand requests that the factor loadings be ordered by magnitude.
- The first ROTATION subcommand produces an orthogonal varimax rotation. The second ROTATION subcommand requests an oblique oblimin rotation.

3 Cluster Analysis

Despite the old adage that opposites attract, it appears instead that likes attract. Birds of a feather and many other animate and inanimate objects that share similar characteristics tend to cluster together. You can form groups of similar objects using a statistical procedure called **cluster analysis**.

In biology, cluster analysis is used to classify animals and plants. This is called numerical taxonomy. In medicine, cluster analysis is used to identify diseases and their stages. For example, by examining patients who are diagnosed as depressed, you might find that there are several distinct subgroups of patients with different types of depression. In marketing, cluster analysis is used to identify people with similar buying habits. By examining their characteristics, you may be able to target future marketing strategies more efficiently. See Romesburg (1984) for more examples of the use of cluster analysis.

Although both cluster analysis and discriminant analysis classify objects, or cases, into categories, discriminant analysis requires you to know group membership for the cases used to derive the classification rule. For example, if you are interested in distinguishing among several disease groups, cases with known diagnoses must be available. Then, based on cases whose group membership is known, discriminant analysis derives a rule for allocating undiagnosed patients. In cluster analysis, group membership for all cases is unknown. In fact, even the number of groups is often unknown. The goal of cluster analysis is to identify homogeneous groups or clusters.

In this chapter, the fundamentals of cluster analysis are illustrated using a subset of data presented in a Consumer Reports (1983) survey of beer. Each of 20 beers is characterized in terms of cost per 12 ounces, alcohol content, sodium content, and the number of calories per 12-ounce serving. From these variables, it is possible to identify several distinct subgroups of beer.

Basic Steps

As in other statistical procedures, a number of decisions must be made before you embark on the actual analysis. Which variables will serve as the basis for cluster formation? How will the distance between cases be measured? What criteria will be used for combining cases into clusters?

Selecting the variables to include in an analysis is always crucial. If important variables are excluded, poor or misleading findings may result. For example, in a regression analysis of salary, if variables such as education and experience are not included, the results may be questionable. In cluster analysis, the initial choice of variables determines the characteristics that can be used to identify subgroups. If you are interested in clustering schools within a city and do not include variables such as the number of students or the number of teachers, size is automatically excluded as a criterion for establishing clusters. By excluding all measures of taste or quality from the beer data, only physical characteristics and price will determine which beers are deemed similar.

How Alike Are the Cases?

The concepts of distance and similarity are basic to many statistical techniques. **Distance** is a measure of how far apart two objects are, and **similarity** measures closeness. Distance measures are small and similarity measures are large for cases that are similar. In cluster analysis, these concepts are especially important, since cases are grouped on the basis of their "nearness." There are many different definitions of distance and similarity. Selection of a distance measure should be based both on the properties of the measure and on the algorithm for cluster formation. See "More on Calculating Distances and Similarities" on p. 109 for further discussion of distance measures.

To see how a simple distance measure is computed, consider Table 3.1, which shows the values for calories and cost for two of the beers. There is a 13-calorie and a 5-cent difference between the two beers. This information can be combined into a single index or distance measure in many different ways. A commonly used index is the **squared Euclidean distance**, which is the sum of the squared differences over all of the variables. In this example, the squared Euclidean distance is $13^2 + 5^2$, or 194.

Table 3.1   Values for calories and cost for two beers

	Calories	Cost
Budweiser	144	43
Lowenbrau	157	48

The squared Euclidean distance has the disadvantage that it depends on the units of measurement for the variables. For example, if the cost were given in pennies per ounce instead of pennies per 12 ounces, the computed distance would change. Another disadvantage is that when variables are measured on different scales, as in this example, variables that are measured in larger numbers will contribute more to the computed distance than variables that are recorded in smaller numbers. For example, the 13-calorie difference contributes much more to the distance score than the 5-cent difference in cost does.

One means of circumventing this problem is to express all variables in standardized form. That is, transform all variables to have a mean of 0 and a standard deviation of 1. This is not always the best strategy, however, since the variability of a particular measure can provide useful information (see Sneath & Sokal, 1973). (See the Descriptive Statistics chapter in the *SPSS/PC+ Base System User's Guide* for further discussion.)

Table 3.2 shows the Z scores for calories and cost for Budweiser and Lowenbrau beers based on the means and standard deviations for all 20 beers. The squared Euclidean distance based on the standardized variables is $(0.38 - 0.81)^2 + (-0.46 - (-0.11))^2$, or 0.307. The differences in calories and cost are now weighted equally.

Table 3.2   Z scores for calories and cost for two beers

	Calories	Cost
Budweiser	0.38	–0.46
Lowenbrau	0.81	–0.11

Forming Clusters

Just as there are many methods for calculating distances between objects, there are many methods for combining objects into clusters. A commonly used method for forming clusters is agglomerative hierarchical cluster analysis. In **agglomerative hierarchical clustering**, clusters are formed by grouping cases into bigger and bigger clusters until all cases are members of a single cluster. For a discussion of nonhierarchical clustering methods, see Everitt (1980).

Agglomerative Clustering

Before discussing the rules for forming clusters, let's consider what happens at each step of agglomerative hierarchical cluster analysis. Before the analysis begins, all cases are considered separate clusters: there are as many clusters as there are cases. At the first step, two of the cases are combined into a single cluster. At the second step, either a third case is added to the cluster already containing two cases, or two other cases are merged into a new cluster. At every step, either individual cases are added to existing clusters or two existing clusters are combined. Once a cluster is formed, it cannot be split; it can only be combined with other clusters. Thus, the agglomerative hierarchical clustering method does not allow cases to separate from clusters to which they have been assigned. For example, if two beers are deemed members of the same cluster at the first step, they will always be members of the same cluster, although they may be combined with additional cases at a later step.

Criteria for Combining Clusters

There are many criteria for deciding which cases or clusters should be combined at each step. All of these criteria are based on a matrix of either distances or similarities between pairs of cases. One of the simplest methods is **single linkage**, sometimes called the **nearest neighbor method**. The first two cases combined are those that have the smallest distance (or largest similarity) between them. The distance between the new cluster and individual cases is then computed as the minimum distance between an individual case and a case in the cluster. The distances between cases that have not been joined do not change. At every step, the distance between two clusters is the distance between their two closest points.

Another commonly used method is called **complete linkage**, or the **furthest neighbor technique**. In this method, the distance between two clusters is calculated as the distance between their two furthest points. Other methods for combining clusters are described in "Methods for Combining Clusters" on p. 110.

Performing a Cluster Analysis

Before considering other distance measures and methods of combining clusters, consider Figure 3.1, which shows the original and standardized values for calories, sodium content, alcohol content, and cost for the 20 beers, and Figure 3.2, which displays the squared Euclidean distance coefficients for all possible pairs of the 20 beers, based on the standardized values.

Figure 3.1   Original and standardized values for the 20 beers

```
DATA LIST
   /ID 1-2 RATING 3 BEER 4-24 (A) ORIGIN 25 AVAIL 26
    PRICE 27-30 COST 31-34 CALORIES 35-37 SODIUM 38-39
    ALCOHOL 40-42 CLASS 43 LIGHT 44.
VARIABLE LABEL CALORIES 'CALORIES PER 12 FLUID OUNCES'
               COST 'COST PER 12 FLUID OUNCES'
               ALCOHOL 'ALCOHOL BY VOLUME (IN %)'
               SODIUM 'SODIUM PER 12 FLUID OUNCES IN MG'.
FORMATS PRICE COST (F4.2) ALCOHOL (F3.1).
MISSING VALUES CLASS(0).
BEGIN DATA
lines of data
END DATA.
DESCRIPTIVES CALORIES SODIUM ALCOHOL COST
   /OPTIONS=3.
FORMATS ZCALORIE ZSODIUM ZALCOHOL ZCOST (F5.2).
LIST VAR=ID BEER CALORIES SODIUM ALCOHOL
           COST ZCALORIE ZSODIUM ZALCOHOL ZCOST.
```

ID	BEER	CALORIES	SODIUM	ALCOHOL	COST	ZCALORIE	ZSODIUM	ZALCOHOL	ZCOST
1	BUDWEISER	144	15	4.7	.43	.38	.01	.34	-.46
2	SCHLITZ	151	19	4.9	.43	.61	.62	.61	-.46
3	LOWENBRAU	157	15	4.9	.48	.81	.01	.61	-.11
4	KRONENBOURG	170	7	5.2	.73	1.24	-1.21	1.00	1.62
5	HEINEKEN	152	11	5.0	.77	.65	-.60	.74	1.90
6	OLD MILWAUKEE	145	23	4.6	.28	.42	1.22	.21	-1.51
7	AUGSBERGER	175	24	5.5	.40	1.41	1.38	1.40	-.67
8	STROHS BOHEMIAN STYLE	149	27	4.7	.42	.55	1.83	.34	-.53
9	MILLER LITE	99	10	4.3	.43	-1.10	-.75	-.18	-.46
10	BUDWEISER LIGHT	113	8	3.7	.44	-.64	-1.06	-.97	-.39
11	COORS	140	18	4.6	.44	.25	.46	.21	-.39
12	COORS LIGHT	102	15	4.1	.46	-1.00	.01	-.45	-.25
13	MICHELOB LIGHT	135	11	4.2	.50	.09	-.60	-.32	.02
14	BECKS	150	19	4.7	.76	.58	.62	.34	1.83
15	KIRIN	149	6	5.0	.79	.55	-1.36	.74	2.04
16	PABST EXTRA LIGHT	68	15	2.3	.38	-2.13	.01	-2.82	-.81
17	HAMMS	136	19	4.4	.43	.12	.62	-.05	-.46
18	HEILEMANS OLD STYLE	144	24	4.9	.43	.38	1.38	.61	-.46
19	OLYMPIA GOLD LIGHT	72	6	2.9	.46	-2.00	-1.36	-2.03	-.25
20	SCHLITZ LIGHT	97	7	4.2	.47	-1.17	-1.21	-.32	-.18

Figure 3.2   The squared Euclidean distance coefficient matrix

```
SET WIDTH=WIDE.
CLUSTER ZCALORIE ZSODIUM ZALCOHOL ZCOST
    /PRINT=DISTANCE
    /METHOD=COMPLETE.
```

Squared Euclidean Dissimilarity Coefficient Matrix

Case	1	2	3	4	5	6	7	8
2	.4922							
3	.3749	.5297						
4	7.0040	8.2298	4.8424					
5	6.1889	7.0897	4.4835	.8700				
6	2.5848	1.6534	3.7263	17.0154	15.2734			
7	4.0720	1.8735	3.1573	12.1251	11.5371	3.1061		
8	3.3568	1.5561	3.6380	14.8000	12.0038	1.3526	2.0742	
9	3.0662	5.4473	4.9962	11.4721	9.5339	7.4577	13.3723	9.6850
10	3.9181	6.8702	5.8179	11.5391	10.0663	8.9551	15.7993	11.5019
11	.2474	.3160	.7568	8.4698	6.8353	1.8432	3.6498	1.9953
12	2.5940	4.1442	4.4322	12.1519	9.1534	5.4981	11.2604	6.4385
13	1.1281	2.8432	1.7663	5.9995	4.9519	6.0530	9.0610	6.8673
14	5.6782	5.3399	4.2859	4.2382	1.6427	11.5628	8.6397	7.0724
15	8.3245	10.1947	6.6075	.7483	.6064	19.5528	16.0117	16.9620
16	16.4081	19.7255	20.8463	33.3380	28.0650	17.6015	32.1339	20.5466
17	.5952	.6788	1.4051	10.0509	7.9746	1.6159	4.3782	1.8230
18	1.9394	.6307	2.1757	11.9216	9.5828	1.2688	1.7169	.3092
19	13.1887	17.6915	16.7104	23.2048	19.8574	19.0673	30.9530	22.3479
20	4.4010	7.4360	6.2635	10.8241	9.1372	10.4511	16.4825	12.7426

Case	9	10	11	12	13	14	15	16
10	.9349							
11	3.4745	4.5082						
12	.6999	1.5600	2.2375					
13	1.6931	1.3437	1.6100	1.6536				
14	10.2578	10.9762	5.1046	7.8646	5.4275			
15	10.2201	10.3631	9.6179	10.9556	5.9694	4.1024		
16	8.6771	6.9127	15.2083	7.1851	12.2231	24.6793	29.7992	
17	3.3828	4.2251	.1147	1.8315	1.7851	5.6395	10.9812	13.1806
18	7.3607	9.4595	1.0094	4.9491	5.0762	5.9553	13.7962	20.0105
19	4.6046	3.0565	13.4011	5.3477	7.9175	20.5149	19.3851	2.8209
20	.3069	.7793	5.1340	1.5271	1.9902	10.8954	9.0403	9.0418

Case	17	18	19
18	1.0802		
19	12.3170	20.1156	
20	5.1327	10.0114	3.6382

The first entry in Figure 3.2 is the distance between the first two cases, Budweiser and Schlitz (case 1 and case 2 in Figure 3.1). Cases form the rows and columns of the distance matrix. The rows and columns are labeled with the first eight characters of the values for the variable *beer*. The distance between Budweiser and Schlitz can be calculated from the standardized values in Figure 3.1 as:

$$D^2 = (0.38 - 0.61)^2 + (0.01 - 0.62)^2$$
$$+ (0.34 - 0.61)^2 + (-0.46 - (-0.46))^2 = 0.49$$

Equation 3.1

Since the distance between pairs of cases is symmetric (that is, the distance between Budweiser and Schlitz is the same as the distance between Schlitz and Budweiser), SPSS/PC+ displays only the lower half of the distance matrix in the output. Redundant values are excluded from the matrix.

Icicle Plots

Once the distance matrix has been calculated, the actual formation of clusters can commence. Figure 3.3 summarizes a cluster analysis that uses the complete linkage method. This type of figure is sometimes called a **vertical icicle plot** because it resembles a row of icicles hanging from eaves.

Figure 3.3   Vertical icicle plot for the 20 beers

```
SET WIDTH=WIDE.
CLUSTER ZCALORIE ZSODIUM ZALCOHOL ZCOST
   /PLOT=VICICLE
   /ID=BEER
   /METHOD=COMPLETE.


   Vertical Icicle Plot using Complete Linkage

      (Down) Number of Clusters   (Across) Case Label and number
```

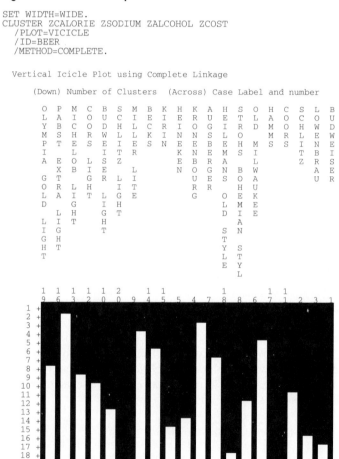

The columns in Figure 3.3 correspond to the objects being clustered (in this instance, the 20 beers). They are identified by a sequential number corresponding to their order or location in the file and by their labels. (If labels are not defined, then only the case number is used.) Thus, the first column in the figure represents the last beer in the file, beer 19, Olympia Gold Light, and the last column represents the first beer in the file, Budweiser. Rows represent steps in the cluster analysis; the figure is read from bottom to top. Row 19 represents step 1 in the analysis and row 1 represents the last step, where all cases form a single cluster. (In step 0 of the cluster analysis, not pictured in the figure, each case is a separate cluster.)

As previously described, initially each case is considered an individual cluster. Since there are twenty beers in this example, there are 20 clusters. At the first step of the analysis (row 19 in the figure), the two closest cases are combined into a single cluster, resulting in 19 clusters. (The step number corresponds to the number of clusters in the solution.) Each case is represented by a solid dark bar and cases are separated by a blank space. The two cases that have been merged into a single cluster, Coors and Hamms, do not have a space separating them and are represented by consecutive solid bars. Row 18 in Figure 3.3 corresponds to the solution at the next step, when 18 clusters are present. At this step, Miller Lite and Schlitz Light are merged into a single cluster. At this point, there are 18 clusters, 16 consisting of individual beers and 2 consisting of pairs of beers. At each subsequent step, an additional cluster is formed either by joining a case to an existing multicase cluster, by joining two separate cases into a single cluster, or by joining two multicase clusters.

For example, row 5 in Figure 3.3 corresponds to a solution that has five clusters. Beers 19 and 16, the very light beers, form one cluster. Beers 13, 12, 10, 20, and 9 form the next cluster. These beers—Michelob Light, Coors Light, Budweiser Light, Schlitz Light, and Miller Light—are all light beers, but not as light as the two in the first cluster. The third cluster consists of Becks, Kirin, Heineken, and Kronenbourg; these are all imported beers. Although no variable in this example explicitly indicates whether beers are domestic or imported, the cost variable (see Figure 3.1) causes the imported beers to cluster together, since they are quite a bit more expensive than the domestic ones. A fourth cluster consists of Augsberger, Heilemans Old Style, Strohs Bohemian Style, and Old Milwaukee; Figure 3.4, produced with the SPSS/PC+ Tables option, shows that all of these beers are distinguished by high sodium content. The last cluster consists of five beers, Hamms, Coors, Schlitz, Lowenbrau, and Budweiser. These beers share the distinction of being average; they are neither particularly high nor particularly low on the variables measured. Note from Figure 3.4 that, based on the standard deviations, beers in the same cluster, when compared to all beers, are more homogeneous on the variables measured.

Figure 3.4   Cluster characteristics

```
CLUSTER ZCALORIE ZSODIUM ZALCOHOL ZCOST
  /ID=BEER
  /METHOD=COMPLETE(CLUSMEM)
  /SAVE=CLUSTER(5).
VALUE LABELS CLUSMEM5 1 'AVERAGE' 2 'EXPENSIVE' 3 'HIGH NA'
   4 'LIGHT' 5 'VERY LIGHT'.
TABLES OBSERVATION=COST CALORIES ALCOHOL SODIUM
  /FTOTAL=TOTAL
  /FORMAT=CWIDTH(10,9)
  /TABLE=CLUSMEM5+TOTAL BY CALORIES+COST+ALCOHOL+SODIUM
  /STATISTICS=MEAN STDDEV.
```

	CALORIES PER 12 FLUID OUNCES		COST PER 12 FLUID OUNCES		ALCOHOL BY VOLUME (IN %)		SODIUM PER 12 FLUID OUNCES IN MG	
	Mean	Standard Deviation	Mean	Standard Deviation	Mean	Standard Deviation	Mean	Standard Deviation
CLUSMEM5								
AVERAGE	146	8	.44	.02	4.7	.2	17	2
EXPENSIVE	155	10	.76	.03	5.0	.2	11	6
HIGH NA	153	15	.38	.07	4.9	.4	25	2
LIGHT	109	16	.46	.03	4.1	.2	10	3
VERY LIGHT	70	3	.42	.06	2.6	.4	11	6
TOTAL	132	30	.50	.14	4.4	.8	15	7

Cluster formation continues until all cases are merged into a single cluster, as in row 1 in Figure 3.3. Thus, all steps of the cluster analysis are displayed. If we were clustering people instead of beers, the last row would represent individuals and earlier rows would perhaps represent individuals merged into families, families merged into neighborhoods, and so forth. Often there is no single, meaningful cluster solution, but many, depending on what characteristic is of interest.

The Agglomeration Schedule

The results of the cluster analysis are summarized in the **agglomeration schedule** in Figure 3.5, which identifies the cases or clusters being combined at each stage. The first row of the schedule represents stage 1, the 19-cluster solution. At this stage, beers 11 and 17 are combined, as indicated in the *Cluster 1* and *Cluster 2* columns under the heading *Clusters Combined* (in this column, *cluster* can refer to either an individual case or a multicase cluster). The squared Euclidean distance between these two beers is displayed in the column labeled *Coefficient*. (This coefficient is identical to the distance measure for cases 11 and 17—Coors and Hamms—in Figure 3.2.) The column entitled *Stage Cluster 1st Appears* indicates at which stage a multicase cluster is first formed. For example, looking at the row for stage 5, the 4 in the *Cluster 1* column indicates that case 1 was first involved in a merge in the previous step, stage 4. Reading across the row for stage 4, you can see that case 1 was involved in a merge with case 3. The last column, labeled *Next Stage*, indicates the next stage at which another case or cluster is combined with this one. Looking at stage 5, we see that the new cluster (cases 1, 2, and 3), numbered cluster 1, is next involved in a merge at stage 10, where it combines with cases 11 and 17. (The cluster number is always the same as the number of its earliest case; thus, the cluster formed by cases 1, 2, and 3 is called cluster 1, and the cluster formed by cases 11 and 17 is called cluster 11.)

Figure 3.5   Agglomeration schedule using complete linkage

```
CLUSTER ZCALORIE ZSODIUM ZALCOHOL ZCOST
 /ID=BEER
 /PRINT=SCHEDULE
 /METHOD=COMPLETE.
```

Agglomeration Schedule using Complete Linkage

Stage	Clusters Cluster 1	Combined Cluster 2	Coefficient	Stage Cluster 1st Appears Cluster 1	Cluster 2	Next Stage
1	11	17	.114695	0	0	10
2	9	20	.306903	0	0	8
3	8	18	.309227	0	0	9
4	1	3	.374859	0	0	5
5	1	2	.529696	4	0	10
6	5	15	.606378	0	0	7
7	4	5	.870016	0	6	15
8	9	10	.934909	2	0	11
9	6	8	1.352618	0	3	14
10	1	11	1.405148	5	1	16
11	9	12	1.559987	8	0	12
12	9	13	1.990205	11	0	17
13	16	19	2.820897	0	0	19
14	6	7	3.106108	9	0	16
15	4	14	4.238165	7	0	17
16	1	6	4.378198	10	14	18
17	4	9	12.151937	15	12	18
18	1	4	19.552841	16	17	19
19	1	16	33.338039	18	13	0

The information in Figure 3.5 that is not available in the icicle plot is the value of the distance between the two most dissimilar points of the clusters being combined at each stage, or the coefficient. By examining these values, you can get an idea of how unlike the clusters being combined are. Small coefficients indicate that fairly homogeneous clusters are being merged. Large coefficients indicate that clusters containing quite dissimilar members are being combined. The actual value depends on the clustering method and the distance measure used.

These coefficients can also be used for guidance in deciding how many clusters are needed to represent the data. You usually want to stop agglomeration as soon as the increase between two adjacent steps becomes large. For example, in Figure 3.5 there is a fairly large increase in the value of the distance measure from a four-cluster to a three-cluster solution (stages 16 and 17).

The Dendrogram

Another way of visually representing the steps in a hierarchical clustering solution is with a display called a **dendrogram**. The dendrogram identifies the clusters being combined and the values of the coefficients at each step. The dendrogram produced by SPSS/PC+ does not plot actual distances but rescales them to numbers between 0 and

25. Thus, the ratio of the distances between steps is preserved, but the scale displayed at the top of the figure does not correspond to actual distance values.

To understand how a dendrogram is constructed, consider a simple four-beer example. Figure 3.6 contains the icicle plot for clustering Kirin, Becks, Old Milwaukee, and Budweiser. From the icicle plot, you can see that at the first step Budweiser and Old Milwaukee are combined, at the second step Becks and Kirin are merged, and at the last step all four beers are merged into a single cluster.

Figure 3.6   Vertical icicle plot for the four-beer example

```
CLUSTER ZCALORIE ZSODIUM ZALCOHOL ZCOST
 /ID=BEER
 /METHOD=COMPLETE
 /PLOT=VICICLE.


    Vertical Icicle Plot using Complete Linkage

        (Down) Number of Clusters  (Across) Case Label and number

            K   B   O   B
            I   E   L   U
            R   C   D   D
            I   K       W
            N   S   M   E
                    I   I
                    L   S
                    W   E
                    A   R
                    U
                    K
                    E
                    E


            4  3  2  1
         1 +
         2 +
         3 +
```

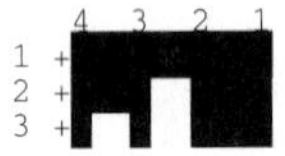

The distances at which the beers are combined are shown in the agglomeration schedule in Figure 3.7. From this schedule, we see that the distance between Budweiser and Old Milwaukee (cases 1 and 2) is 2.017 when they are combined. Similarly, when Becks and Kirin (cases 3 and 4) are combined, their distance is 6.323. Since the method of complete linkage is used, the distance coefficient displayed for the last stage is the largest distance between a member of the Budweiser–Milwaukee cluster and a member of the Becks–Kirin cluster. This distance is 16.789.

Figure 3.7   Agglomeration schedule for the four-beer example

```
CLUSTER ZCALORIE ZSODIUM ZALCOHOL ZCOST
 /ID=BEER
 /PRINT=SCHEDULE
 /METHOD=COMPLETE.
```

Agglomeration Schedule using Complete Linkage

Stage	Clusters Cluster 1	Combined Cluster 2	Coefficient	Stage Cluster Cluster 1	1st Appears Cluster 2	Next Stage
1	1	2	2.017019	0	0	3
2	3	4	6.323440	0	0	3
3	1	3	16.789230	1	2	0

The information in Figure 3.7 is displayed in the dendrogram in Figure 3.8, which is read from left to right. Vertical lines denote joined clusters. The position of the line on the scale indicates the distance at which clusters were joined. Since the distances are re-scaled to fall in the range of 1 to 25, the largest distance, 16.8, corresponds to the value of 25. The smallest distance, 2.017, corresponds to the value 1. The second distance, 6.32, corresponds to a value of about 8. Note that the ratio of the rescaled distances is, after the first, the same as the ratios of the original distances.

The first two clusters that are joined are Budweiser and Old Milwaukee. They are connected by a line that is one unit from the origin, since this is the rescaled distance between these points. When Becks and Kirin are joined, the line that connects them is 8 units from the origin. Similarly, when these two clusters are merged into a single cluster, the line that connects them is 25 units from the origin. Thus, the dendrogram indicates not only which clusters are joined but also the distance at which they are joined.

Figure 3.8   Dendrogram for the four-beer example

```
CLUSTER ZCALORIE ZSODIUM ZALCOHOL ZCOST
 /ID=BEER
 /METHOD=COMPLETE
 /PLOT=DENDROGRAM.
```

Dendrogram using Complete Linkage

```
                                       Rescaled Distance Cluster Combine

               C A S E            0         5        10        15        20        25
         Label                Seq  +---------+---------+---------+---------+---------+

         BUDWEISER             1
         OLD MILWAUKEE         2
         BECKS                 3
         KIRIN                 4
```

Figure 3.9 contains the dendrogram for the complete 20-beer example. Since many of the distances at the beginning stages are similar in magnitude, you cannot tell the sequence in which some of the early clusters are formed. However, at the last three stages, the distances at which clusters are being combined are fairly large. Looking at the dendrogram, it appears that the five-cluster solution (very light beers, light beers, imported beers, high-sodium beers, and "average" beers) may be appropriate, since it is easily interpretable and occurs before the distances at which clusters are combined become too large.

Figure 3.9   Dendrogram using complete linkage for the 20 beers

```
CLUSTER ZCALORIE ZSODIUM ZALCOHOL ZCOST
 /ID=BEER
 /METHOD=COMPLETE
 /PLOT=DENDROGRAM.
```

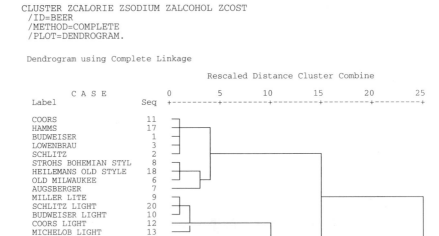

Some Additional Displays and Modifications

The agglomeration schedule, icicle plot, and dendrogram illustrate the results produced by a hierarchical clustering solution. Several variations of these plots may also be useful. For example, when there are many cases, the initial steps of the cluster analysis may not be of particular interest. You might want to display solutions for only certain numbers of clusters. Or you might want to see the results at every kth step. Figure 3.10 shows the icicle plot of results at every fifth step.

Figure 3.10 Icicle plot with results at every fifth step

```
CLUSTER ZCALORIE ZSODIUM ZALCOHOL ZCOST
 /ID=BEER
 /METHOD=COMPLETE
 /PLOT=VICICLE(1,19,5).
```

Vertical Icicle Plot using Complete Linkage

(Down) Number of Clusters (Across) Case Label and number

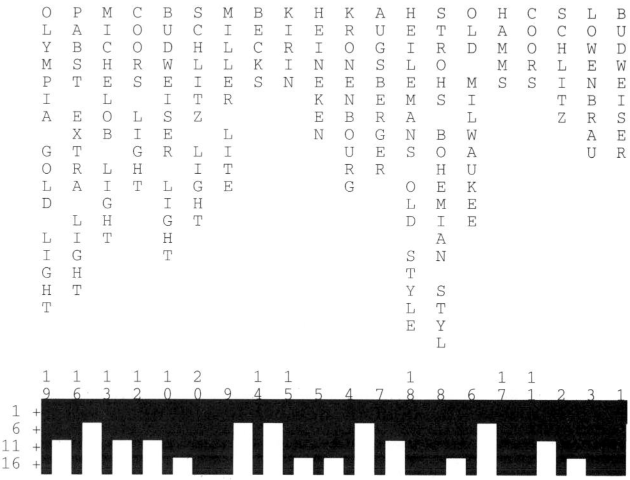

When there are many cases, all of them may not fit across the top of a single page. In this situation, it may be useful to turn the icicle plot on its side. This is called a **horizontal icicle plot**. Figure 3.11 contains the horizontal icicle plot corresponding to Figure 3.3.

Figure 3.11   Horizontal icicle plot

```
CLUSTER ZCALORIE ZSODIUM ZALCOHOL ZCOST
 /ID=BEER
 /METHOD=COMPLETE
 /PLOT=HICICLE.
```

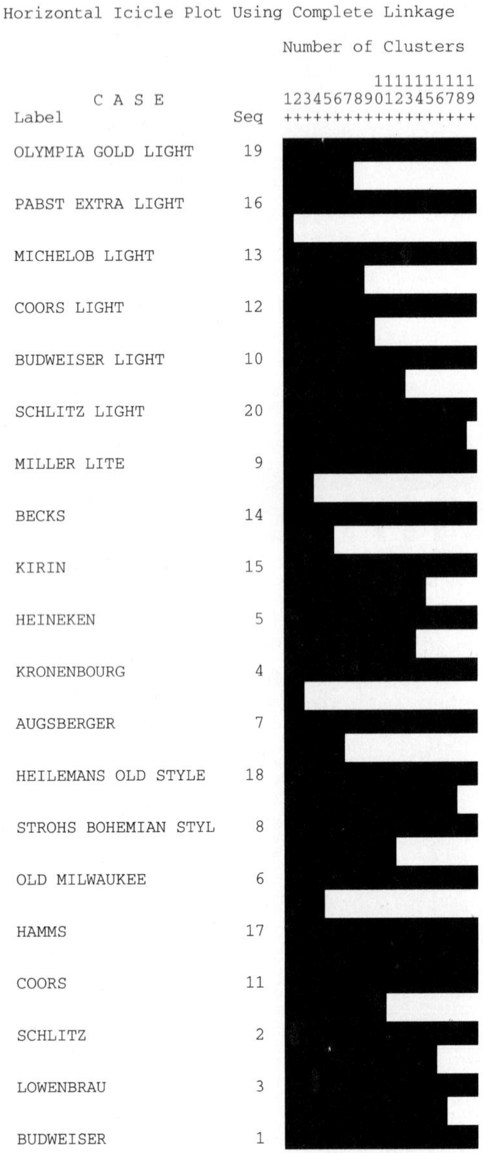

Horizontal Icicle Plot Using Complete Linkage

Number of Clusters

Although the composition of clusters at any stage can be discerned from the icicle plots, it is often helpful to display the information in tabular form. Figure 3.12 contains the cluster memberships for the cases at different stages of the solution. From Figure 3.12, you can easily tell to which clusters cases belong in the two- to five-cluster solutions.

Figure 3.12   Cluster membership at different stages

```
CLUSTER ZCALORIE ZSODIUM ZALCOHOL ZCOST
 /ID=BEER
 /PRINT=CLUSTER(2,5)
 /METHOD=COMPLETE.
```

```
Cluster Membership of Cases using Complete Linkage
```

| | | Number of Clusters | | | |
Label	Case	5	4	3	2
BUDWEISER	1	1	1	1	1
SCHLITZ	2	1	1	1	1
LOWENBRAU	3	1	1	1	1
KRONENBOURG	4	2	2	2	1
HEINEKEN	5	2	2	2	1
OLD MILWAUKEE	6	3	1	1	1
AUGSBERGER	7	3	1	1	1
STROHS BOHEMIAN STYL	8	3	1	1	1
MILLER LITE	9	4	3	2	1
BUDWEISER LIGHT	10	4	3	2	1
COORS	11	1	1	1	1
COORS LIGHT	12	4	3	2	1
MICHELOB LIGHT	13	4	3	2	1
BECKS	14	2	2	2	1
KIRIN	15	2	2	2	1
PABST EXTRA LIGHT	16	5	4	3	2
HAMMS	17	1	1	1	1
HEILEMANS OLD STYLE	18	3	1	1	1
OLYMPIA GOLD LIGHT	19	5	4	3	2
SCHLITZ LIGHT	20	4	3	2	1

More on Calculating Distances and Similarities

There are many methods for estimating the distance or similarity between two cases. But even before these measures are computed, you must decide whether the variables need to be rescaled. When the variables have different scales, such as cents and calories, and they are not standardized, any distance measure will reflect primarily the contributions of variables measured in the large units. For example, the beer data variables were standardized prior to cluster analysis to have a mean of 0 and a standard deviation of 1. Besides standardization to Z scores, variables can be standardized by dividing them by just the standard deviation, the range, the mean, or the maximum. See Romesburg (1984) or Anderberg (1973) for further discussion.

Based on the transformed data, it is possible to calculate many different types of distance and similarity measures. Different distance and similarity measures weight data characteristics differently. The choice among the measures should be based on which differences or similarities in the data are important for a particular application. For example, if one is clustering animal bones, what may matter is not the actual differences in bone size but relationships among the dimensions, since we know that even animals of the same species differ in size. Bones with the same relationship between length and diameter should be judged as similar, regardless of their absolute magnitudes. See Romesburg (1984) for further discussion.

The most commonly used distance measure, the squared Euclidean distance, has been discussed previously. Sometimes its square root, the **Euclidean distance**, is also used. A distance measure that is based on the absolute values of differences is the **city-block distance**, or **Manhattan distance**. For two cases it is just the sum of the absolute differences of the values for all variables. Since the differences are not squared, large differences are not weighted as heavily as in the squared Euclidean distances. The **Chebychev distance** defines the distance between two cases as the maximum absolute difference in the values over all variables. Thus, it ignores much of the available information.

When variables are binary, special distance and similarity measures are required. Many are based on the familiar measures of association for contingency tables.

Methods for Combining Clusters

Many methods can be used to decide which cases or clusters should be combined at each step. In general, clustering methods fall into three groups: linkage methods, error sums of squares or variance methods, and centroid methods. All are based on either a matrix of distances or a matrix of similarities between pairs of cases. The methods differ in how they estimate distances between clusters at successive steps. Since the merging of clusters at each step depends on the distance measure, different distance measures can result in different cluster solutions for the same clustering method. See Milligan (1980) for comparisons of the performance of some of the different clustering methods.

One of the simplest methods for joining clusters is single linkage, sometimes called nearest neighbor. The first two cases combined are those with the smallest distance, or greatest similarity, between them. The distance between the new cluster and individual cases is then computed as the minimum distance between an individual case and a case in the cluster. The distances between cases that have not been joined do not change. At every step, the distance between two clusters is taken to be the distance between their two closest points.

Another commonly used method is called complete linkage, or the furthest neighbor technique. In this method, the distance between two clusters is calculated as the distance between their two furthest points.

The **average linkage between groups method**, often called **UPGMA** (unweighted pair-group method using arithmetic averages), defines the distance between two clusters as the average of the distances between all pairs of cases in which one member of the pair is from each of the clusters. For example, if cases 1 and 2 form cluster A and cases 3, 4, and 5 form cluster B, the distance between clusters A and B is taken to be the average of the distances between the following pairs of cases: (1,3) (1,4) (1,5) (2,3) (2,4) (2,5). This differs from the other linkage methods in that it uses information about all pairs of distances, not just the nearest or the furthest. For this reason, it is usually preferred to the single and complete linkage methods for cluster analysis.

The UPGMA method considers only distances between pairs of cases in different clusters. A variant of it, the **average linkage within groups method**, combines clusters so that the average distance between all cases in the resulting cluster is as small as possible. Thus, the distance between two clusters is taken to be the average of the distances between all possible pairs of cases in the resulting cluster.

Another frequently used method for cluster formation is **Ward's method**. For each cluster, the means for all variables are calculated. Then for each case, the squared Euclidean distance to the cluster means is calculated. These distances are summed for all of the cases. At each step, the two clusters that merge are those that result in the smallest increase in the overall sum of the squared within-cluster distances.

The **centroid method** calculates the distance between two clusters as the distance between their means for all of the variables. One disadvantage of the centroid method is that the distance at which clusters are combined can actually decrease from one step to the next. Since clusters merged at later stages are more dissimilar than those merged at early stages, this is an undesirable property.

In the centroid method, the centroid of a merged cluster is a weighted combination of the centroids of the two individual clusters, where the weights are proportional to the sizes of the clusters. In the **median method**, the two clusters being combined are weighted equally in the computation of the centroid, regardless of the number of cases in each. This allows small groups to have equal effect on the characterization of larger clusters into which they are merged.

When similarity measures are used, the criteria for combining is reversed. That is, clusters with large similarity-based measures are merged.

Clustering Variables

In the previous example, the units used for cluster analysis were individual cases (the different brands of beer). Cluster analysis can also be used to find homogeneous groups of variables. For example, consider the 14 community variables described in Chapter 2. We could use cluster analysis to group the 88 counties included in the study and then examine the resulting clusters to establish what characteristics they share. Another approach is to cluster the 14 variables used to describe the communities. In this case, the unit used for analysis is the variable. The distance or similarity measures are computed for all pairs of variables.

Figure 3.13 shows the results of clustering the community variables using the absolute value of the correlation coefficient as a measure of similarity. The absolute value of the coefficient is used, since it is a measure of the strength of the relationship. The sign indicates only the direction. If you want clusters for positively correlated variables only, the sign of the coefficient should be maintained.

Figure 3.13   Cluster analysis of the community variables

```
DATA LIST MATRIX FREE /
    POPSTABL NEWSCIRC FEMEMPLD FARMERS RETAILNG
    COMMERCL INDUSTZN HEALTH CHLDNEGL COMMEFFC
    DWELGNEW MIGRNPOP UNEMPLOY MENTALIL.
N 88.
BEGIN DATA
1.000
 .175 1.000
 .276  .616 1.000
 .369  .625  .637 1.000
 .127  .624  .736  .519 1.000
 .069  .652  .589  .306  .727 1.000
 .106  .712  .742  .545  .785  .911 1.000
 .149  .030  .241  .068  .100  .123  .129 1.000
 .039  .171  .589  .257  .557  .357  .424  .407 1.000
 .005  .100  .471  .213  .452  .287  .357  .732  .660 1.000
 .670  .188  .413  .579  .030  .203  .290  .138  .311 1.000
 .476  .086  .064  .198  .007  .068  .024  .083  .148  .067  .505 1.000
 .137  .373  .689  .450  .650  .424  .528  .348  .733  .601  .266  .181
1.000
 .237  .046  .237  .121  .190  .055  .095  .279  .247  .324  .266  .307
 .217 1.000
END DATA.
CLUSTER POPSTABL TO MENTALIL
   /READ=TRIANGLE SIMILAR.
```

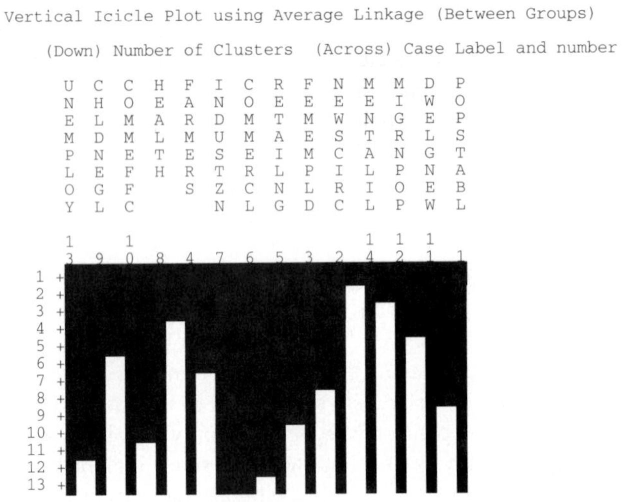

```
Vertical Icicle Plot using Average Linkage (Between Groups)

(Down) Number of Clusters   (Across) Case Label and number
```

The clustering procedure is the same whether variables or cases are clustered. It starts out with as many clusters as there are variables. At each successive step, variables or clusters of variables are merged, as shown in the icicle plot in Figure 3.13.

Consider the four-cluster solution (in row 4). The *unemploy, chldnegl, commeffc,* and *health* variables form one cluster; the *farmers, industzn, commercl, retailng, femempld,* and *newscirc* variables form the second cluster; *mentalil* is a cluster by itself; and *migrnpop, dwelgnew,* and *popstabl* form the fourth cluster.

If you've read Chapter 2, this solution should appear familiar. The groupings of the variables are exactly those established by the factor analysis. The first cluster is the *welfare* factor; the second, the *urbanism* factor; and the fourth, the *influx* factor. In both cases, the extent of mental illness does not appear to be related to the remainder of the variables.

This is not a chance occurrence. Although factor analysis has an underlying theoretical model and cluster analysis is much more ad hoc, both identify related groups of variables. However, factor analysis allows variables to be either positively or negatively related to a factor. Cluster analysis can be restricted to search only for positive associations between variables. Thus, if the absolute values of the correlation coefficients are not taken, variables that correlate negatively with a factor do not appear in the same cluster with variables that correlate positively. For example, the *farmers* variable would not appear with the other urbanism variables. Factor analysis and cluster analysis need not always arrive at the same variable groupings, but it is comforting when they do.

Running the Cluster Procedure

Use the Cluster procedure to obtain hierarchical clusters for cases when the number of cases is not too large. Variables can also be clustered if the data are in the appropriate format (for example, if you have a correlation matrix or some other measure of distance). The Cluster procedure provides several measures of dissimilarity and allows you to specify missing-value treatment. A matrix of similarity or dissimilarity coefficients can be entered and used to cluster cases or variables.

Specifying the Variables

The first specification on CLUSTER is a list of variables to use in computing similarities or distances between cases, as in

```
CLUSTER ZCALORIE ZSODIUM ZALCOHOL ZCOST.
```

The variable list is the only required specification and must precede any optional subcommands. When a matrix is read, the variable list identifies the variables represented in the similarity or distance matrix. These variables are then clustered.

Selecting the Clustering Method

The METHOD subcommand specifies the clustering method. If you do not specify a method, CLUSTER uses the average-linkage-between-groups method (see "Methods for Combining Clusters" on p. 110). You can specify one or more of the following keywords on a single METHOD subcommand:

BAVERAGE	*Average linkage between groups (UPGMA).* This is the default.
WAVERAGE	*Average linkage within groups.*
SINGLE	*Single linkage or nearest neighbor.*
COMPLETE	*Complete linkage or furthest neighbor.*
CENTROID	*Centroid clustering (UPGMC).* Squared Euclidean distances should be used with this method.
MEDIAN	*Median clustering (WPGMC).* Squared Euclidean distances should be used with this method.
WARD	*Ward's method.* Squared Euclidean distances should be used with this method.
DEFAULT	*Same as BAVERAGE.*

For example, the command

```
CLUSTER ZCALORIE ZSODIUM ZALCOHOL ZCOST
  /METHOD=SINGLE COMPLETE.
```

requests clustering with both the single and complete methods.

Specifying the Distance Measure

Use the MEASURE subcommand to specify the distance measure to use for clustering cases (see "How Alike Are the Cases?" on p. 96 and "More on Calculating Distances and Similarities" on p. 109). If you omit the MEASURE subcommand, CLUSTER uses squared Euclidean distances. You can specify only one of the following keywords on MEASURE:

SEUCLID   *Squared Euclidean distances.* This is the default. This measure should be used with the centroid, median, and Ward's methods of clustering. The distance between two cases is the sum of the squared differences in values for each variable:

$$\text{Distance}\,(X, Y)\;=\;\sum_i (X_i - Y_i)^2$$

EUCLID   *Euclidean distances.* The distance between two cases is the square root of the sum of the squared differences in values for each variable:

$$\text{Distance}\,(X, Y)\;=\;\sqrt{\sum_i (X_i - Y_i)^2}$$

COSINE   *Cosine of vectors of variables.* This is a pattern similarity measure:

$$\text{Similarity}\,(X, Y)\;=\;\left(\sum_i X_i Y_i\right) \Big/ \sqrt{\left(\sum X_i^2\right)\left(\sum Y_i^2\right)}$$

BLOCK *City-block or Manhattan distances.* The distance between two cases is the sum of the absolute differences in values for each variable:

$$\text{Distance } (X, Y) \ = \ \sum_i |X_i - Y_i|$$

CHEBYCHEV *Chebychev distance metric.* The distance between two cases is the maximum absolute difference in values for any variable:

$$\text{Distance } (X, Y) \ = \ MAX_i |X_i - Y_i|$$

POWER(p,r) *Distances in an absolute power metric.* The distance between two cases is the *r*th root of the sum of the absolute differences to the *p*th power in values on each variable:

$$\text{Distance } (X, Y) \ = \ (\sum_i |X_i - Y_i|^p)^{\frac{1}{r}}$$

Appropriate selection of integer parameters *p* and *r* yields Euclidean, squared Euclidean, Minkowski, city-block, minimum, maximum, and many other distance metrics.

DEFAULT *Same as SEUCLID.*

Specifying Output

CLUSTER automatically displays the clustering method, the similarity or distance measure used for clustering, and the number of cases. The following additional output is controlled by the PRINT subcommand:

SCHEDULE *Agglomeration schedule.* Display the order or stage at which cases or clusters were combined and their distance coefficient (see Figure 3.5 and Figure 3.7). The agglomeration schedule is displayed by default if you do not specify PRINT or if you specify PRINT without any keywords. If you specify any other keywords on PRINT, you must request SCHEDULE explicitly.

CLUSTER(min,max) *Cluster membership.* You must specify the minimum and maximum numbers of clusters in the cluster solutions. For each case, CLUSTER displays an identifying label and values indicating which cluster the case belongs to in a given cluster solution (see Figure 3.12). For example, PRINT=CLUSTER(3,5) displays the clusters to which each case belongs when three, four, and five clusters are produced. Cases are identified by case number plus the value of any string variable specified on the ID subcommand (see "Identifying Cases" on p. 116).

DISTANCE	*Matrix of distances or similarities between items.* The type of matrix produced (similarities or dissimilarities) depends upon the measure selected. For a large number of cases, DISTANCE uses considerable computer processing time.
DEFAULT	*Same as SCHEDULE.*
NONE	*None of the above.* Use keyword NONE when you want to suppress all display output, for example, when you are using SAVE.

Requesting Plots

CLUSTER produces the vertical icicle plot by default. Use the PLOT subcommand to obtain a horizontal icicle plot or a dendrogram. When you specify PLOT, only the requested plots are produced.

VICICLE(n1,n2,n3)	*Vertical icicle plot* (see Figure 3.3, Figure 3.6, and Figure 3.10). You can specify the maximum and minimum numbers of cluster solutions to plot and the increment between cluster levels. The values you specify for *n1*, *n2*, and *n3* must be integers. By default, the increment is 1 and all cluster solutions are plotted. For example, `PLOT=VICICLE (2,10,2)` plots cluster solutions with two, four, six, eight, and ten clusters. VICICLE is the default if the PLOT subcommand is omitted or is specified by itself.
HICICLE(n1,n2,n3)	*Horizontal icicle plot* (see Figure 3.11). You can specify the minimum and maximum cluster numbers and the increment as with VICICLE.
DENDROGRAM	*Dendrogram* (see Figure 3.8 and Figure 3.9). The dendrogram is scaled by the distances at which clusters are joined.
NONE	*No plots.*

If there is insufficient memory to plot a dendrogram or icicle plot, CLUSTER performs the cluster analysis, skips the plot, and displays an error message. To obtain a plot when this occurs, specify an increment for VICICLE or HICICLE.

Identifying Cases

By default, CLUSTER identifies cases by case number. Name a string variable on the ID subcommand to identify cases with string values. For example, `/ID=BEER` produces the beer name labels in Figure 3.3, Figure 3.6, Figure 3.8, Figure 3.9, Figure 3.10, Figure 3.11, and Figure 3.12.

Missing Values

CLUSTER uses listwise deletion as the default missing-value treatment. A case with missing values for any clustering variable is excluded from the analysis. Use the MISS-ING subcommand to treat user-missing values as valid.

LISTWISE   *Delete cases with missing values listwise.* This is the default.

INCLUDE   *Include user-missing values.*

DEFAULT   *Same as LISTWISE.*

Cases with system-missing values for clustering variables are never included in the analysis.

Matrix Materials

The Cluster procedure can read and write similarity and distance matrices. Use the READ subcommand to read a matrix (such as a correlation matrix created by CORRE-LATION). This allows you to cluster variables or cases using a distance measure not available in CLUSTER. Three keywords indicate the type of matrix to read:

SIMILAR   *Matrix of similarity values.* By default, CLUSTER assumes that a dissim-ilarity or distance matrix is read.

TRIANGLE   *Matrix in lower-triangular form.* By default, CLUSTER assumes that a square matrix is read.

LOWER   *Matrix in lower-subdiagonal form.* The matrix is in lower-triangular form but without the diagonal elements.

It may be necessary to use more than one of the above keywords to correctly indicate the type of matrix being read. For example, since CLUSTER assumes that a square ma-trix is read, if you have a similarity matrix which is in lower-triangular form, you would have to specify /READ=TRIANGLE SIMILAR, as shown in Figure 3.13. Only one similarity or distance matrix can be read in a single procedure.

To save a computed similarity or distance matrix in a file, use the WRITE subcom-mand. The output file must first be specified on a previous PROCEDURE OUTPUT com-mand. The optional DISTANCE keyword indicates that the saved matrix is a distance matrix:

DISTANCE   *Write a distance matrix.* This is the default.

Saving Cluster Memberships

You can use the SAVE subcommand to save cluster memberships at specified cluster levels as new variables on the active file. You must specify a rootname on the METHOD subcommand for each cluster method for which you wish to save cluster membership; for example,

```
CLUSTER A B C
  /METHOD=BAVERAGE(CLUSMEM)
  /SAVE=CLUSTERS(3,5).
```

This command saves each case's cluster memberships for the three-, four-, and five-cluster solutions. The names for the new variables are *clusmem5*, *clusmem4*, and *clusmem3*, and they will appear in the active file in that order. CLUSTER prints the names of variables it adds to the active file.

Annotated Example

The following commands produce the output in Figure 3.1, Figure 3.3, Figure 3.5, Figure 3.9, Figure 3.11, and Figure 3.12.

```
SET WIDTH=WIDE.
DATA LIST
  /ID 1-2 RATING 3 BEER 4-24 (A) ORIGIN 25 AVAIL 26
    PRICE 27-30 COST 31-34 CALORIES 35-37 SODIUM 38-39
    ALCOHOL 40-42 CLASS 43 LIGHT 44.
FORMATS PRICE COST (F4.2) ALCOHOL (F3.1).
MISSING VALUES CLASS(0).
BEGIN DATA.
lines of data
END DATA.
DESCRIPTIVES CALORIES SODIUM ALCOHOL COST
 /OPTIONS=3.
FORMATS ZCALORIE ZSODIUM ZALCOHOL ZCOST (F8.6).
CLUSTER ZCALORIE ZSODIUM ZALCOHOL ZCOST
 /ID=BEER
 /PRINT=CLUSTER(2,5) DISTANCE SCHEDULE
 /METHOD=COMPLETE
 /PLOT=HICICLE VICICLE DENDROGRAM.
```

- The SET command tells SPSS/PC+ to change the width to 132 characters.

- The DATA LIST command gives the variable names and column locations for the variables in the analysis.

- The FORMATS command assigns display and write formats to the variables *price*, *cost*, and *alcohol*.

- The MISSING VALUES command assigns the value 0 user-missing status for the variable *class*.

- The DESCRIPTIVES command adds the Z scores for *calories, sodium, alcohol*, and *cost* to the active file so they can be used by CLUSTER.

- The FORMATS command assigns print and write formats for the new variables *zcalorie, zsodium, zalcohol,* and *zcost.*
- The CLUSTER command requests a cluster analysis of the standardized values for calories, sodium content, alcohol content, and cost.
- The ID subcommand requests that the values for the string variable *beer* be used to identify cases.
- The PRINT subcommand gives the values 2 and 5 as the minimum and maximum numbers of clusters in the cluster membership display. It also requests that a matrix of distances between items and an agglomeration schedule be displayed.
- The METHOD subcommand asks for complete linkage.
- The PLOT subcommand requests a horizontal icicle plot and a dendrogram, in addition to the vertical icicle plot.

4 Cluster Analysis for Large Files

Chapter 3 discusses the basics of cluster analysis and describes a commonly used method for cluster formation—agglomerative hierarchical clustering. This is but one of many methods available for cluster formation. For a particular problem, selection of a method to use depends not only on the characteristics of the various methods but also on the data set to be analyzed. For example, when the number of cases is large, algorithms that require many computations or storage of all cases in memory may pose difficulties in terms of either the time required to perform the computations or available memory.

This chapter describes the Quick Cluster procedure, which can be used to cluster large numbers of cases (200 or more) efficiently without requiring substantial computer resources. Unlike the Cluster procedure, which results in a series of solutions corresponding to different numbers of clusters, the Quick Cluster procedure, which uses the k-means algorithm, produces only one solution for the number of clusters requested. The number of clusters must be specified by the user.

The Method

The algorithm used for determining cluster membership in the Quick Cluster procedure is based on **nearest centroid sorting** (Anderberg, 1973). That is, a case is assigned to the cluster with the smallest distance between the case and the center of the cluster (centroid). The actual mechanics of the procedure depend on the information available. If the cluster centers are known, they can be specified, and case assignment is based on them. Otherwise, cluster centers are iteratively estimated from the data.

Since k-means cluster analysis requires a user-specified number of clusters, you may want to use hierarchical cluster analysis on a random sample or subset of cases to help determine the number of clusters before using k-means cluster analysis on all cases. Hierarchical cluster analysis can also be used to determine the initial cluster centers for k-means cluster analysis.

Classification When Cluster Centers Are Known

Consider again the beer data described in Chapter 3. Using hierarchical cluster analysis, we identified five interpretable clusters for twenty beers. If there are additional beers that we want to classify into one of these five clusters, we can use the Quick Cluster procedure as a quick and efficient means of doing so. Each of the new beers is assigned to the cluster to whose center it is closest. For each cluster, the center is simply the mean of the four variables for cases in the cluster; these values, standardized, are shown in Figure 4.1. (The unstandardized values are shown in Figure 3.1 in Chapter 3.)

Figure 4.1   Standardized means for the five clusters

```
CLUSTER ZCALORIE ZSODIUM ZALCOHOL ZCOST
 /SAVE CLUSTER(5)
  /METHOD=COMPLETE(CLUSMEM).
VALUE LABELS CLUSMEM5 1 'AVERAGE' 2 'EXPENSIVE'
 3 'HIGH NA' 4 'LIGHT' 5 'VERY LIGHT'.
MEANS TABLES=ZCALORIE ZCOST ZALCOHOL ZSODIUM BY CLUSMEM5
 /OPTIONS=5 7.


Summaries of    ZCALORIE    Zscore(CALORIES)
By levels of    CLUSMEM5

Variable      Value  Label                      Mean

For Entire Population                    -1.016E-13

CLUSMEM5            1  AVERAGE                  .4363
CLUSMEM5            2  EXPENSIVE                .7552
CLUSMEM5            3  HIGH NA                  .6891
CLUSMEM5            4  LIGHT                   -.7668
CLUSMEM5            5  VERY LIGHT             -2.0623

   Total Cases =      20

Summaries of    ZCOST       Zscore(COST)
By levels of    CLUSMEM5

Variable      Value  Label                      Mean

For Entire Population                    -9.271E-14

CLUSMEM5            1  AVERAGE                 -.3791
CLUSMEM5            2  EXPENSIVE               1.8503
CLUSMEM5            3  HIGH NA                 -.7930
CLUSMEM5            4  LIGHT                   -.2539
CLUSMEM5            5  VERY LIGHT              -.5321

   Total Cases =      20

Summaries of    ZALCOHOL    Zscore(ALCOHOL)
By levels of    CLUSMEM5

Variable      Value  Label                      Mean

For Entire Population                    -1.772E-14

CLUSMEM5            1  AVERAGE                  .3422
CLUSMEM5            2  EXPENSIVE                .7042
CLUSMEM5            3  HIGH NA                  .6383
CLUSMEM5            4  LIGHT                   -.4475
CLUSMEM5            5  VERY LIGHT             -2.4218
```

(Continued on following page)

(Continued from previous page)

```
 Total Cases =        20

Summaries of    ZSODIUM      Zscore(SODIUM)
By levels of    CLUSMEM5

Variable       Value  Label                        Mean

For Entire Population                         -8.368E-14

CLUSMEM5          1  AVERAGE                        .3419
CLUSMEM5          2  EXPENSIVE                     -.6382
CLUSMEM5          3  HIGH NA                       1.4511
CLUSMEM5          4  LIGHT                         -.7217
CLUSMEM5          5  VERY LIGHT                    -.6762

  Total Cases =        20
```

The 15 cases in the new data set are standardized using the means and standard deviations from the original data set (see Chapter 3). The original and standardized values are shown in Figure 4.2.

Figure 4.2   Original and standardized values for the 15 new beers

```
COMPUTE ZCALORIE=(CALORIES-132.4)/30.26.
COMPUTE ZCOST=(COST-49.65)/14.38.
COMPUTE ZALCOHOL=(ALCOHOL-4.44)/.76.
COMPUTE ZSODIUM=(SODIUM-14.95)/6.58.
PROCESS IF (SELECT EQ 0)
LIST VAR=BEER CALORIES SODIUM ALCOHOL COST
          ZCALORIE ZSODIUM ZALCOHOL ZCOST.
```

BEER	CALORIES	SODIUM	ALCOHOL	COST	ZCALORIE	ZSODIUM	ZALCOHOL	ZCOST
MILLER HIGH LIFE	149	17	4.7	42.0	.55	.31	.34	-.53
MICHELOB	162	10	5.0	50.0	.98	-.75	.74	.02
LABATTS	147	17	5.0	53.0	.48	.31	.74	.23
MOLSON	154	17	5.1	56.0	.71	.31	.87	.44
HENRY WEINHARD	149	7	4.7	61.0	.55	-1.21	.34	.79
ANCHOR STEAM	154	17	4.7	120	.71	.31	.34	4.89
SCHMIDTS	147	7	4.7	30.0	.48	-1.21	.34	-1.37
PABST BLUE RIBBON	152	8	4.9	38.0	.65	-1.06	.61	-.81
OLYMPIA	153	27	4.6	44.0	.68	1.83	.21	-.39
DOS EQUIS	145	14	4.5	70.0	.42	-.14	.08	1.42
SCOTCH BUY (SAFEWAY)	145	18	4.5	27.0	.42	.46	.08	-1.58
BLATZ	144	13	4.6	30.0	.38	-.30	.21	-1.37
ROLLING ROCK	144	8	4.7	36.0	.38	-1.06	.34	-.95
TUBORG	155	13	5.0	43.0	.75	-.30	.74	-.46
ST PAULI GIRL	144	21	4.7	77.0	.38	.92	.34	1.90

To classify the cases, the Euclidean distance (see Chapter 3) from each new case to each of the cluster centers is calculated. The cluster centers are simply the means from Figure 4.1. To use these values as initial centers in the Quick Cluster procedure, enter them on the INITIAL subcommand or save them into an SPSS/PC+ data file and read them in using the FILE subcommand. Figure 4.3 shows these centers as they appear in output from the Quick Cluster procedure.

Figure 4.3   Initial cluster centers

```
QUICK CLUSTER ZCALORIE ZCOST ZALCOHOL ZSODIUM
  /CRITERIA=CLUSTERS(5)
  /INITIAL=(.436  -.379    .342     .342
            .755   1.85    .704    -.639
            .689  -.793    .638    1.45
           -.767  -.254   -.447    -.722
           -2.06  -.532   -2.42    -.676).
```

```
Initial Cluster Centers.

   Cluster      ZCALORIE        ZCOST        ZALCOHOL        ZSODIUM

      1           .4360        -.3790          .3420          .3420
      2           .7550        1.8500          .7040         -.6390
      3           .6890        -.7930          .6380         1.4500
      4          -.7670        -.2540         -.4470         -.7220
      5         -2.0600        -.5320        -2.4200         -.6760
```

The first new beer to be classified is Miller High Life. From Figure 4.2, its standardized value for calories is 0.55, for cost is −0.53, for alcohol is 0.34, and for sodium is 0.31. Its Euclidean distance to cluster 1 is:

$$\sqrt{(0.55-0.44)^2 + (-0.53-(-0.38))^2 + (0.34-0.34)^2 + (0.31-0.34)^2} = 0.19$$

Equation 4.1

Distances to the other cluster centers are computed in the same way. The distance to cluster 2 is 2.6, to cluster 3 is 1.21, to cluster 4 is 1.87, and to cluster 5 is 3.92. Since the distance is smallest to cluster 1, Miller High Life is assigned to cluster 1.

Figure 4.4 shows the clusters to which the new beers are assigned, as well as the Euclidean distance from the case to the center of its assigned cluster. As shown in Figure 4.5, ten beers are assigned to cluster 1, four beers to cluster 2, and one beer to cluster 3. No beers are assigned to the last two clusters.

Once the beers have been assigned to clusters, it is possible to calculate the actual centers of the resulting clusters, which are simply the average values of the variables for cases in the cluster. These values, called the final cluster centers, are shown in Figure 4.6. Since no cases were assigned to the last two clusters, system-missing values are displayed. From this table, we can see that the clusters do not differ much in average calories, since all three have similar standardized values. Cluster 2 has the beers with the highest cost, while cluster 3 contains the high-sodium beers.

Figure 4.4   Case listing of cluster membership

```
PROCESS IF (SELECT EQ 0).
QUICK CLUSTER ZCALORIE ZCOST ZALCOHOL ZSODIUM
 /CRITERIA=CLUSTERS(5)
 /METHOD=CLASSIFY
 /INITIAL=(.436   -.379    .342     .342
           .755   1.85     .704    -.639
           .689   -.793    .638    1.45
          -.767   -.254   -.447    -.722
          -2.06   -.532   -2.42    -.676)
 /PRINT=ID(BEER) CLUSTER.
```

```
Case listing of Cluster membership.

BEER                        Cluster      Distance

  MILLER HIGH LIFE             1            .192
  MICHELOB                     1           1.345
  LABATTS                      1            .730
  MOLSON                       1           1.014
  HENRY WEINHARD               2           1.274
  ANCHOR STEAM                 2           3.208
  SCHMIDTS                     1           1.839
  PABST BLUE RIBBON            1           1.502
  OLYMPIA                      3            .699
  DOS EQUIS                    2            .969
  SCOTCH BUY (SAFEWAY)         1           1.231
  BLATZ                        1           1.184
  ROLLING ROCK                 1           1.511
  TUBORG                       1            .817
  ST PAULI GIRL                2           1.643
```

Figure 4.5   Number of cases in each cluster

```
PROCESS IF (SELECT EQ 0).
QUICK CLUSTER ZCALORIE ZCOST ZALCOHOL ZSODIUM
 /CRITERIA=CLUSTERS(5)
 /METHOD=CLASSIFY
 /INITIAL=(.436   -.379    .342     .342
           .755   1.85     .704    -.639
           .689   -.793    .638    1.45
          -.767   -.254   -.447    -.722
          -2.06   -.532   -2.42    -.676).
```

```
Number of Cases in each Cluster.

  Cluster      unweighted cases    weighted cases

     1              10.0              10.0
     2               4.0               4.0
     3               1.0               1.0
     4                .0                .0
     5                .0                .0

Missing                 0
Valid cases          15.0              15.0
```

Figure 4.6   Final cluster centers

```
Final Cluster Centers.

  Cluster    ZCALORIE     ZCOST     ZALCOHOL     ZSODIUM

     1          .5783      -.6363      .5000       -.3267
     2          .5155      2.2497      .2763       -.0304
     3          .6808      -.3929      .2105       1.8313
     4            .           .          .           .
     5            .           .          .           .
```

Once clusters have been formed, you can assess how "well separated" they are by calculating the distances between their centers. Hopefully, the clusters will have centers that are far apart, with cases within a cluster hovering fairly closely to the cluster's center.

Euclidean distances between pairs of final cluster centers are displayed in Figure 4.7. For example, the distance between clusters 1 and 2 is:

$$\sqrt{(0.58 - 0.52)^2 + (-0.64 - 2.25)^2 + (0.50 - 0.28)^2 + (-0.33 - (-0.03))^2} = 2.91$$

Equation 4.2

Similarly, the distance between clusters 1 and 3 is 2.19, while the distance between clusters 2 and 3 is 3.24.

Figure 4.7   Euclidean distances between final cluster centers

```
PROCESS IF (SELECT EQ 0).
QUICK CLUSTER ZCALORIE ZCOST ZALCOHOL ZSODIUM
 /CRITERIA=CLUSTERS(5)
 /METHOD=CLASSIFY
 /INITIAL=(.436  -.379   .342    .342
           .755  1.85    .704   -.639
           .689  -.793   .638   1.45
          -.767  -.254  -.447   -.722
          -2.06  -.532  -2.42   -.676)
 /PRINT=DISTANCE.


Distances between Final Cluster centers.

   Cluster            1            2            3            4

      1            .0000
      2           2.9104        .0000
      3           2.1933       3.2374       .0000
      4             .            .            .         .0000
      5             .            .            .           .
```

The table of final cluster centers (Figure 4.6) contains the average values of the variables for each cluster but provides no idea of the variability. One way of assessing the between-cluster to within-cluster variability is to compute a one-way analysis of variance for each of the variables and examine the ratio of the between-cluster to within-cluster mean squares.

Figure 4.8 contains the mean squares for examining differences between the clusters. The between-clusters mean square is labeled *Cluster MS*, and the within-cluster mean square is labeled *Error MS*. Their ratio is displayed in the column labeled *F*. Large ratios and small observed significance levels are associated with variables that differ between the clusters. However, the *F* tests should be used only for descriptive purposes, since the clusters have been chosen to maximize the differences among cases in different clusters. The observed significance levels are not corrected for this and, thus, cannot be interpreted as tests of the hypothesis that the cluster means are equal.

Figure 4.8   Cluster mean squares

```
PROCESS IF (SELECT EQ 0).
QUICK CLUSTER ZCALORIE ZCOST ZALCOHOL ZSODIUM
 /CRITERIA=CLUSTERS(5)
 /METHOD=CLASSIFY
 /INITIAL=(.436  -.379   .342    .342
           .755   1.85   .704   -.639
           .689  -.793   .638   1.45
          -.767  -.254  -.447   -.722
          -2.06  -.532  -2.42   -.676)
 /PRINT=ANOVA.

Analysis of Variance.

  Variable      Cluster MS   DF      Error MS      DF          F    Prob

  ZCALORIE         .0124      2         .033      12.0      .3712   .698
  ZCOST         12.0558       2        1.200      12.0    10.0438   .003
  ZALCOHOL         .0952      2         .058      12.0     1.6256   .237
  ZSODIUM         2.1316      2         .524      12.0     4.0665   .045
```

As expected from Figure 4.6, the calories variable (*zcalorie*) does not differ between the clusters. The *F* value is small and the associated significance level is large. Beers in the three clusters also have fairly similar alcohol content (*zalcohol*). However, they do seem to be different in sodium (*zsodium*) and cost (*zcost*).

Classification When Cluster Centers Are Unknown

In the previous example, the cluster centers for classifying cases were already known. The initial cluster solution and the center values were obtained from the hierarchical cluster solution. In many situations, the center values for the clusters are not known in advance. Instead, they too must be estimated from the data. Several different methods for estimating cluster centers are available. Most of them involve examining the data several times.

Good cluster centers separate the cases well. One strategy is to choose cases that have large distances between them and use their values as initial estimates of the cluster centers. The number of cases selected is the number of clusters specified.

The algorithm for this strategy proceeds as follows. The first *k* cases in the data file, where *k* is the number of clusters requested, are selected as temporary centers. As subsequent cases are processed, a case replaces a center if its smallest distance to a center is greater than the distance between the two closest centers. The center that is closest to the case is replaced. A case also replaces a center if the smallest distance from the case to a center is larger than the smallest distance between that center and all other centers. Again, it replaces the center closest to it.

To illustrate the basics of the *k*-means cluster analysis when centers are estimated from the data, let's consider the beer data again, this time using *k*-means clustering to cluster all 35 beers into five clusters.

Selecting Initial Cluster Centers

The first step of cluster formation, as previously described, is making a first guess at cluster centers. Figure 4.9 contains the values of five centers selected by the program, the *initial cluster centers*. Each center corresponds to a beer. The first center is Schlitz Light, the second, Kronenbourg, the third, Pabst Extra Light, the fourth, Anchor Steam, and the fifth, Heileman's Old Style. In terms of the variables under consideration, these are clearly differentiated beers. Schlitz Light is a low-calorie beer; Kronenbourg is a low-sodium beer; Pabst Extra Light is a very light beer; Anchor Steam is a very expensive beer; and Heileman's Old Style is an average beer, though somewhat higher in sodium than most of the beers.

Figure 4.9   Initial cluster centers for all 35 beers

```
DESCRIPTIVES CALORIES (ZCAL) SODIUM (ZSOD) ALCOHOL (ZALC) COST(ZCST)
 /OPTIONS=3.
QUICK CLUSTER ZCAL ZSOD ZALC ZCST
 /METHOD=KMEANS
 /CRITERIA=CLUSTER (5).


   Initial Cluster Centers.

      Cluster      ZCAL         ZSOD         ZALC         ZCST

           1     -1.7496      -1.2461       -.6255       -.1907
           2      1.2365      -1.2461       1.0330       1.1973
           3     -2.9358        .0558      -3.7765       -.6711
           4       .5820        .3813        .2038       3.7064
           5       .1730       1.5204        .5354       -.4042
```

After the initial cluster centers have been selected, cluster centers are updated in an iterative process. All cases are grouped into the cluster with the closest center. Then, average values for the variables are computed from the cases that have been assigned to each cluster and the cases that were the initial cluster centers. This process of assigning cases and recomputing cluster centers is repeated until no further changes occur in cluster centers or until the maximum number of iterations has been reached. The resulting centers are used to classify the cases. The changes in cluster centers at each iteration are displayed in Figure 4.10.

Figure 4.10   Iteration history

```
QUICK CLUSTER ZCAL ZSOD ZALC ZCST
 /METHOD=KMEANS
 /CRITERIA=CLUSTER (5).


Convergence achieved due to no or small distance change.
The maximum distance by which any center has changed is .0542
Current iteration is   3

Minimum distance between initial centers is 3.1717

Iteration      Change in Cluster Centers
                  1        2        3        4        5
        1      6.18E-01 1.09E+00 6.10E-01    .0000  1.07E+00
        2      1.03E-01 1.21E-01 2.03E-01    .0000  5.36E-02
        3      1.72E-02 1.34E-02 6.77E-02    .0000  2.68E-03
```

The results of assigning cases based on the cluster centers when iteration stops is shown in Figure 4.11. Beer names, cluster assignment, and distances to the cluster centers used for classification are shown for the first ten beers. The number of cases in each cluster is shown in Figure 4.12.

Figure 4.11   Case listing of cluster membership

```
QUICK CLUSTER ZCAL ZSOD ZALC ZCST
  /METHOD=KMEANS
  /CRITERIA=CLUSTER (5)
  /PRINT=ID(BEER) CLUSTER.

Case listing of Cluster membership.

BEER                    Cluster      Distance

  MILLER HIGH LIFE         5            .172
  BUDWEISER                5            .470
  SCHLITZ                  5            .361
  LOWENBRAU                5            .660
  MICHELOB                 2           1.218
  LABATTS                  5            .751
  MOLSON                   5            .989
  HENRY WEINHARD           2            .981
  KRONENBOURG              2           1.219
  HEINEKEN                 2            .455
  .
  .
  .
```

Figure 4.12   Number of cases in each cluster

```
Number of Cases in each Cluster.

  Cluster       unweighted cases      weighted cases

      1               5.0                  5.0
      2               8.0                  8.0
      3               2.0                  2.0
      4               1.0                  1.0
      5              19.0                 19.0

  Missing             0
  Valid cases        35.0                 35.0
```

Once the cases have been classified, average values of the variables are again computed. These are termed **final cluster centers** and are shown in Figure 4.13. The resulting five clusters are quite similar to those obtained with hierarchical cluster analysis in Chapter 3 using a subset of the beers. Cluster 1 contains the light beers, cluster 3 contains the very light beers, and cluster 5 contains the average beers. Anchor Steam, which was not included in the previous analysis, constitutes a separate cluster (cluster 4).

Figure 4.13   Final cluster centers

```
Final Cluster Centers.

  Cluster      ZCAL         ZSOD         ZALC         ZCST

      1       -1.2505      -.7253       -.7913       -.2440
      2         .5258      -.4527        .4525       1.0572
      3       -2.8540      -.6765      -3.2790       -.4576
      4         .5820       .3813        .2038       3.7064
      5         .3775       .4327        .3521       -.5278
```

Euclidean distances between the final cluster centers are shown in Figure 4.14. Based on this, you can assess how different the final clusters are. The largest distance is between the very light beers and Anchor Steam. From Figure 4.15, it appears that for all of the variables, variability within a cluster is less than the variability between the clusters.

Figure 4.14   Euclidean distances between final cluster centers

```
QUICK CLUSTER ZCAL ZSOD ZALC ZCST
  /METHOD=KMEANS
  /CRITERIA=CLUSTER (5)
  /PRINT=DISTANCE.

 Distances between Final Cluster Centers.

   Cluster             1             2             3             4

       1          .0000
       2         2.5436         .0000
       3         2.9678        5.2623         .0000
       4         4.6020        2.7890        6.5110         .0000
       5         2.3193        1.8243        4.9862        4.2420
```

Figure 4.15   Cluster mean squares

```
QUICK CLUSTER ZCAL ZSOD ZALC ZCST
  /CRITERIA=CLUSTER (5)
  /PRINT=ANOVA.

 Analysis of Variance.
```

Variable	Cluster MS	DF	Error MS	DF	F	Prob
ZCAL	7.3419	4	.1544	30.0	47.5448	.000
ZSOD	2.2219	4	.8371	30.0	2.6543	.052
ZALC	7.1675	4	.1777	30.0	40.3421	.000
ZCST	7.1720	4	.1771	30.0	40.5044	.000

Running the Quick Cluster Procedure

The Quick Cluster procedure allocates cases to clusters when the number of clusters to be formed is known. It is particularly useful when the number of cases is large, since it requires substantially less computer memory and computation time than does the Cluster procedure. The algorithm classifies cases into clusters based on distances to the cluster centers. Cluster centers can either be specified by the user or estimated from the data.

Available output from QUICK CLUSTER includes estimates of initial, updated, and final cluster centers, distances between all pairs of final cluster centers, cluster membership and distance to the cluster center for all cases, and analysis-of-variance tables for variables used in the clustering. For each case, cluster membership and distance can be saved as new variables in the active file.

Specifying the Variables

The only required specification for QUICK CLUSTER is the list of variables to be used for forming the clusters. The variable list must precede any optional subcommands.

Example

```
QUICK CLUSTER ZCALORIE ZCOST ZALCOHOL ZSODIUM.
```

- This command produces a default clustering of cases into two groups based on the values of the four variables.

Specifying Initial Cluster Centers

Use the INITIAL subcommand to specify initial cluster centers. For each cluster requested, you must include one value for each clustering variable (see "Classification When Cluster Centers Are Known" on p. 122). If initial cluster centers are not known, you can use the CRITERIA subcommand to control the selection of initial cluster centers (see "Classification When Cluster Centers Are Unknown" on p. 127 and "Controlling Clustering Algorithm" on p. 132).

Example

```
QUICK CLUSTER ZCALORIE ZCOST ZALCOHOL ZSODIUM
 /CRITERIA=CLUSTERS(5)
 /METHOD=CLASSIFY
 /INITIAL=(.436   -.379    .342     .342
           .755   1.85     .704    -.639
           .689   -.793    .638    1.45
          -.767   -.254   -.447    -.722
          -2.06   -.532   -2.42    -.676).
```

- This command requests five clusters. The values for the initial cluster centers are given. In the example, the columns correspond to the variables specified on QUICK CLUSTER and the rows to the clusters requested. The matrix format is optional but the order of the cluster centers must be maintained.

- The METHOD subcommand specifies that these initial cluster centers be used for classification.

Updating Cluster Centers

By default, QUICK CLUSTER recalculates cluster centers after assigning all the cases and repeats the process until one of the criteria is met. You can use the METHOD subcommand to recalculate cluster centers after each case is assigned or to suppress recalculation until after classification is complete.

KMEANS (NOUPDATE) *Recalculate cluster centers after all cases are assigned for each iteration.* This is the default.

KMEANS(UPDATE) *Recalculate a cluster center each time a case is assigned.* QUICK CLUSTER calculates the mean of cases currently in the cluster and uses this new cluster center in subsequent case assignment.

CLASSIFY *Do not recalculate cluster centers.* QUICK CLUSTER uses the initial cluster centers for classification and computes the final cluster centers as the means of all the cases assigned to the same cluster. When CLASSIFY is specified, the CONVERGE or MXITER specifications on CRITERIA are ignored.

Controlling Clustering Algorithm

Use the CRITERIA subcommand to specify various options for the clustering algorithm. The following keywords are available:

CLUSTER(n) *Number of clusters.* QUICK CLUSTER assigns cases to *n* clusters. The default is 2.

NOINITIAL *No initial cluster center selection.* By default, initial cluster centers are formed by choosing one case (with valid data for the clustering variables) for each cluster requested. The initial selection requires a pass through the data to ensure that the centers are well separated from one another. If NOINITIAL is specified, QUICK CLUSTER selects the first *n* cases without missing values as initial cluster centers. See "Selecting Initial Cluster Centers" on p. 128.

MXITER(n) *Maximum number of iterations for updating cluster centers.* The default is 10. Iteration stops when maximum number of iterations has been reached. MXITER is ignored when METHOD=CLASSIFY.

CONVERGE(n) *Convergence criterion controlling maximum change in cluster centers.* The default value for *n* is 0.02. The maximum change value equals the convergence value (*n*) times the minimum distance between initial centers. Iteration stops when the largest change of any cluster center is less than or equal to the maximum change value. CONVERGE is ignored when METHOD=CLASSIFY.

Displaying Optional Output

By default, QUICK CLUSTER prints the centers used for classification (the initial cluster centers), the mean values of the cases in each cluster when clustering is complete (final cluster centers), and the number of cases in each cluster. Use the PRINT subcommand with the following keywords to obtain additional output:

CLUSTER   *Display for each case an identifying number or label, the number of the cluster to which it is assigned, and its Euclidean distance to the center of the cluster.* (See Figure 4.4 and Figure 4.11.)

ID(varname)   *Identify cases on output by the values of the variable specified.* By default, cases are identified by their sequential number in the active file. (See Figure 4.4 and Figure 4.11.)

DISTANCE   *Display Euclidean distances between all pairs of final cluster centers.* (See Figure 4.7 and Figure 4.14.)

ANOVA   *Display an analysis-of-variance table for each variable used for classification.* (See Figure 4.8 and Figure 4.15.)

Missing Values

By default, QUICK CLUSTER eliminates from the analysis cases with system- or user-missing values for any variable on the variable list. Use the MISSING subcommand with one of the following four keywords to change the missing-value treatment:

LISTWISE   *Delete cases with missing values on any variable.* This is the default.

PAIRWISE   *Assign cases to clusters based on distances computed from all variables with nonmissing values.* Only cases with missing values for all clustering variables are deleted. PAIRWISE and LISTWISE are mutually exclusive, but either can be specified with INCLUDE.

INCLUDE   *Treat user-missing values as nonmissing.*

DEFAULT   *Same as LISTWISE.*

Saving Cluster Membership and Distance

Use the SAVE subcommand to save cluster membership and distance as new variables in the active file. To use these results in subsequent sessions, you must save the active file using the SAVE or EXPORT command. You can save cluster membership or distance, or both, and assign variable names to the new variables:

CLUSTER(varname)   *The number of the cluster to which a case belongs.* Specify a variable name in parentheses.

DISTANCE(varname)   *For each case the distance to the cluster center is stored in the variable specified in parentheses.*

If you do not assign a variable name, QUICK CLUSTER creates default names beginning with *QCL_* with a sequential number to make the new variable unique in the active file.

Example

```
QUICK CLUSTER A B C D
  /CRITERIA=CLUSTER(6)
  /SAVE=CLUSTER DISTANCE.
```

- This command forms six clusters on the basis of the four variables *a*, *b*, *c*, and *d*.
- *QCL_1* is created to hold the class membership for each case. The values of *QCL_1* are integers ranging from 1 to 6.
- *QCL_2* is created to hold the Euclidean distance between a case and the center of the cluster to which it is assigned.

Writing the Final Cluster Centers

Use the WRITE subcommand to write the final cluster centers to the results file specified on the SET command (the default is *spss.prc*). You can edit this file and use these cluster centers on an INITIAL subcommand in a subsequent session. The WRITE subcommand has no specifications.

Annotated Example

The following SPSS/PC+ commands created the output in Figure 4.3 through Figure 4.8.

```
DATA LIST FREE /SELECT RATING BEER (A21) ORIGIN AVAIL
       PRICE COST CALORIES SODIUM ALCOHOL CLASS LIGHT.
COMPUTE ZCALORIE=(CALORIES-132.4)/30.26.
COMPUTE ZCOST=(COST-49.65)/14.38.
COMPUTE ZALCOHOL=(ALCOHOL-4.44)/.76.
COMPUTE ZSODIUM=(SODIUM-14.95)/6.58.
BEGIN DATA.
data lines
END DATA.
PROCESS IF (SELECT EQ 0).
QUICK CLUSTER ZCALORIE ZCOST ZALCOHOL ZSODIUM
  /CRITERIA=CLUSTERS(5)
  /METHOD=CLASSIFY
  /INITIAL=(.436   -.379    .342     .342
            .755    1.85    .704    -.639
            .689   -.793    .638     1.45
           -.767   -.254   -.447    -.722
           -2.06   -.532   -2.42    -.676)
  /PRINT=ID(BEER) CLUSTER DISTANCE ANOVA.
```

- The DATA LIST command defines the variables and tells SPSS/PC+ that the data are in freefield format.

- The four COMPUTE commands create the standardized variables needed for input to the QUICK CLUSTER command. COMPUTE statements are used so that the standardized values are based on the means and standard deviations of the original 20 beers analyzed in Chapter 8.

- PROCESS IF command temporarily selects only those beers that were not analyzed in Chapter 8. The variable *select* is coded 0 for the new beers and 1 for the beers previously analyzed.

- The QUICK CLUSTER command names the four standardized variables as the variables to be used for forming clusters. The CRITERIA subcommand tells SPSS/PC+ to form five clusters.

- Since the values of the initial cluster centers are given on the INITIAL subcommand, CLASSIFY is specified on the METHOD subcommand so that the initial cluster centers are used for classification.

- The PRINT subcommand asks for all available output, using the values of string variable *beer* to label cases.

5 Measuring Scales: Reliability Analysis

From the moment we are born, the world begins to "score" us. One minute after birth, we are rated on the ten-point Apgar scale, followed closely by the five-minute Apgar scale, and then on to countless other scales that will track our intelligence, creditworthiness, likelihood of hijacking a plane, and so on. A dubious mark of maturity is when we find ourselves administering these scales.

Constructing a Scale

When we want to measure characteristics such as driving ability, mastery of course materials, or the ability to function independently, we must construct some type of measurement device. Usually we develop a **scale** or test that is composed of a variety of related items. The responses to each item can be graded and summed, resulting in a score for each case. A question that frequently arises is, How good is our scale? To answer this question, consider some of the characteristics of a scale or test.

When we construct a test to measure how well college students have learned the material in an introductory psychology course, the questions actually included on the test are a small sample from all of the items that may have been selected. Although we have selected a limited number of items for inclusion on the test, we want to draw conclusions about the students' mastery of the entire course content. In fact, we'd like to think that even if we changed the actual items on the test, there would be a strong relationship between students' scores on the test actually given and the scores they would have received on other tests we could have given. A good test is one that yields stable results—that is, it is reliable.

Reliability and Validity

Everyone knows the endearing qualities of a reliable car. It goes anytime, anywhere, for anybody. It behaves the same way under a variety of circumstances. Its performance is repeatable. A **reliable** measuring instrument behaves similarly. A reliable test yields similar results when different people administer it and when alternative forms are used. When conditions for making the measurement change, the results of the test should not.

A test must be reliable to be useful. But it is not enough for a test to be reliable; it must also be **valid**. That is, the instrument must measure what it is intended to measure. A test that requires students to do mirror drawing and memorize nonsense syllables may be quite reliable, but it is a poor indicator of mastery of the concepts of psychology. Such a test has poor validity.

There are many different ways to assess both reliability and validity. In this chapter, we will be concerned only with measures of reliability.

Describing Test Results

Before discussing measures of reliability, let's look at some of the descriptive statistics that are useful for characterizing a scale. We will analyze a scale whose goal is to assess an elderly person's competence in the physical activities of daily living.[1] Three hundred and ninety-five people were rated on the eight items shown in Figure 5.1. For each item, a score of 1 was assigned if the patient was unable to perform the activity, 2 if the patient was able to perform the activity with assistance, and 3 if the patient required no assistance to perform the activity.

Figure 5.1   Physical activity items

```
RELIABILITY VARIABLES=ITEM1 TO ITEM8.

1.      ITEM1       Can eat
2.      ITEM2       Can dress and undress
3.      ITEM3       Can take care of own appearance
4.      ITEM4       Can walk
5.      ITEM5       Can get in and out of bed
6.      ITEM6       Can take a bath or shower
7.      ITEM7       Can get to bathroom on time
8.      ITEM8       Has been able to do tasks for 6 months
```

When we summarize a scale, we want to look at the characteristics of the individual items, the characteristics of the overall scale, and the relationship between the individual items and the entire scale. Figure 5.2 contains descriptive statistics for the individual items. You see that the average scores for the items range from 2.93 for item 1 to 1.66 for item 8. Item 7 has the largest standard deviation, 0.5190.

---

1. Thanks to Dr. Michael Counte of Rush–Presbyterian—St. Luke's Medical Center, Chicago, Principal Investigator of the National Institute of Aging Panel Study of Elderly Health Beliefs and Behavior, for making these data available.

Figure 5.2   Univariate descriptive statistics

```
RELIABILITY VARIABLES=ITEM1 TO ITEM8
   /STATISTICS=DESCRIPTIVES.

                              MEAN        STD DEV       CASES

1.      ITEM1             2.9266          .3593        395.0
2.      ITEM2             2.8962          .4116        395.0
3.      ITEM3             2.9165          .3845        395.0
4.      ITEM4             2.8684          .4367        395.0
5.      ITEM5             2.9114          .3964        395.0
6.      ITEM6             2.8506          .4731        395.0
7.      ITEM7             2.7873          .5190        395.0
8.      ITEM8             1.6582          .4749        395.0
```

The correlation coefficients between the items are shown in Figure 5.3. The only item that appears to have a small correlation with the other items is item 8. Its highest correlation is 0.26, with item 6.

Figure 5.3   Inter-item correlation coefficients

```
RELIABILITY VARIABLES=ITEM1 TO ITEM8
   /STATISTICS=CORRELATIONS.

                    CORRELATION MATRIX

                ITEM1       ITEM2       ITEM3       ITEM4       ITEM5

ITEM1         1.0000
ITEM2          .7893     1.0000
ITEM3          .8557      .8913     1.0000
ITEM4          .7146      .7992      .7505     1.0000
ITEM5          .8274      .8770      .8173      .8415     1.0000
ITEM6          .6968      .8326      .7684      .8504      .7684
ITEM7          .5557      .5736      .5340      .5144      .5497
ITEM8          .0459      .1427      .0795      .2108      .0949

                ITEM6       ITEM7       ITEM8

ITEM6         1.0000
ITEM7          .5318     1.0000
ITEM8          .2580      .1883     1.0000
```

Additional statistics for the scale as a whole are shown in Figure 5.4 and Figure 5.5. The average score for the scale is 21.82 and the standard deviation is 2.7 (Figure 5.4). The average score on an item (Figure 5.5) is 2.73, with a range of 1.27. Similarly, the average of the item variances is 0.19, with a minimum of 0.13 and a maximum of 0.27.

Figure 5.4   Scale statistics

```
RELIABILITY VARIABLES=ITEM1 TO ITEM8
   /STATISTICS=SCALE.

                                                  # OF
STATISTICS FOR        MEAN    VARIANCE    STD DEV  VARIABLES
        SCALE      21.8152     7.3896     2.7184        8
```

Figure 5.5   Summary statistics for items

```
RELIABILITY VARIABLES=ITEM1 TO ITEM8
 /SUMMARY=MEANS VARIANCES CORRELATIONS.
```

```
          # OF CASESE =          395.0

ITEM MEANS          MEAN    MINIMUM    MAXIMUM     RANGE    MAX/MIN    VARIANCE
                  2.7269     1.6582     2.9266    1.2684     1.7649       .1885

ITEM VARIANCES      MEAN    MINIMUM    MAXIMUM     RANGE    MAX/MIN    VARIANCE
                   .1891      .1291      .2694     .1403     2.0864       .0022

INTER-ITEM
CORRELATIONS        MEAN    MINIMUM    MAXIMUM     RANGE    MAX/MIN    VARIANCE
                   .5843      .0459      .8913     .8454    19.4033       .0790
```

The correlations between items range from 0.046 to 0.891. The ratio between the largest and smallest correlation is $0.891/0.046$, or 19.4. The average correlation is 0.584.

Relationship Between the Scale and the Items

Now let's look at the relationship between the individual items and the composite score (see Figure 5.6).

Figure 5.6   Item-total summary statistics

```
RELIABILITY VARIABLES=ITEM1 TO ITEM8
 /SUMMARY=TOTAL.
```

```
ITEM-TOTAL STATISTICS
```

	SCALE MEAN IF ITEM DELETED	SCALE VARIANCE IF ITEM DELETED	CORRECTED ITEM- TOTAL CORRELATION	SQUARED MULTIPLE CORRELATION	ALPHA IF ITEM DELETED
ITEM1	18.8886	5.8708	.7981	.7966	.8917
ITEM2	18.9190	5.5061	.8874	.8882	.8820
ITEM3	18.8987	5.7004	.8396	.8603	.8873
ITEM4	18.9468	5.4718	.8453	.8137	.8848
ITEM5	18.9038	5.6202	.8580	.8620	.8852
ITEM6	18.9646	5.3084	.8520	.8029	.8833
ITEM7	19.0278	5.6414	.5998	.3777	.9095
ITEM8	20.1570	6.7316	.1755	.1331	.9435

For each item, the first column of Figure 5.6 shows what the average score for the scale would be if the item were excluded from the scale. For example, we know from Figure 5.4 that the average score for the scale is 21.82. If item 1 were eliminated from the scale, the average score would be 18.89. This is computed by simply subtracting the average score for the item from the scale mean. In this case, it is $21.82 - 2.93 = 18.89$. The next column is the scale variance if the item were eliminated. The column labeled *COR-RECTED ITEM–TOTAL CORRELATION* is the Pearson correlation coefficient between the score on the individual item and the sum of the scores on the remaining items. For example, the correlation between the score on item 8 and the sum of the scores on items

1 through 7 is only 0.176. This indicates that there is not much of a relationship between the eighth item and the other items. On the other hand, item 2 has a very high correlation, 0.887, with the other items.

Another way to look at the relationship between an individual item and the rest of the scale is to try to predict a person's score on an item based on the scores obtained on the other items. We can do this by calculating a multiple regression equation with the item of interest as the dependent variable and all other items as independent variables. The multiple R^2 from this regression equation is displayed for each item in the column labeled *SQUARED MULTIPLE CORRELATION*. We can see that almost 80% of the observed variability in the responses to item 1 can be explained by the other items. As expected, item 8 is poorly predicted from the other items. Its multiple R^2 is only 0.13.

The Reliability Coefficient

By looking at the statistics shown above, we've learned quite a bit about our scale and the individual items it includes. However, we still haven't come up with an index of how reliable the scale is. There are several different ways to measure reliability (see Lord & Novick, 1968; Nunnally, 1978):

- You can compute an estimate of reliability based on the observed correlations or covariances of the items with each other.
- You can correlate the results from two alternate forms of the same test or split the same test into two parts and look at the correlation between the two parts.

One of the most commonly used reliability coefficients is **Cronbach's alpha**. Alpha (or α) is based on the "internal consistency" of a test. That is, it is based on the average correlation of items within a test, if the items are standardized to a standard deviation of 1; or on the average covariance among items on a scale, if the items are not standardized. We assume that the items on a scale are positively correlated with each other because they are measuring, to a certain extent, a common entity. If items are not positively correlated with each other, we have no reason to believe that they are correlated with other possible items we may have selected. In this case, we do not expect to see a positive relationship between this test and other similar tests.

Interpreting Cronbach's Alpha

Cronbach's α has several interpretations. It can be viewed as the correlation between this test or scale and all other possible tests or scales containing the same number of items, which could be constructed from a hypothetical universe of items that measure the characteristic of interest. In the physical activities scale, for example, the eight questions actually selected for inclusion can be viewed as a sample from a universe of many possible items. The patients could have been asked whether they can walk up a flight of stairs, get up from a chair, cook a meal, or perform a myriad of other activities related to daily living. Cronbach's α tells us how much correlation we expect between our scale and all other possible eight-item scales measuring the same thing.

Another interpretation of Cronbach's α is the squared correlation between the score a person obtains on a particular scale (the observed score) and the score he or she would have obtained if questioned on *all* of the possible items in the universe (the true score).

Since α can be interpreted as a correlation coefficient, it ranges in value from 0 to 1. (Negative α values can occur when items are not positively correlated among themselves and the reliability model is violated.)

Cronbach's α for the physical activity scale is shown in Figure 5.7. Note that the value, 0.91, is large, indicating that our scale is quite reliable. The other entry in Figure 5.7, labeled *STANDARDIZED ITEM ALPHA*, is the α value that would be obtained if all items were standardized to have a variance of 1. Since the items on our scale have fairly comparable variances, there is little difference between the two α's. If items on the scale have widely differing variances, the two α's may differ substantially.

Figure 5.7   Cronbach's alpha

```
RELIABILITY VARIABLES=ITEM1 TO ITEM8
 /SUMMARY=MEANS.

RELIABILITY COEFFICIENTS      8 ITEMS

ALPHA =    .9089           STANDARDIZED ITEM ALPHA =    .9183
```

Cronbach's α can be computed using the following formula:

$$\alpha = \frac{k\overline{cov}/\overline{var}}{1 + (k-1)\,\overline{cov}/\overline{var}}$$

Equation 5.1

where k is the number of items in the scale, $\overline{cov}$ is the average covariance between items, and $\overline{var}$ is the average variance of the items. If the items are standardized to have the same variance, the formula can be simplified to

$$\alpha = \frac{k\overline{r}}{1 + (k-1)\,\overline{r}}$$

Equation 5.2

where $\overline{r}$ is the average correlation between items.

Looking at Equation 5.2, we can see that Cronbach's α depends on both the length of the test (k in the formula) and the correlation of the items on the test. For example, if the average correlation between items is 0.2 on a 10-item scale, α is 0.71. If the number of items is increased to 25, α is 0.86. You can have large reliability coefficients, even when the average inter-item correlation is small, if the number of items on the scale is large enough.

Alpha If Item Deleted

When we are examining individual items, as in Figure 5.6, you may want to know how each of the items affects the reliability of the scale. This can be accomplished by calculating Cronbach's α when each of the items is removed from the scale. These α's are shown in the last column of Figure 5.6. You can see that eliminating item 8 from the physical activity scale causes α to increase from 0.91 (as in Figure 5.7) to 0.94 (Figure 5.6). From the correlation matrix in Figure 5.3, we saw that item 8 is not strongly related to the other items, so we would expect that eliminating it from the scale would increase the overall reliability of the scale. Elimination of any of the other items from the scale causes little change in α.

The Split-Half Reliability Model

Cronbach's α is based on correlations of items on a single scale. It is a measure based on the internal consistency of the items. Other measures of reliability are based on splitting the scale into two parts and looking at the correlation between the two parts. Such measures are called **split-half coefficients**. One of the disadvantages of this method is that the results depend on the allocation of items to halves. The coefficient you get depends on how you split your scale. Sometimes split-half methods are applied to situations in which two tests are administered or the same test is administered twice.

Figure 5.8 contains summary statistics that would be obtained if we split the physical ability scale into two equal parts. The first four items are part 1, while the second four items are part 2. Note that separate descriptive statistics are given for each of the parts, as well as for the entire scale. Reliability statistics for the split model are shown in Figure 5.9.

Figure 5.8   Split-half statistics

```
RELIABILITY /VARIABLES = ITEM1 TO ITEM8
  /STATISTICS SCALE
  /SUMMARY = MEANS VARIANCES CORRELATIONS
  /MODEL = SPLIT.
       # OF CASES =        395.0

                                             # OF
STATISTICS FOR     MEAN    VARIANCE  STD DEV  VARIABLES
       PART 1    11.6076    2.1527   1.4672      4
       PART 2    10.2076    1.8959   1.3769      4
       SCALE     21.8152    7.3896   2.7184      8

ITEM MEANS         MEAN    MINIMUM  MAXIMUM   RANGE   MAX/MIN   VARIANCE
       PART 1    2.9019    2.8684   2.9266   .0582   1.0203    .0007
       PART 2    2.5519    1.6582   2.9114  1.2532   1.7557    .3575
       SCALE     2.7269    1.6582   2.9266  1.2684   1.7649    .1885

ITEM VARIANCES     MEAN    MINIMUM  MAXIMUM   RANGE   MAX/MIN   VARIANCE
       PART 1    .1593     .1291    .1907    .0616   1.4774    .0007
       PART 2    .2190     .1571    .2694    .1123   1.7147    .0021
       SCALE     .1891     .1291    .2694    .1403   2.0864    .0022

INTER-ITEM
CORRELATIONS       MEAN    MINIMUM  MAXIMUM   RANGE   MAX/MIN   VARIANCE
       PART 1    .8001     .7146    .8913    .1768   1.2474    .0039
       PART 2    .3985     .0949    .7684    .6735   8.0973    .0606
       SCALE     .5843     .0459    .8913    .8454  19.4033    .0790
```

Figure 5.9   Split-half reliability

```
RELIABILITY COEFFICIENTS      8 ITEMS

CORRELATION BETWEEN FORMS =         .8269

EQUAL LENGTH SPEARMAN-BROWN =       .9052

GUTTMAN SPLIT-HALF =                .9042

UNEQUAL-LENGTH SPEARMAN-BROWN =     .9052

ALPHA FOR PART 1 =          .9387    ALPHA FOR PART 2 =          .7174
   4 ITEMS IN PART 1                    4 ITEMS IN PART 2
```

The correlation between the two halves, labeled on the output as *CORRELATION BE-TWEEN FORMS*, is 0.8269. This is an estimate of the reliability of the test if it has four items. The equal-length **Spearman-Brown coefficient**, which has a value of 0.9052 in this case, tells us what the reliability of the eight-item test would be if it were made up of two equal parts that have a four-item reliability of 0.8269. (Remember, the reliability of a test increases as the number of items on the test increase, provided that the average correlation between items does not change.) If the number of items on each of the two parts is not equal, the unequal-length Spearman-Brown coefficient can be used to esti-mate what the reliability of the overall test would be. In this case, since the two parts are of equal length, the two Spearman-Brown coefficients are equal. The **Guttman split-half coefficient** is another estimate of the reliability of the overall test. It does not as-sume that the two parts are equally reliable or have the same variance. Separate values of Cronbach's α are also shown for each of the two parts of the test.

Other Reliability Models

In the previous models, we didn't make any assumptions about item means or variances. If we have information about item means and variances, we can incorporate this addi-tional information into the estimation of reliability coefficients. Two commonly used models are the **strictly parallel model** and the **parallel model**. In the strictly parallel model, all items are assumed to have the same means, the same variances for the true (unobservable) scores, and the same error variances over replications. When the as-sumption of equal means is relaxed, we have what is known as a parallel model.

Additional statistics can be obtained from a strictly parallel or parallel model. Figure 5.10 contains a test of the goodness of fit for the parallel model applied to the physical activity data. (This model is not appropriate for these data. We'll use it, however, to il-lustrate the output for this type of model.)

Figure 5.10   Goodness of fit for parallel model

```
RELIABILITY /VARIABLES = ITEM1 TO ITEM8
  /MODEL = PARALLEL.


TEST FOR GOODNESS OF FIT OF MODEL         PARALLEL

CHI SQUARE =      1660.1597      DEGREES OF FREEDOM =       34
LOG OF DETERMINANT OF UNCONSTRAINED MATRIX =     -21.648663
LOG OF DETERMINANT OF CONSTRAINED MATRIX    =     -17.403278
PROBABILITY =    .0000
```

As you can see, the chi-square value is very large and we must reject the hypothesis that the parallel model fits. If the parallel model were appropriate, we could consider the results, which are shown in Figure 5.11.

Figure 5.11   Maximum-likelihood reliability estimate

```
    PARAMETER ESTIMATES

ESTIMATED COMMON VARIANCE =          .1891
         ERROR VARIANCE =          .0842
          TRUE VARIANCE =          .1049
ESTIMATED COMMON INTERITEM CORRELATION =       .5549

ESTIMATED RELIABILITY OF SCALE   = .9089
UNBIASED ESTIMATE OF RELIABILITY = .9093
```

The first entry is an estimate of the common variance for an item. It is the sum of the true variance and the error variance, which are displayed below it. An estimate of the common inter-item correlation, based on the model, is also shown. Figure 5.11 also shows two reliability coefficients. The first is a **maximum-likelihood estimate** of the reliability coefficient, while the second is the maximum-likelihood estimate corrected for bias. If either the parallel or the strictly parallel model fits the data, then the best linear combination of the items is simply their sum.

Running the Reliability Procedure

The Reliability procedure analyzes **additive scales**, which are scales formed by simply adding a number of component variables, or items. Using RELIABILITY, you can efficiently analyze different groups of items in order to choose the best scale. RELIABILITY does not create the scale for you. After choosing the items that you want, on the basis of the reliability analysis, use the COMPUTE command to form the scale as the sum of the items.

Specifying Variables

Use the VARIABLES subcommand to specify a group of variables for subsequent analyses. It must be the first subcommand. You can enter more than one VARIABLES subcommand; each one specifies variables for the following SCALE subcommands, up to the next VARIABLES subcommand (if any). You can specify ALL to use all variables in your active file as scale components.

Specifying a Scale

After a VARIABLES subcommand, enter one or more SCALE subcommands. Each SCALE subcommand defines a scale for analysis. Specifications on SCALE consist of a scale name of up to eight characters, in parentheses, and a list of the variables making up the scale.

- Specify ALL to use all the variables on the VARIABLES subcommand.
- Use multiple SCALE subcommands to analyze different subsets of items specified on the preceding VARIABLES subcommand.
- Keyword TO on the SCALE subcommand refers to the order in which variables were listed on the preceding VARIABLES subcommand—not to their order in the active file.

Example

```
RELIABILITY VARIABLES=ITEM1 TO ITEM8
   /SCALE (SUM) = ALL.
```

- The scale name *SUM* will be used to label the reliability analysis.
- The scale includes all the variables from *item1* to *item8*.

Example

```
RELIABILITY VARIABLES=ITEM1 TO ITEM8
 /SCALE (ALL) = ALL
 /SCALE (ALLBUT8) = ITEM1 TO ITEM7
 /SCALE (FIRST4) = ITEM1 TO ITEM4.
```

- This command analyzes three groups of items, two of which are different subsets of the first.

Choosing a Model

The default model for reliability analysis is ALPHA, which calculates Cronbach's α coefficient for each SCALE subcommand. To use a different model, specify the MODEL subcommand after the SCALE to which the model applies. Available models are:

ALPHA   *Cronbach's α. This is the default.*

SPLIT(n)	*Split-half coefficients.* A split-half reliability analysis is performed, based on the order in which you named the items on the preceding SCALE subcommand. The first half of the items (rounding up if the number of items is odd) form the first part, and the remaining items form the second part. After the keyword SPLIT, you can specify in parentheses the number of items to be placed in the *second* part. Thus, /MODEL=SPLIT(5) indicates that the last five items on the SCALE subcommand should form the second part, and the items that precede them should form the first part.
GUTTMAN	*Guttman's lower bounds for true reliability.*
PARALLEL	*Maximum-likelihood reliability estimate under parallel assumptions.* This model assumes that the items all have equal variance.
STRICTPARALLEL	*Maximum-likelihood reliability estimate under strictly parallel assumptions.* This model assumes that the items have the same variance and the same mean.

You can specify MODEL only once after a single SCALE subcommand. To use more than one model on the same scale, specify several SCALE subcommands, each followed by MODEL.

Example

```
RELIABILITY VARIABLES=ITEM1 TO ITEM8
 /SCALE (ALPHA)=ALL /MODEL=ALPHA
 /SCALE (SPLIT)=ALL /MODEL=SPLIT
 /SCALE (ML)=ALL    /MODEL=PARALLEL.
```

Obtaining Statistics

Use the STATISTICS and SUMMARY subcommands for additional statistics from RELIABILITY. Use these subcommands only once; they apply to all the SCALE subcommands that you enter.

Requesting Comparisons

Use the SUMMARY subcommand to request comparisons of various statistics over all items on a scale and/or comparisons of each item to the others taken as a group. Available keywords are:

MEANS	*Summary statistics for item means.* The average item mean, the largest, smallest, range, and variance of item means, and the ratio of the largest to the smallest item mean.

VARIANCES	*Summary statistics for item variances.* Same statistics as those displayed for MEANS.
COVARIANCES	*Summary statistics for inter-item covariances.* Same statistics as those displayed for MEANS.
CORRELATIONS	*Summary statistics for inter-item correlations.* Same statistics as those displayed for MEANS.
TOTAL	*Summary statistics comparing each item to the scale composed of the other items.* Scale mean and variance if the item were deleted; correlation between the item and the scale if it were deleted; squared multiple correlation with the other items; Cronbach's α if the item were deleted.
ALL	*All available summary statistics.*

Example

```
RELIABILITY /VARIABLES = ITEM1 TO ITEM8
   /SUMMARY = MEANS VARIANCES CORRELATIONS TOTAL.
```

- This command produces Figure 5.5 and Figure 5.6.

Requesting Additional Statistics

Use the STATISTICS subcommand to compute descriptive and diagnostic statistics. You can request the following statistics:

DESCRIPTIVES	*Item means and standard deviations.*
COVARIANCES	*Inter-item variance–covariance matrix.*
CORRELATIONS	*Inter-item correlation matrix.*
SCALE	*Scale mean and variance.*
ANOVA	*Repeated measures analysis-of-variance table.*
TUKEY	*Tukey's estimate of the power to which the scale must be raised to achieve additivity.* This tests the assumption that there is no multiplicative interaction among the items.
HOTELLING	*Hotelling's* T^2. This tests for violations of the assumption that item means are equal, for scales with more than two items.
FRIEDMAN	*Friedman's chi-square and Kendall's coefficient of concordance.* Request this in addition to ANOVA if your items have the form of ranks. The chi-square test replaces the usual F test in the ANOVA table.

COCHRAN   *Cochran's* Q. You can request this in addition to ANOVA if your items are all dichotomies. The *Q* statistic replaces the usual *F* test in the ANOVA table.

ALL   *All available statistics.*

Example

```
RELIABILITY /VARIABLES = ITEM1 TO ITEM8
  /STATISTICS DESCRIPTIVES CORRELATIONS SCALE.
```

- This command produces Figure 5.2, Figure 5.3, and Figure 5.4.

Annotated Example

The following commands produced the output in Figure 5.1 through Figure 5.11.

```
DATA LIST FREE/ ID ITEM1 TO ITEM8.
VARIABLE LABELS ITEM1 'Can eat'
   ITEM2 'Can dress and undress'
   ITEM3 'Can take care of own appearance'
   ITEM4 'Can walk'
   ITEM5 'Can get in and out of bed'
   ITEM6 'Can take a bath or shower'
   ITEM7 'Can get to bathroom on time'
   ITEM8 'Has been able to do tasks for 6 months'.
VALUE LABELS ITEM1 TO ITEM8 1 'Unable to perform'
   2 'Needs assistance' 3 'Needs no assistance'.
BEGIN DATA.
3433 3 3 3 3 3 3 2 2
1418 3 3 3 3 3 3 3 2
2180 3 2 3 2 3 2 3 1
 ...
END DATA.
RELIABILITY VARIABLES = ITEM1 TO ITEM8
  /STATISTICS = DESCRIPTIVES CORRELATIONS SCALE
  /SUMMARY = MEANS VARIANCES CORRELATIONS TOTAL
  /SCALE (DEFAULT) ALL /MODEL ALPHA
  /SCALE (SPLIT) ALL    /MODEL SPLIT
  /SCALE (ML) ALL       /MODEL PARALLEL.
```

- The DATA LIST command indicates that the variables *id* and *item1* to *item8* are to be read in freefield format.
- The VARIABLE LABELS and VALUE LABELS commands provide descriptive labels.
- The RELIABILITY command names all eight items on the VARIABLES subcommand.
- The STATISTICS subcommand requests descriptive statistics (Figure 5.2), the correlation matrix (Figure 5.3), and scale statistics (Figure 5.4).
- The SUMMARY subcommand requests summary tables of means, variances, and correlations (Figure 5.5), as well as item-total summary statistics (Figure 5.6).

- A series of SCALE subcommands follows. Each provides a scale name (in parentheses) and specifies that all eight variables should be included in the scale. Scale names are arbitrary (although limited to 8 letters or numbers); these were chosen to indicate the model used for each scale.
- Each SCALE subcommand is followed by a MODEL subcommand that specifies the model for that scale.

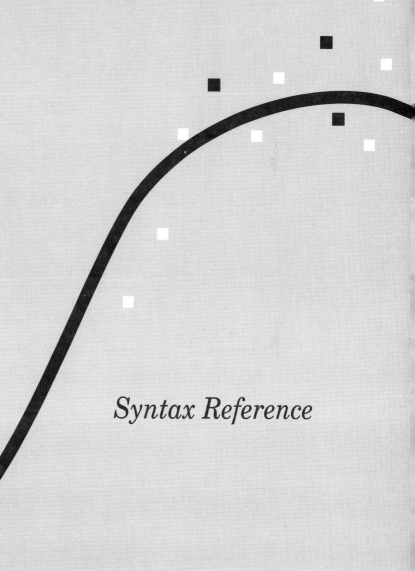

Syntax Reference

CLUSTER

```
CLUSTER varlist [/MISSING=LISTWISE**] [INCLUDE]

[/READ=[SIMILAR] [{TRIANGLE}]] [/WRITE=[DISTANCE]]
                  {LOWER   }

[/MEASURE={SEUCLID** }] [/METHOD={BAVERAGE**}[(rootname)] [...]]
          {EUCLID    }           {WAVERAGE  }
          {COSINE    }           {SINGLE    }
          {POWER(p,r)}           {COMPLETE  }
          {BLOCK     }           {CENTROID  }
          {CHEBYCHEV }           {MEDIAN    }
          {DEFAULT** }           {WARD      }
                                 {DEFAULT** }

[/SAVE=CLUSTER({level  })]   [/ID=varname]
              {min,max}

[/PRINT=[SCHEDULE**] [CLUSTER({level  })] [DISTANCE] [NONE]]
                             {min,max}

[/PLOT=[VICICLE**[({1,n-1,1**    })] [DENDROGRAM] [NONE]]
                 {min[,max[,inc]]}
       [HICICLE[({1,n-1,1**    })]
                {min[,max[,inc]]}
```

** Default if subcommand or keyword is omitted.

Example:
```
CLUSTER V1 TO V4
 /PLOT=DENDROGRAM
 /PRINT=CLUSTER (2,4).
```

Overview

CLUSTER produces hierarchical clusters of items based on distance measures of dissimilarity or similarity. The items being clustered are usually cases from the active file, and the distance measures are computed from their values for one or more variables. You can also cluster variables if you read in a matrix measuring distances between variables. Cluster analysis is discussed in Anderberg (1973).

Options

Cluster Measures and Methods. You can specify one of six similarity or distance measures on the MEASURE subcommand, and you can cluster items using any one of seven methods using the METHOD subcommand: single linkage, complete linkage, between- and within-groups average linkage, and median, centroid, and Ward's methods. You can request more than one clustering method on a single CLUSTER command.

New Variables. You can save cluster membership for specified solutions as new variables in the active file using the SAVE subcommand.

Display and Plots. You can display cluster membership, the distance or similarity matrix used to cluster variables or cases, and the agglomeration schedule for the cluster solution with the PRINT subcommand. You can request either a horizontal or vertical icicle plot or a dendrogram of the cluster solution, and you can control the cluster levels displayed on the icicle plot with the PLOT subcommand. You can also specify a variable to be used as a case identifier in the display on ID.

Writing and Reading Matrices. Using the WRITE subcommand, you can write out the distance matrix and use it in subsequent CLUSTER analyses. Using the READ subcommand (along with DATA LIST MATRIX), you can read in matrices produced by other procedures (for example, CORRELATION) to cluster different items, such as variables instead of cases.

Basic Specification

The basic specification is a variable list. CLUSTER assumes that the items being clustered are cases and uses the squared Euclidean distances between cases on the variables in the analysis as the measure of distance. Cases are clustered using the method of average linkage between groups.

The default display includes the number of cases in the analysis, the agglomeration schedule for the clustering, and a vertical icicle plot. Cases are identified by case number. By default, CLUSTER omits cases with missing values for any variable in the analysis.

Subcommand Order

- The variable list must be specified first.
- The remaining subcommands can be specified in any order.

Syntax Rules

- The variable list and subcommands can each be specified once.
- More than one clustering method can be specified.

Operations

The Cluster procedure involves four steps:
- First, CLUSTER obtains distance measures of similarities between or distances separating initial clusters (or separating individual cases or individual variables if the input is a matrix measuring distances between variables).
- Second, it combines the two nearest clusters to form a new cluster.
- Third, it recomputes similarities or distances of existing clusters to the new cluster.
- It then returns to the second step until all items are combined into one cluster.

This process yields a hierarchy of cluster solutions, ranging from one overall cluster to as many clusters as there are items being clustered. Clusters at a higher level can contain several lower-level clusters. Within each level, the clusters are disjoint (each item belongs to only one cluster).

- CLUSTER identifies clusters in solutions by sequential integers (1, 2, 3, and so on).
- When a narrow width is defined on the SET command, plots exceeding the defined width are broken into two sections and are displayed one after the other.
- The BOX specification on the SET command controls the character used in dendrograms.

Limitations

- CLUSTER stores cases and a lower-triangular matrix of proximities in memory. Storage requirements increase rapidly with the number of cases. You should be able to cluster 100 cases using a small number of variables in an 80K workspace.
- CLUSTER does not use case weights.

Example

```
CLUSTER V1 TO V4
 /PLOT=DENDROGRAM
 /PRINT=CLUSTER (2,4).
```

- This example clusters cases based on their values for all variables between and including *V1* and *V4* in the SPSS/PC+ active file.
- The analysis uses the default measure of distance (squared Euclidean) and the default clustering method (average linkage between groups).
- PLOT requests a dendrogram.
- PRINT displays a table of the cluster membership of each case for the two-, three-, and four-cluster solutions.

Variable List

The variable list identifies the variables used to compute similarities or distances between cases.

- The variable list is required. It must be specified before the optional subcommands.
- You can use ALL to refer to all user-defined variables in the active file.
- You can use keyword TO to refer to consecutive variables in the active file.

MEASURE Subcommand

MEASURE specifies the distance or similarity measure used to cluster cases.

- If the MEASURE subcommand is omitted or included without specifications, squared Euclidean distances are used.
- Only one measure can be specified.

SEUCLID   *Squared Euclidean distances.* The distance between two cases is the sum of the squared differences in their values for each variable. SEUCLID is the measure commonly used with centroid, median, and Ward's methods of clustering. SEUCLID is the default and can also be requested with keyword DEFAULT.

EUCLID   *Euclidean distances.* The distance between two cases is the square root of the sum of the squared differences in their values for each variable.

COSINE   *Cosine of vectors of variables.* This is a pattern similarity measure.

BLOCK   *City-block or Manhattan distances.* The distance between two cases is the sum of the absolute differences in their values for each variable.

CHEBYCHEV   *Chebychev distance metric.* The distance between two cases is the maximum absolute difference in their values for any variable.

POWER(p,r) *Distances in an absolute power metric.* The distance between two cases is the *r*th root of the sum of the absolute differences to the *p*th power of their values for each variable. Appropriate selection of integer parameters *p* and *r* yields Euclidean, squared Euclidean, Minkowski, city-block, and many other distance metrics.

METHOD Subcommand

METHOD specifies one or more clustering methods.

- If the METHOD subcommand is omitted or included without specifications, the method of average linkage between groups is used.
- Only one METHOD subcommand can be used, but more than one method can be specified on it.
- When the number of items is large, CENTROID and MEDIAN require significantly more CPU time than other methods.

BAVERAGE   *Average linkage between groups (UPGMA).* BAVERAGE is the default and can also be requested with keyword DEFAULT.

WAVERAGE   *Average linkage within groups.*

SINGLE   *Single linkage or nearest neighbor.*

COMPLETE   *Complete linkage or furthest neighbor.*

CENTROID   *Centroid clustering (UPGMC).* Squared Euclidean distances are commonly used with this method.

MEDIAN   *Median clustering (WPGMC).* Squared Euclidean distances are commonly used with this method.

WARD   *Ward's method.* Squared Euclidean distances are commonly used with this method.

Example

```
CLUSTER V1 V2 V3
 /METHOD=SINGLE COMPLETE WARDS.
```

- This example clusters cases based on their values for variables *V1*, *V2*, and *V3*, and uses three clustering methods: single linkage, complete linkage, and Ward's method.

SAVE Subcommand

SAVE allows you to save cluster membership at specified solution levels as new variables in the SPSS/PC+ active file.

- The specification on SAVE is the CLUSTER keyword, followed by either a single number indicating the level (number of clusters) of the cluster solution or a range separated by a comma indicating the minimum and maximum numbers of clusters when membership of more than one solution is to be saved. The number or range must be enclosed in parentheses and applies to all methods specified on METHOD.
- Both the CLUSTER keyword and a solution number or range are required. There are no default specifications.
- For each method for which you want to save cluster membership, you must specify a rootname on the METHOD subcommand. Therefore, the METHOD subcommand is required when you use the SAVE subcommand.
- Specify the rootname in parentheses after the method keyword. You can specify only one rootname for a method. If you do not supply a rootname for a specified method, cluster membership for that method is not saved. If you do not supply any rootname, CLUSTER displays a warning.
- The solution number or range specified on the SAVE subcommand applies to all methods for which you supply a rootname.
- The new variables derive their names from the rootname and the number of the cluster solution.

Example

```
CLUSTER A B C
 /METHOD=BAVERAGE (BMEM) SINGLE (SINMEM) WARD
 /SAVE=CLUSTERS(3,5).
```

- This command creates six new variables: *BMEM5*, *BMEM4*, and *BMEM3* for BAVERAGE and *SINMEM5*, *SINMEM4*, and *SINMEM3* for SINGLE. Cluster membership is not saved for WARD.
- The order of the new variables in the active file is the same as listed above, since the solutions are obtained in the order from 5 to 3.

ID Subcommand

ID names a string variable to be used as the case identifier in cluster membership tables, icicle plots, and dendrograms. If the ID subcommand is omitted, cases are identified by case number.

PRINT Subcommand

PRINT controls the display of cluster output (except plots, which are controlled by the PLOT subcommand).

- If the PRINT subcommand is omitted or included without specifications, an agglomeration schedule is displayed. If any keywords are specified on PRINT, the agglomeration schedule is displayed only if explicitly requested.

- CLUSTER automatically displays summary information (the method and measure used, the number of cases) for each method named on the METHOD subcommand. This summary is displayed regardless of specifications on PRINT.

You can specify any or all of the following on the PRINT subcommand:

SCHEDULE
: *Agglomeration schedule.* The agglomeration schedule shows the order and distances at which items and clusters combine to form new clusters. It also shows the cluster level at which an item joins a cluster. SCHEDULE is the default and can also be requested with keyword DEFAULT.

CLUSTER(min,max)
: *Cluster membership.* For each item, the display includes the value of the case identifier (or the variable name if matrix input is used), the case sequence number, and a value (1, 2, 3, etc.) identifying the cluster to which that case belongs in a given cluster solution. Specify either a single integer value in parentheses indicating the level of a single solution or a minimum and a maximum value indicating a range of solutions for which display is desired. If the number of clusters specified exceeds the number produced, the largest number of clusters is used (the number of items minus 1). If CLUSTER is specified more than once, the last specification is used.

DISTANCE
: *Matrix of distances or similarities between items.* DISTANCE displays either the matrix computed by CLUSTER or the input matrix if one is specified on MATRIX. The type of matrix produced (similarities or dissimilarities) depends upon the measure selected. DISTANCE produces a large volume of output and uses significant CPU time when the number of cases is large.

NONE
: *None of the above.* NONE overrides any other keywords specified on the PRINT subcommand.

Example

```
CLUSTER V1 V2 V3 /PRINT=CLUSTER(3,5).
```

- This command displays cluster membership for each case for the three-, four-, and five-cluster solutions.

PLOT Subcommand

PLOT controls the plots produced for each method specified on the METHOD subcommand. For icicle plots, PLOT allows you to control the cluster solution at which the plot begins and ends and the increment for displaying intermediate cluster solutions.

- If the PLOT subcommand is omitted or included without specifications, a vertical icicle plot is produced.
- If any keywords are specified on PLOT, only those plots requested are produced.
- If there is not enough memory for a dendrogram or an icicle plot, the plot is skipped and a warning is issued.
- The size of an icicle plot can be controlled by specifying range values or an increment for VICICLE or HICICLE. Smaller plots require significantly less workspace and time.

VICICLE(min,max,inc) *Vertical icicle plot.* This is the default. The range specifications are optional. If used, they must be integer and must be enclosed in parentheses. The specification *min* is the cluster solution at which to start the display (the default is 1); the specification *max* is the cluster solution at which to end the display (the default is the number of cases minus 1). If *max* is greater than the number of cases minus 1, the default is used. The increment to use between cluster solutions is *inc* (the default is 1). If *max* is specified, *min* must be specified, and if *inc* is specified, both *min* and *max* must be specified. If VICICLE is specified more than once, only the last range specification is used.

HICICLE(min,max,inc) *Horizontal icicle plot.* The range specifications are the same as for VICICLE. If both VICICLE and HICICLE are specified, the last range specified is used for both. If a range is not specified on the last instance of VICICLE or HICICLE, the defaults are used even if a range is specified earlier.

DENDROGRAM *Tree diagram.* The dendrogram is scaled by the distances at which clusters join.

NONE *No plots.*

Example

```
CLUSTER V1 V2 V3 /PLOT=VICICLE(1,20).
```

- This example produces a vertical icicle plot for the one-cluster through the twenty-cluster solution.

Example

```
CLUSTER V1 V2 V3 /PLOT=VICICLE(1,151,5).
```

- This example produces a vertical icicle plot for every fifth cluster solution starting with 1 and ending with 151 (1 cluster, 6 clusters, 11 clusters, and so on).

MISSING Subcommand

MISSING controls the treatment of cases with missing values. By default, a case that has a missing value for any variable on the variable list is omitted from the analysis.

LISTWISE   *Delete cases with missing values listwise.* Only cases with nonmissing values for all variables on the variable list are used. LISTWISE is the default and can also be requested with keyword DEFAULT.

INCLUDE   *Include cases with user-missing values.* Only cases with system-missing values are excluded.

WRITE Subcommand

The WRITE subcommand allows you to write a computed distance or similarity matrix to the results file named on the SET command.

- If the WRITE subcommand is omitted, no file is written.
- If the WRITE subcommand is included without specifications, a square distance matrix of similarities or dissimilarities (depending on the measure selected) is written. You can request the default explicitly by specifying DISTANCE on the WRITE subcommand.
- Matrix elements are written in fixed 16-column fields with five decimal places. Thus, there are five matrix elements on each 80-character record.
- The dimensions of the matrix depend on the number of items clustered. If cases are read, the distance matrix is dimensioned by the number of cases clustered.
- Each row of the matrix begins on a new line.
- The WRITE subcommand writes the matrix to the results file named on the SET command or to the default results file (*SPSS.PRC*). Any existing contents of the results file are overwritten.

Example

```
SET RESULTS='GSS80.MAT'.
DATA LIST FILE='GSS80.DAT'/SUICIDE1 TO SUICIDE4 2-9.
N 35.
CLUSTER  SUICIDE1 TO SUICIDE4
/WRITE DISTANCE.
```

- This example produces a default clustering of 35 cases. It uses all variables between and including *SUICIDE1* to *SUICIDE4* in the active file.
- A matrix of squared Euclidean distances is written to the file *GSS80.MAT*.

READ Subcommand

By default, CLUSTER assumes that the data file it uses contains cases. Use the READ subcommand to indicate that the data file contains a matrix. The general conventions for matrix materials are described in DATA LIST: Matrix Materials (see the Syntax Reference section of the *SPSS/PC+ Base System User's Guide*).

- If the READ subcommand is included without specifications, the matrix is assumed to be a square distance matrix. This is the default matrix written by CLUSTER. Specify one or more keywords to read a matrix other than the default.
- If you use the READ subcommand on CLUSTER, you must first use a DATA LIST command specifying matrix input. The DATA LIST command also assigns a variable name to each item that dimensions the matrix.
- All items named on the CLUSTER variable list must be defined on the DATA LIST command.
- The order in which items are named on the variable list must be the same as their order in the matrix.
- The MEASURE subcommand is ignored with matrix input.
- All methods specified on METHOD will accept either similarity or dissimilarity distance matrices as input. Incorrect results will be obtained for all methods if a similarity matrix is read and not identified as such.
- CLUSTER can read more than one distance matrix from the same file. Each matrix must be of the same type (similarity or dissimilarity) and must have the same dimensions.
- CLUSTER can also read other matrices such as a correlation matrix created by CORRELATION or another SPSS/PC+ procedure. This allows you to cluster variables as well as cases or to use a distance or similarity measure not available in CLUSTER.

The following keywords are available on the READ subcommand:

SIMILAR   *Distance matrix based on a similarity measure.* By default, the distance matrix is assumed to be based on a measure of dissimilarity, or distance.

TRIANGLE   *Lower-triangular matrix.* Same as LOWER but includes the diagonal elements. By default, the matrix is assumed to be square.

LOWER   *Lower-subdiagonal matrix.* Same as TRIANGLE but without the diagonal elements. By default, the matrix is assumed to be square.

Example

```
DATA LIST MATRIX FILE='GSS80.MAT'/CASE1 TO CASE35.
CLUSTER CASE1 TO CASE35/READ.
```

- The DATA LIST command names the file and the items in the matrix. The matrix is assumed to be in the fixed format written by CLUSTER.
- The variable list indexes the matrix to be read by naming the variable that stands for each matrix item. In this case, the items are the cases on which the matrix was calculated.
- The READ subcommand specifies that a matrix is to be read. By default, CLUSTER assumes that the matrix was based on a measure of distance.

Example

```
* The following commands compute correlations among three
 variables and write the correlation matrix to a file.

SET RESULTS='VARS.MAT'.
DATA LIST FILE='VARS.DAT'/VA VB VC 1-3.
CORRELATION VARIABLES=VA VB VC/OPTIONS=2 4.

* The following commands read the matrix into CLUSTER.

DATA LIST MATRIX FREE FILE='VARS.MAT'/VA VB VC.
CLUSTER VA VB VC
 /PRINT=DISTANCE /READ=SIMILAR.
```

- The DATA LIST command specifies that a matrix will be read in freefield format (keyword FREE) from *VARS.MAT* and assigns variable names to the items in the matrix. FREE is specified because the matrix to be read is not in the default format produced by CLUSTER. In this example, the items being clustered are variables.
- The variable list on CLUSTER names the same variables as the DATA LIST command and in the same order. This identifies the entries of the input matrix.
- The PRINT subcommand allows you to verify that the matrix is being read properly.
- The READ subcommand specifies that a matrix will be read instead of cases. The matrix is a square matrix and contains a measure of similarity.
- The CLUSTER command will read both the correlation matrix and the matrix of N's written by the CORRELATION command. You should ignore the warning message and analysis produced by the matrix of N's.
- This analysis clusters variables by the default between-groups average-linkage method.

Annotated Example

For a complete example with output, see the Annotated Examples following the Syntax Reference section of this manual.

DSCRIMINANT

```
DSCRIMINANT GROUPS=varname(min,max) /VARIABLES=varlist
  [/SELECT=varname(value)] [/ANALYSIS=varlist(level) [varlist...]]
  [/METHOD={DIRECT  }] [/TOLERANCE={0.001}] [/MAXSTEPS={2v}]
           {WILKS   }             {t    }              {m }
           {MAHAL   }
           {MAXMINF }
           {MINRESID}
           {RAO     }
  [/FIN={1.0**}] [/FOUT={1.0**}] [/PIN=n] [/POUT=n] [/VIN={0 }]
        {n    }        {n    }                            {vi}
  [/FUNCTIONS={g-1,100.0,1.0}] [/PRIORS={EQUAL     }]
             {n1 ,n2 ,n3   }           {SIZE      }
                                        {value list}
  [/SAVE=[CLASS varname] [PROBS rootname] [SCORES rootname]]
  [/ANALYSIS=...]
  [/OPTIONS=option numbers]
  [/STATISTICS={statistic numbers}]
               {ALL              }
```

**Default if subcommand or keyword is omitted.

Options:

1 Include missing values
4 Suppress step output
5 Suppress summary table
6 Varimax rotation of function matrix
7 Varimax rotation of structure matrix

8 Substitute means for missing values during classification
9 Classify only unselected cases
10 Classify only unclassified cases
11 Use individual covariance matrices for classification

Statistics:

1 Group means
2 Group standard deviations
3 Pooled within-groups covariance matrix
4 Pooled within-groups correlation matrix
5 Matrix of pairwise *F* ratios
6 Univariate *F* ratios
7 Box's *M*
8 Group covariance matrices

9 Total covariance matrix
10 Territorial map
11 Unstandardized function coefficients
12 Classification function coefficients
13 Classification results table
14 Casewise materials
15 Combined plot
16 Separate plot

Example:

```
DSCRIMINANT GROUPS=OUTCOME (1,4)
  /VARIABLES=VAR1 TO VAR7
  /SAVE CLASS=PREDOUT.
```

Overview

DSCRIMINANT performs linear discriminant analysis for two or more groups. The goal of discriminant analysis is to classify cases into one of several mutually exclusive groups based on their values for a set of predictor variables. In the analysis phase, a classification rule is developed using cases for which group membership is known. In the classification phase, the rule is used to classify cases for which group membership is not known. The grouping variable must be categorical, and the independent (predictor) variables must be interval or dichotomous, since they will be used in a regression-type equation.

Options

Variable Selection Method. In addition to the direct-entry method, you can specify any of several stepwise methods for entering variables into the discriminant analysis using the METHOD subcommand. You can also specify the maximum number of steps in a stepwise analysis using the MAXSTEPS subcommand.

Statistical Criteria. You can set the values for the statistical criteria used to enter variables into the equation using the TOLERANCE, FIN, PIN, FOUT, POUT, and VIN subcommands, and you can specify inclusion levels on the ANALYSIS subcommand.

Case Selection. You can select a subset of cases for analysis using the SELECT subcommand.

Prior Probabilities. You can specify prior probabilities for membership in the different groups using the PRIORS subcommand. These are used in classifying cases but not in the analysis leading to the discriminant functions.

Saving Discriminant Statistics. You can use the SAVE subcommand to add new variables to the active file containing the predicted group membership, the probabilities of membership in each of the groups, and the scores on the discriminant functions.

Classification Options. With the OPTIONS subcommand, you can request that DSCRIMINANT classify only those cases that were not selected for inclusion in the discriminant analysis, or only those cases whose code for the grouping variable fell outside the range analyzed. In addition, you can classify cases on the basis of the separate-group covariance matrices rather than the pooled within-groups covariance matrix.

Statistical Display. Using the STATISTICS subcommand, you can request any of a variety of statistics.   You can compare actual with predicted group membership using a classification results table or any of several types of plots or histograms. In addition, you can display the discriminant scores and the actual and predicted group membership for each case. You can also rotate the pattern or structure matrix using the OPTIONS subcommand.

Missing Values. With the OPTIONS subcommand, you can include user-missing values in the analysis. During the classification phase, you can substitute means for missing values so that cases with missing data will be classified.

Basic Specifications

The basic specification requires two subcommands:

- GROUPS specifies the variable used to group cases.
- VARIABLES specifies the predictor variables.

By default, DSCRIMINANT enters all variables simultaneously into the discriminant equation (the DIRECT method) provided that they are not so highly correlated that collinearity problems arise. Default output consists of counts of cases in the groups, the method used and associated parameters, and a summary of results including eigenvalues, standardized discriminant function coefficients, and within-groups correlations between the discriminant functions and the predictor variables.

Syntax Rules

- Only one GROUPS, one VARIABLES, and one SELECT subcommand can be specified per DSCRIMINANT command.
- An ANALYSIS subcommand specifies the predictor variables to be used in a single analysis. The variables must have been named on the VARIABLES subcommand.

Subcommand Order

- GROUPS, VARIABLES, and SELECT subcommands can be entered in any order but each must precede any other subcommands.
- All other subcommands may be entered in any order and apply only to the preceding ANALYSIS subcommand. If any of these subcommands is entered before the first ANALYSIS subcommand or if there is no ANALYSIS subcommand, DSCRIMINANT performs a default discriminant analysis using the entire set of variables named on the VARIABLES subcommand.

Operations

- The procedure first determines one or more discriminant functions that best distinguish between the groups.
- Using these functions, the procedure then classifies cases into the group predicted by the predictor variables.
- If more than one ANALYSIS command is supplied, these steps are repeated for each requested group of variables.

Limitations

- The number of predictor variables that may be used is limited by available memory.
- A maximum of 10 ANALYSIS subcommands may be entered.
- Pairwise deletion of missing data is not available.

Example

```
DSCRIMINANT GROUPS=OUTCOME (1,4)
  /VARIABLES=VAR1 TO VAR7
  /STATISTICS=3 8 9 11
  /SAVE CLASS=PREDOUT.
```

- Only cases for which the grouping variable *OUTCOME* has values 1, 2, 3, or 4 will be used to compute the discriminant functions.
- The variables in the active file between and including *VAR1* and *VAR7* will be used to compute the discriminant functions and to classify cases.
- In addition to the default output, the STATISTICS subcommand requests the display of the pooled within-groups covariance matrix, the group and total covariance matrices, and the unstandardized discriminant function coefficients.
- Predicted group membership will be saved in the variable *PREDOUT*, which will be added to the active file if it does not already exist.

GROUPS Subcommand

The GROUPS subcommand specifies the name of the grouping variable, which defines the categories or groups among which the discriminant function should distinguish. Along with the variable name, you must specify a range of categories. The discriminant analysis will attempt to predict membership in the categories of this variable.

- The GROUPS subcommand is required and may be used only once.
- The specification consists of a variable name followed by a range of values in parentheses.
- You can specify only one grouping variable, and its values must be integers.
- Empty groups are ignored and do not affect calculations. For example, if there are no cases in group 2, the value range (1,5) will define only four groups.
- Cases with values outside the value range or with missing values are ignored during the analysis phase but will be classified during the classification phase.

VARIABLES Subcommand

The VARIABLES subcommand identifies the predictor variables, which are used to classify cases into the groups defined on the GROUPS subcommand. The list of variables follows the usual SPSS/PC+ conventions for variable lists.

- The VARIABLES subcommand is required and may be used only once. Use the ANALYSIS subcommand to obtain multiple analyses.
- Only numeric variables may be used.
- Variables should be suitable for use in a regression-type equation: either measured at the interval level, or dichotomous.

ANALYSIS Subcommand

Use the ANALYSIS subcommand to request several different discriminant analyses using the same grouping variable, or to control the order in which variables are entered into a stepwise analysis.

- The ANALYSIS subcommand is optional. By default, all variables on the VARIABLES subcommand are included in the analysis.
- The variables named on ANALYSIS must first be specified on the VARIABLES subcommand.
- Keyword ALL can be used to explicitly include all variables on the VARIABLES subcommand.
- Keyword TO on an ANALYSIS subcommand refers to the order of variables on the VARIABLES subcommand, which is not necessarily that in the active file.

Example

```
DSCRIMINANT GROUPS=SUCCESS(0,1)
  /VARIABLES=VAR10 TO VAR15, AGE, VAR5
  /ANALYSIS=VAR15 TO VAR5
  /ANALYSIS=ALL.
```

- The first ANALYSIS uses variables *VAR15, AGE,* and *VAR5* to discriminate between cases where *SUCCESS*=0 and the cases where *SUCCESS*=1.
- The second ANALYSIS uses all variables named on the VARIABLES subcommand.

Inclusion Levels

When you specify a stepwise method (any method other than the default DIRECT method), you can control the order in which variables are considered for entry or removal by specifying inclusion levels on the ANALYSIS subcommand. By default, all variables in the analysis are entered according to the criterion requested on the METHOD subcommand.

- An inclusion level is an integer between 0 and 99, specified in parentheses after a variable or list of variables on an ANALYSIS subcommand.
- The default inclusion level is 1.
- Variables with higher inclusion levels are considered for entry before variables with lower inclusion levels.
- Variables with even inclusion levels are entered as a group.
- Variables with odd inclusion levels are entered individually, according to the stepwise method specified on the METHOD subcommand.
- Only variables with an inclusion level of 1 are considered for removal. To make a variable with a higher inclusion level eligible for removal, name it twice on the ANALYSIS subcommand, first specifying the desired inclusion level and then an inclusion level of 1.
- Variables with an inclusion level of 0 are never entered. However, the statistical criterion for entry is computed and displayed.
- Variables that fail the TOLERANCE criterion are not entered regardless of their inclusion level.

Example

```
DSCRIMINANT GROUPS=SUCCESS(0,1)
  /VARIABLES=A, B, C, D, E
  /ANALYSIS=A TO C (2) D, E (1)
  /METHOD=WILKS.
```

- Variables *A*, *B*, and *C* are entered into the analysis first, assuming that they pass the tolerance criterion. Since their inclusion level is even, they are entered together.
- Variables *D* and *E* are then entered stepwise. Whichever of the two minimizes the overall value of Wilks' lambda is entered first, if it meets entry criteria.
- After entering *D* and *E*, SPSS/PC+ checks whether the partial *F* for either one justifies removal from the equation (see the discussion under FOUT and POUT).

Example

```
DSCRIMINANT GROUPS=SUCCESS(0,1)
  /VARIABLES=A, B, C, D, E
  /ANALYSIS=A TO C (2) D, E (1).
```

- Since no stepwise method is specified, inclusion levels have no effect and all variables are entered into the model at once.

SELECT Subcommand

With the SELECT subcommand, you can limit the discriminant analysis to cases with a specified value on any one variable.

- Only one SELECT subcommand is allowed. It may follow the GROUPS and VARIABLES subcommands but must precede any other subcommands.
- Specifications for the SELECT subcommand consist of a variable name and a single value in parentheses. Multiple variables or values are not permitted.
- The selection variable need not have been named on the GROUPS or VARIABLES subcommand.
- Only cases with the specified value on the selection variable are used in the analysis phase.
- By default, all cases will be classified whether selected or not. You can use Option 9 to classify only the unselected cases.
- When you use the SELECT subcommand, classification statistics are reported separately for selected and unselected cases, unless you use Option 9 to restrict classification.

Example

```
DSCRIMINANT GROUPS=APPROVAL(1,5)
  /VARIABLES=Q1 TO Q10
  /SELECT=COMPLETE(1)
  /OPTIONS=9.
```

- This command uses only the cases where variable *COMPLETE* has a value of 1.
- DSCRIMINANT forms a discriminant function out of *Q1* to *Q10* that discriminates between the categories 1 to 5 of the grouping variable *APPROVAL*.

- Because Option 9 is requested, the discriminant function will be used to classify only the unselected cases, namely, the cases for which *COMPLETE* does not equal 1.

METHOD Subcommand

Use the METHOD subcommand to select any one of six methods for entering variables into the analysis phase.

- A variable will never be entered into the analysis if it does not pass the tolerance criterion specified on the TOLERANCE subcommand (or the default).
- A METHOD subcommand applies only to the *preceding* ANALYSIS subcommand or to an analysis using all predictor variables if no ANALYSIS subcommand has been specified.
- Only one METHOD command may be entered per ANALYSIS.

Any one of the following methods may be entered on the METHOD subcommand:

DIRECT *All variables passing the tolerance criteria are entered simultaneously.* This is the default.

WILKS *The variable that minimizes the Wilks' lambda is entered.*

MAHAL *The variable that maximizes the Mahalanobis distance between the two closest groups is entered.*

MAXMINF *The variable that maximizes the smallest F ratio between pairs of groups is entered.*

MINRESID *The variable that minimizes the sum of the unexplained variation for all pairs of groups is entered.*

RAO *The variable that produces the largest increase in Rao's V is entered.*

Subcommands Controlling Statistical and Iteration Criteria

In addition to naming a method for variable selection on the METHOD subcommand, you can specify a number of optional subcommands to set other parameters controlling the selection algorithm.

- These subcommands must follow the METHOD subcommand to which they apply and may be entered in any order.
- All of these subcommands except TOLERANCE apply only to the stepwise methods.

TOLERANCE Subcommand

The **tolerance** of a variable that is a candidate for inclusion in the analysis is the proportion of its within-group variance that is not accounted for by other variables currently in the analysis. A variable with very low tolerance is nearly a linear function of the other variables; its inclusion in the analysis would make the calculations unstable. The TOLERANCE subcommand specifies the minimum tolerance a variable can have and still be entered into the analysis.

- The default tolerance is 0.001.
- You can specify any decimal value between 0 and 1 as the minimum tolerance.

FIN Subcommand

FIN specifies the minimum partial F value a variable must have to enter the analysis.

- The default is 1.0.
- You can set FIN to any non-negative number.
- PIN overrides FIN if both are specified.
- FIN is ignored if the METHOD subcommand is omitted or if METHOD specifies DIRECT.

PIN Subcommand

PIN specifies the minimum probability of F a variable must have to enter the analysis. Since the probability of F depends upon the degrees of freedom and the variables in the equation, it can change at each step. Use the PIN subcommand to keep the minimum F's at a minimum significance level.

- If the PIN subcommand is omitted, the value of FIN is used.
- You can set PIN to any decimal value between 0 and 1.
- If PIN is specified, FIN is ignored.
- PIN is ignored if the METHOD subcommand is omitted or if METHOD specifies DIRECT.

FOUT Subcommand

As additional variables are entered into the analysis, the partial F for variables already in the equation changes. FOUT is the maximum partial F a variable can have before it is removed from the analysis.

- The default is 1.0.
- You can set FOUT to any non-negative number. However, FOUT should be less than FIN if FIN is also specified.
- To be removed, variables must also have an inclusion level of 1, if an inclusion level is specified.
- POUT overrides FOUT if both are specified.
- FOUT is ignored if the METHOD subcommand is omitted or if METHOD specifies DIRECT.

POUT Subcommand

POUT is the maximum probability of F a variable can have before it is removed from the analysis.

- By default, a variable is removed if its partial F falls below the FOUT specification.

- You can set POUT to any decimal value between 0 and 1. However, POUT should be greater than PIN if PIN is also specified.
- To be removed, variables must also have an inclusion level of 1, if an inclusion level is specified.
- POUT overrides FOUT if both are specified.
- POUT is ignored if the METHOD subcommand is omitted or if METHOD specifies DIRECT.

VIN Subcommand

VIN specifies the minimum Rao's V a variable must have to enter the analysis. When you specify RAO on METHOD, variables satisfying one of the other criteria for entering the equation may actually cause a decrease in Rao's V for the equation. The default VIN prevents this, but does not prevent variables that provide no additional separation between groups from being added.

- The default is 0.
- You can specify any value for VIN.
- VIN should be used only when you have specified RAO on METHOD. Otherwise, it is ignored.

MAXSTEPS Subcommand

By default, the maximum number of steps allowed in a stepwise analysis is the number of variables with inclusion levels greater than 1 plus twice the number of variables with inclusion levels equal to 1. This is the maximum number of steps possible without a loop in which a variable is repeatedly cycled in and out. Use the MAXSTEPS subcommand to decrease the maximum number of steps allowed.

- MAXSTEPS applies only to the stepwise methods. MAXSTEPS is ignored if the METHOD subcommand is omitted or if METHOD specifies DIRECT.
- MAXSTEPS must be specified after the METHOD subcommand to which it applies.
- Specify the maximum number of steps desired after an optional equals sign following the MAXSTEPS subcommand.

FUNCTIONS Subcommand

By default, DSCRIMINANT computes the maximum number of functions that are mathematically possible. This is either the number of groups minus 1 or the number of predictor variables, whichever is less. Use the FUNCTIONS subcommand to set more restrictive criteria for the extraction of functions.

The FUNCTIONS subcommand has three parameters:

n1   *Maximum number of functions.* The default is the number of groups minus 1 or the number of predictor variables, whichever is less.

n2   *Cumulative percentage of eigenvalues.* The default is 100.

n3   *Significance level of function.* The default is 1.0.

You can restrict the number of functions by modifying one and only one parameter at a time. When you modify $n2$, you must explicitly specify the default for $n1$. Similarly, when you modify $n3$, you must specify the defaults for $n1$ and $n2$. If more than one nondefault restriction is specified on the FUNCTIONS subcommand, SPSS/PC+ uses the first one encountered.

Example

```
DSCRIMINANT  GROUPS=CLASS(1,5)
  /VARIABLES=SCORE1 TO SCORE20
  /FUNCTIONS=4,100,.80.
```

- The first two specifications on the FUNCTIONS subcommand are defaults: the default for $n1$ is 4 (5, the number of groups, minus 1) and the default for $n2$ is 100.
- The third specification tells DSCRIMINANT to use fewer than four discriminant functions if the significance level of a function is greater than 0.80.

STATISTICS Subcommand

STATISTICS controls statistic display during both analysis and classification phases. Specify the appropriate number after an optional equals sign following the subcommand keyword to request desired output.

The Analysis Phase

By default, the following statistics are produced during the analysis phase:

- *Summary table.* A table showing the action taken at every step (for stepwise methods only).
- *Summary statistics.* Eigenvalues, percentage of variance, cumulative percentage of variance, canonical correlations, Wilks' lambda, chi-square, degrees of freedom, and significance of chi-square are reported for the functions. (Summary statistics can be suppressed with Option 5.)
- *Step statistics.* Wilks' lambda, equivalent F, degrees of freedom, and significance of F are reported for each step. Tolerance, F-to-remove, and the stepping criterion value are reported for each variable in the equation. Tolerance, minimum tolerance, F-to-enter, and the stepping criterion value are reported for each variable not in the equation. (Step statistics can be suppressed with Option 4.)
- *Final statistics.* Standardized canonical discriminant function coefficients, the structure matrix of discriminant functions and all variables named in the analysis (whether they were entered into the equation or not), and functions evaluated at group means, are reported following the last step. (These statistics cannot be suppressed.)

You can request additional statistics by specifying the appropriate number(s) on the STATISTICS subcommand:

Statistic 1   *Means.* Overall and group means for all variables named on the ANALYSIS subcommand.

Statistic 2   *Standard deviations.* Overall and group standard deviations for all variables named on the ANALYSIS subcommand.

Statistic 3   *Pooled within-groups covariance matrix.*

Statistic 4   *Pooled within-groups correlation matrix.*

Statistic 5   *Matrix of pairwise* F *ratios.* The *F* ratio for each pair of groups. This *F* is the significance test for the Mahalanobis distance between groups. Available only with the stepwise methods.

Statistic 6   *Univariate* F *ratios.* *F* for each variable. This is a one-way analysis-of-variance test for equality of group means on a single predictor variable.

Statistic 7   *Box's* M *test.* This is a test for equality of group covariance matrices.

Statistic 8   *Group covariance matrices.*

Statistic 9   *Total covariance matrix.*

Statistic 11   *Unstandardized canonical discriminant functions.*

Statistic 12   *Classification function coefficients.* Although DSCRIMINANT does not directly use the Fisher linear discriminant functions to classify cases, you can use these coefficients to classify other samples.

The Classification Phase

With the STATISTICS subcommand, you can request a classification results table and three types of plots to help you examine the effectiveness of the discriminant analysis. You can also display discriminant scores and related information for each case.

Statistic 10   *Territorial map.* A territorial map uses the first two discriminant functions as its axes and displays the boundaries between the territories predicted to fall into each group. It is not available for an analysis producing a single discriminant function. Only the first two discriminant functions can be used as axes. Group centroids are plotted as asterisks. Individual cases are not plotted on this map.

Statistic 13   *Classification results table.* This table reports the proportion of cases that are classified correctly and enables you to judge whether cases are systematically misclassified. If you include a SELECT subcommand, two tables are produced—one for selected cases and one for unselected cases.

Statistic 14   *Casewise classification information.* Statistic 14 displays the following information for each case classified: case sequence number; number of missing values in the case; value specified for the variable on the SELECT subcommand, if any; actual group; highest group classification (G); the probability of a case which is in group G being that far from the group centroid ($P(D/G)$); the probability of a case with these discriminant scores being in group G ($P(G/D)$); the second-highest group classification and its $P(G/D)$; and the discriminant scores.

Statistic 15   *All-groups plot.* Cases in all groups are plotted on a single scatter plot, using the first two discriminant functions as axes. The plotting symbol for each case is the group number. Group centroids are plotted as asterisks. If the analysis yields only one discriminant function, a stacked histogram is plotted instead.

Statistic 16   *Separate-groups plots.* Cases in each group are plotted separately on plots that are otherwise the same as those produced by Statistic 15. If the analysis yields only one discriminant function, a histogram is plotted for each group.

PRIORS Subcommand

By default, DSCRIMINANT assumes equal probabilities for group membership when classifying cases. You can provide different prior probabilities with the PRIORS subcommand.

Any one of the following can be specified on PRIORS:

EQUAL   *Equal prior probabilities.* This is the default.

SIZE   *Proportion of the cases analyzed that fall into each group.* If 50% of the cases included in the analysis fall into the first group, 25% in the second, and 25% in the third, the prior probabilities are 0.5, 0.25, and 0.25, respectively. Group size is determined after cases with missing values for the predictor variables are deleted.

value list   *User-specified prior probabilities.* Specify a list of probabilities summing to 1.0.

- Prior probabilities are used only during classification.
- If you provide unequal prior probabilities, DSCRIMINANT adjusts the classification coefficients to reflect this prior knowledge.
- If adjacent groups have the same prior probability, you can use the notation $n*c$ on the value list to indicate that n adjacent groups have the same prior probability c.
- The value list must name or imply as many prior probabilities as groups.
- You can specify a prior probability of 0. No cases are classified into such a group.
- If the sum of the prior probabilities is not 1, SPSS/PC+ rescales the probabilities to sum to 1 and issues a warning.

Example

```
DSCRIMINANT  GROUPS=TYPE(1,5)
  /VARIABLES=A TO H
  /PRIORS=4*.15,.4.
```

- The PRIORS subcommand establishes prior probabilities of 0.15 for the first four groups and 0.4 for the fifth group.

OPTIONS Subcommand

Use the OPTIONS subcommand to control missing-value treatment, to reduce output, to request rotation of pattern or structure matrices, and to specify classification options.

Missing Values

By default, cases missing on any of the predictor variables named on the VARIABLES subcommand are used during neither phase. Cases out of range or missing for the grouping variable are not used during the analysis phase but are classified in the classification phase.

Two options are available for cases that are missing for the predictor variables:

Option 1   *Include user-missing values.* User-missing values are treated as valid values. Only the system-missing value is excluded.

Option 8   *Substitute means for missing values during classification.* Cases with missing values are not used during analysis. Cases with missing values on the classification variables are classified, using the mean as a substitute for the missing data.

Display Format

Two options are available to reduce the amount of output produced during stepwise analysis:

Option 4   *Suppress display of step-by-step output.*

Option 5   *Suppress display of the summary table.*

These two options affect only display output, not the computation of intermediate results.

Rotation Options

The pattern and structure matrices displayed during the analysis phase may be rotated to facilitate interpretation of results. To obtain a varimax rotation, specify either Option 6 or 7 on the associated OPTIONS subcommand.

Option 6   *Rotate pattern matrix.*

Option 7   *Rotate structure matrix.*

Neither Option 6 nor Option 7 affects the classification of cases since the rotation is orthogonal.

Classification Options

Three options relating to the classification phase may be requested on the OPTIONS subcommand.

Option 9   *Classify only unselected cases.* If you use the SELECT subcommand, DSCRIMINANT classifies all cases with valid data for the predictor variables.

Option 9 suppresses the classification phase for cases selected for the analysis, classifying only the unselected cases.

Option 10   *Classify only unclassified cases.* The analysis phase includes only cases with values for the grouping variable within the range specified. With Option 10, you can suppress classification of cases used to derive the discriminant functions. Only cases with missing or out-of-range values on the grouping variable will be classified.

Option 11   *Use separate-group covariance matrices of the discriminant functions for classification.* By default, DSCRIMINANT uses the pooled within-groups covariance matrix to classify cases. If you specify Option 11, it will instead use the separate-group covariance matrices.

SAVE Subcommand

The SAVE subcommand allows you to add much of the casewise information produced by Statistic 14 to the active file and to specify new variable names for this information. The following keywords may be specified on the SAVE subcommand:

CLASS   *Save a variable containing the predicted group membership.* Specify a name for this variable after the keyword CLASS.

SCORES   *Save the discriminant scores.* One score is saved for each discriminant function derived. Specify a rootname after the SCORES keyword. The rootname must be less than seven characters long. DSCRIMINANT adds a sequential number at the end of the rootname to form unique variable names for the new variables.

PROBS   *Save each case's probabilities of membership in each group.* As many variables are added to each case as there are groups. Specify a rootname after the PROBS keyword. The rootname must be less than seven characters long. DSCRIMINANT adds a sequential number at the end of the rootname to form unique variable names for the new variables.

- Specify only the keywords for the results you want saved.
- SAVE applies to the previous ANALYSIS subcommand (or to an analysis of all variables if no ANALYSIS subcommand precedes it).
- To save casewise results from more than one analysis, enter a SAVE command after each, using different variable names or rootnames.
- You can specify the keywords CLASS, SCORES, and PROBS in any order, but the new variables are always added to the end of the active file in the following order: first class, then discriminant scores, then probabilities.
- Appropriate variable labels are generated automatically for the new variables.
- The CLASS variable will use the value labels (if any) from the variable specified for analysis on the GROUPS subcommand.

Example

```
DSCRIMINANT GROUPS = WORLD(1,3)
  /VARIABLES = FOOD TO FSALES
  /SAVE CLASS=PRDCLASS SCORES=SCORE PROBS=PRB.
```

With three groups, the following variables are added to each case:

Name	Description
PRDCLASS	Predicted group
SCORE1	Discriminant score for Function 1
SCORE2	Discriminant score for Function 2
PRB1	Probability of being in Group 1
PRB2	Probability of being in Group 2
PRB3	Probability of being in Group 3

Annotated Example

For a complete example with output, see the Annotated Examples following the Syntax Reference section of this manual.

FACTOR

```
FACTOR VARIABLES={varlist} [/MISSING=[{LISTWISE**}] [INCLUDE]]
                 {ALL    }            {PAIRWISE }
                                      {MEANSUB  }
                                      {DEFAULT  }

  [/WIDTH={width on SET**}]
          {132           }
          {n             }

  [/READ=[{CORRELATION [TRIANGLE]}]]
          {DEFAULT               }
          {FACTOR(n)             }

  [/ANALYSIS={ALL**  }]
            {varlist}

  [/PRINT=[INITIAL**] [EXTRACTION**] [ROTATION**]
          [UNIVARIATE] [CORRELATION] [DET] [INV] [REPR] [AIC]
          [KMO] [FSCORE] [SIG] [ALL]] [DEFAULT]

  [/PLOT=[EIGEN] [ROTATION [(n1,n2) (n3 n4)...]]

  [/DIAGONAL={DEFAULT**  }]
            {value list }

  [/FORMAT=[DEFAULT**] [SORT] [BLANK(n)] ]

  [/WRITE=[{CORRELATION}]]
          {DEFAULT    }
          {FACTOR     }

  [/CRITERIA=[FACTORS(n)] [MINEIGEN({1.0**})] [ITERATE({25**})]
                                   {n    }            {n   }

             [RCONVERGE({0.0001**})] [DELTA({0**})] [{KAISER**}]
                       {n       }          {n  }    {NOKAISER}

             [ECONVERGE({0.001**})] [DEFAULT] ]
                       {n      }

  [/EXTRACTION={PC**   }] [/ROTATION={VARIMAX**}]
              {PA1**  }             {EQUAMAX  }
              {PAF    }             {QUARTIMAX}
              {ALPHA  }             {OBLIMIN  }
              {IMAGE  }             {NOROTATE }
              {ULS    }             {DEFAULT  }
              {GLS    }
              {ML     }
              {DEFAULT}

  [/SAVE=[{REG    }  ({ALL}[rootname]))]]
          {BART   }  {n  }
          {AR     }
          {DEFAULT}

  [/ANALYSIS...]

  [/CRITERIA...]    [/EXTRACTION...]

  [/ROTATION...]    [/SAVE...]
```

**Default if subcommand or keyword is omitted.

Example:

```
FACTOR VARIABLES=V1 TO V12.
```

Overview

FACTOR performs factor analysis using one of seven extraction methods. FACTOR accepts matrix input in the form of correlation matrices or factor loading matrices and can also write the matrix materials to a matrix data file.

Options

Analysis Block Display. You can tailor the statistical display for an analysis block to include correlation matrices, reproduced correlation matrices, and other statistics with the PRINT subcommand. You can sort the output in the factor pattern and structure matrices with the FORMAT subcommand. You can also request scree plots and plots of the variables in factor space for all analyses within an analysis block on the PLOT subcommand.

Extraction Phase Options. With the EXTRACTION subcommand, you can specify one of six extraction methods in addition to the default principal components extraction: principal axis factoring, alpha factoring, image factoring, unweighted least squares, generalized least squares, and maximum likelihood. You can supply initial diagonal values for principal axis factoring on the DIAGONAL subcommand. On the CRITERIA subcommand, you can select the statistical criteria used in the extraction.

Rotation Phase Options. You can control the criteria for factor rotation with the CRITERIA subcommand. On the ROTATION subcommand, you can choose among three rotation methods (equamax, quartimax, and oblimin) in addition to the default varimax rotation, or you can specify no rotation.

Factor Scores. You can save factor scores as new variables in the active file with any of the three methods available on the SAVE subcommand.

Display Format. You can control the width of the display within FACTOR using the WIDTH subcommand.

Matrix Input and Output. Using the WRITE and READ subcommands, you can write a correlation matrix or a factor loading matrix to the results file named on SET for use in subsequent SPSS/PC+ sessions and read either type of matrix, instead of a case file, for further analysis.

Basic Specification

The basic specification is the VARIABLES subcommand with a variable list. FACTOR performs principal components analysis with a varimax rotation on all variables in the analysis using default criteria. A case that has a missing value for any variable on the FACTOR command is omitted from all analyses.

The default display includes the initial communalities, eigenvalues of the correlation matrix, and percentage of variance associated with each; communalities, eigenvalues, and unrotated factor loadings; the rotated factor pattern matrix; and the factor transformation matrix.

Subcommand Order

The standard subcommand order is illustrated in Figure 1.

Figure 1   Subcommand order

```
FACTOR VARIABLES=...
     / MISSING=...
     / WIDTH=...
     / READ=...
```

Analysis Block(s)

```
     / ANALYSIS=...
     / PRINT=...
     / PLOT=...
     / DIAGONAL=...
     / FORMAT=...
     / WRITE ...
```

Extraction Block(s)

```
     / CRITERIA=(extraction criteria)
     / EXTRACTION=...
```

Rotation Block(s)

```
     / CRITERIA=(rotation criteria)
     / ROTATION=...
     / SAVE=...
```

- Subcommands listed in the analysis block apply to all extraction and rotation blocks within that analysis block. Subcommands listed in the extraction block apply to all rotation blocks within that extraction block.

- Each analysis block can contain multiple extraction blocks, and each extraction block can contain multiple rotation blocks.

- The CRITERIA and FORMAT subcommands remain in effect until explicitly overridden. Other subcommands affect only the block in which they are contained.

- The order of subcommands can be different from the order shown in Figure 1. However, any analysis that can be performed with procedure FACTOR can be performed using this order, repeating analysis, rotation, and extraction blocks as needed. Specifying commands out of order can produce unexpected results.

- If you enter any subcommand other than the global subcommands (VARIABLES, MISSING, WIDTH, and WRITE) before the first ANALYSIS subcommand, an implicit analysis block including all variables on the VARIABLES subcommand is activated. Factors are extracted and rotated for this implicit block before any explicitly requested analysis block is activated.

- If you enter a SAVE or ROTATION subcommand before the first EXTRACTION in any analysis block, an implicit extraction block using the default method (principal components) is activated. Factors are extracted and rotated for this implicit block before any explicitly requested extraction block is activated.

- If you enter CRITERIA *after* an EXTRACTION or ROTATION subcommand, the criteria do not affect that extraction or rotation.

Example

```
FACTOR VAR=V1 TO V12
  /ANALYSIS=V1 TO V8
  /CRITERIA=FACTORS(3)
  /EXTRACTION=PAF
  /ROTATION=QUARTIMAX.
```

- FACTOR extracts three factors using the principal axis method and quartimax rotation.

Example

```
* Unexpected results in FACTOR.

FACTOR VAR=V1 TO V12
  /CRITERIA=FACTORS(3)
  /ANALYSIS=V1 TO V8
  /EXTRACTION=PAF
  /ROTATION=QUARTIMAX.
```

- The CRITERIA subcommand activates an analysis block of all twelve variables. FACTOR extracts three factors using the default extraction method (principal components) and rotation (varimax) before activating the analysis block with *V1* to *V8*, where different extraction and rotation methods are requested.

Example

```
* Unexpected results in FACTOR.

FACTOR VARIABLES=V1 TO V12
  /SAVE DEFAULT (ALL,FAC)
  /EXTRACTION=PAF
  /ROTATION=OBLIMIN.
```

- The SAVE subcommand activates an extraction block using the default extraction method (principal components) and rotation (varimax). These factors are saved in the active file as *FAC1*, *FAC2*, and so on.

- The next extraction block uses principal axis factoring and oblimin rotation but does not contain a SAVE subcommand, so no factor scores for this extraction block are saved in the active file.

Example

```
* Unexpected results in FACTOR.

FACTOR V1 TO V12
  /EXTRACTION PAF
  /CRITERIA FACTORS(5).
```

- Since no CRITERIA subcommand precedes EXTRACTION, default criteria are used, and the specified CRITERIA subcommand is ignored.

Syntax Rules

- The global subcommands VARIABLES and READ can be specified only once and are in effect for the entire Factor procedure. Multiple specifications of MISSING and WIDTH are allowed, but only the last specified is in effect for the entire procedure.
- VARIABLES, READ, and MISSING must precede any of the other subcommands. WIDTH can be specified anywhere.
- Subcommands ANALYSIS, PRINT, PLOT, DIAGONAL, FORMAT, and WRITE are **analysis block** subcommands. ANALYSIS initiates an analysis block and specifies a subset of variables; the other subcommands apply to analyses performed on those variables.
- The PRINT, PLOT, DIAGONAL, and WRITE subcommands are in effect only for the current analysis block. Defaults are restored when another analysis block is specified. The FORMAT subcommand remains in effect until a new FORMAT subcommand is specified. Defaults are *not* restored when a new analysis block is specified.
- Only one PRINT, PLOT, DIAGONAL, FORMAT, or WRITE subcommand can be in effect for each ANALYSIS subcommand. If any of these is specified more than once in a given analysis block, the last one specified for that block is in effect.
- You can request more than one analysis block within a Factor procedure.
- Subcommands CRITERIA and EXTRACTION are **extraction block** subcommands. EXTRACTION triggers the extraction of factors according to a specified method.
- CRITERIA can be used one or more times in an extraction block to set parameters governing any *subsequent* EXTRACTION and ROTATION subcommands. Specifications on the CRITERIA subcommand carry over from analysis to analysis until explicitly overridden by another CRITERIA subcommand. Defaults are *not* restored when a new analysis block is specified.
- You can request more than one extraction block within an analysis block.
- Subcommands SAVE and ROTATION are **rotation block** subcommands. ROTATION triggers a rotation of the factors in the current extraction block, and SAVE adds factor scores for the following rotation to the active file.
- You can specify SAVE more than once within a rotation block.
- You can request more than one rotation block within an extraction block.

Operations

- VARIABLES calculates a correlation matrix, which is the basis for all further analyses.
- The width specified on the WIDTH subcommand, if any, overrides the width defined on SET.

Example

```
FACTOR VARIABLES=V1 TO V12.
```

- This example produces the default principal components analysis of twelve variables. Those with eigenvalues greater than 1 (the default criterion for extraction) are rotated using varimax rotation (the default).

VARIABLES Subcommand

VARIABLES names all the variables to be used in the Factor procedure. FACTOR computes a correlation matrix that includes all the variables named. This matrix is used by all analysis blocks that follow.

- Subcommand VARIABLES is required.
- The specification on VARIABLES is a list of numeric variables.
- Keyword ALL on VARIABLES refers to all variables in the active file.
- All variables named on subsequent subcommands must first be named on the VARIABLES subcommand.
- Only one VARIABLES subcommand can be specified, and it must precede any analysis or rotation block subcommands. Only the MISSING and WIDTH subcommands can precede it.

MISSING Subcommand

MISSING controls the treatment of cases with missing values.

- If MISSING is omitted or included without specifications, listwise deletion is in effect.
- MISSING must precede any analysis block subcommands.
- The MISSING specification controls all analyses requested on FACTOR.
- The LISTWISE, PAIRWISE, and MEANSUB keywords are alternatives, but any one of them can be used with INCLUDE.

LISTWISE   *Delete cases with missing values listwise.* Only cases with nonmissing values for all variables named on the VARIABLES subcommand are used. Listwise deletion can also be requested with keyword DEFAULT.

PAIRWISE   *Delete cases with missing values pairwise.* All cases with nonmissing values for each pair of variables correlated are used to compute that correlation, regardless of whether the cases have missing values for any other variable.

MEANSUB	*Replace missing values with the variable mean.* All cases are used after the substitution is made. If INCLUDE is also specified, user-missing values are included in the computation of the means, and means are substituted only for the system-missing value.
INCLUDE	*Include user-missing values.* Cases with user-missing values are treated as valid.

WIDTH Subcommand

WIDTH controls the width of the output.

- WIDTH can be specified anywhere and affects all FACTOR output. If more than one width is specified, the last is in effect.
- The specification on WIDTH is an integer ranging from 72 to 132.
- If WIDTH is omitted or if WIDTH specifies DEFAULT, the width specified on the SET command is used.
- If WIDTH is entered without specifications, a width of 132 is used.

ANALYSIS Subcommand

The ANALYSIS subcommand specifies a subset of the variables named on VARIABLES for use in an analysis block. For factor matrix input, however, ANALYSIS must specify the same variable list as on VARIABLES.

- The specification on ANALYSIS is a list of variables, all of which must have been named on the VARIABLES subcommand.
- Each ANALYSIS subcommand initiates an analysis block. The analysis block ends when another ANALYSIS subcommand is specified or the Factor procedure ends.
- Within an analysis block, only those variables named on the ANALYSIS subcommand are available.
- If ANALYSIS is omitted, all variables named on the VARIABLES subcommand are used in all extractions.
- Keyword TO in a variable list on ANALYSIS refers to the order in which variables are named on the VARIABLES subcommand, not to their order in the active file.
- Keyword ALL refers to all variables named on the VARIABLES subcommand.

Example

```
FACTOR VARIABLES=V1 V2 V3 V4 V5 V6
  /ANALYSIS=V1 TO V4
  /ANALYSIS=V4 TO V6.
```

- This example specifies two analysis blocks. Variables *V1*, *V2*, *V3*, and *V4* are included in the first analysis block. Variables *V4*, *V5*, and *V6* are in the second analysis block.
- Keyword TO on ANALYSIS refers to the order of variables on the VARIABLES subcommand, not the order in the active file.

- A default principal components analysis with a varimax rotation will be performed for each analysis block.

FORMAT Subcommand

FORMAT modifies the format of factor pattern and structure matrices.

- FORMAT can be specified once in each analysis block. If more than one FORMAT is encountered in an analysis block, the last is in effect.
- If FORMAT is omitted or included without specifications, variables appear in the order in which they are named and all matrix entries are displayed.
- Once specified, FORMAT stays in effect until it is overridden. Defaults are not automatically restored when a new analysis block is specified.

SORT   *Order the factor loadings in descending order by the magnitude of the first factor.*

BLANK(n)   *Suppress coefficients lower in absolute value than* n.

DEFAULT   *Turn off keywords SORT and BLANK.*

Example

```
FACTOR VARIABLES=V1 TO V12
  /MISSING=MEANSUB
  /FORMAT=SORT BLANK(.3)
  /EXTRACTION=ULS
  /ROTATION=NOROTATE.
```

- This example specifies a single analysis block. All variables between and including *V1* and *V12* in the active file are included.
- The MISSING subcommand substitutes variable means for missing values.
- The FORMAT subcommand orders variables in factor pattern matrices by descending value of loadings. Factor loadings with an absolute value less than 0.3 are omitted.
- Factors are extracted using unweighted least squares and are not rotated.

PRINT Subcommand

PRINT controls the statistical output for an analysis block and all extraction and rotation blocks within it.

- Keywords INITIAL, EXTRACTION, and ROTATION are the defaults if PRINT is omitted or specified without keywords.
- If any keywords are specified, only the output specifically requested is produced for the current analysis block.
- The defaults are reinstated when a new ANALYSIS subcommand is encountered.
- The requested statistics are displayed only for variables in the analysis block.
- PRINT can be specified anywhere within the analysis block. If more than one PRINT subcommand is specified, only the last is in effect.

INITIAL   *Initial communalities for each variable, eigenvalues of the unreduced correlation matrix, and percentage of variance for each factor.*

EXTRACTION   *Factor pattern matrix, revised communalities, the eigenvalue of each factor retained, and the percentage of variance each eigenvalue represents.*

ROTATION   *Rotated factor pattern matrix, factor transformation matrix, and factor correlation matrix.*

UNIVARIATE   *Valid number of cases, means, and standard deviations.* (Not available with matrix input.)

CORRELATION   *Correlation matrix.*

SIG   *Matrix of one-tailed significance levels of correlations.*

DET   *Determinant of the correlation matrix.*

INV   *Inverse of the correlation matrix.*

AIC   *Anti-image covariance and correlation matrices* (Kaiser, 1970). The measure of sampling adequacy for the individual variable is displayed on the diagonal of the anti-image correlation matrix.

KMO   *Kaiser-Meyer-Olkin measure of sampling adequacy and Bartlett's test of sphericity.* Tests of significance are not computed for an input matrix when it does not contain N values.

REPR   *Reproduced correlations and residual correlations.*

FSCORE   *Factor score coefficient matrix.* Factor score coefficients are calculated using the method requested on the SAVE subcommand. The default is the regression method.

ALL   *All available statistics.*

DEFAULT   *INITIAL, EXTRACTION, and ROTATION.*

Example

```
FACTOR VARS=V1 TO V12
  /MISS=MEANSUB
  /PRINT=DEF AIC KMO REPR
  /EXTRACT=ULS
  /ROTATE=VARIMAX.
```

- This example specifies a single analysis block that includes all variables between and including *V1* and *V12* in the active file.
- Variable means are substituted for missing values.
- The output includes the anti-image correlation and covariance matrices, the Kaiser-Meyer-Olkin measure of sampling adequacy, the reproduced correlation and residual matrix, and the default statistics.
- Factors are extracted using unweighted least squares.
- The factor pattern matrix is rotated using the varimax rotation.

PLOT Subcommand

Use PLOT to request scree plots or plots of variables in rotated factor space.

- If PLOT is omitted, no plots are produced. If PLOT is used without specifications, it is ignored.
- PLOT is in effect only for the current analysis block. The default (no plots) is reinstated when a new ANALYSIS subcommand is encountered.
- PLOT can be specified anywhere within the analysis block. If more than one PLOT subcommand is specified, only the last one is in effect.

EIGEN   *Scree plot* (Cattell, 1966). The eigenvalues from each extraction are plotted in descending order.

ROTATION(n1,n2)...   *Plots of variables in factor space.* Specify pairs of factor numbers in parentheses; for example, PLOT ROTATION(1,2)(1,3)(2,3) requests three plots, each defined by two factors. The ROTATION subcommand must be explicitly specified when you request ROTATION on the PLOT subcommand.

DIAGONAL Subcommand

DIAGONAL specifies values for the diagonal in conjunction with principal axis factoring.

- If DIAGONAL is omitted or included without specifications, FACTOR uses the default method for specifying the diagonal.
- DIAGONAL is in effect for all PAF extractions within the analysis block. It is ignored with extraction methods other than PAF.
- The default method for specifying the diagonal is reinstated when a new ANALYSIS subcommand is encountered. DIAGONAL can be specified anywhere within the analysis block. If more than one DIAGONAL subcommand is specified, only the last one is in effect. Default communality estimates for PAF are squared multiple correlations. If these cannot be computed, the maximum absolute correlation between the variable and any other variable in the analysis is used.

value list   *Diagonal values.* The number of values supplied must equal the number of variables in the analysis block. Use the notation n* before a value to indicate the value is repeated *n* times.

DEFAULT   *Initial communality estimates.*

Example

```
FACTOR VARIABLES=V1 TO V12
  /DIAGONAL=.56 .55 .74 2*.56 .70 3*.65 .76 .64 .63
  /EXTRACTION=PAF
  /ROTATION=VARIMAX.
```

- A single analysis block includes all variables between and including *V1* and *V12* in the active file.

- DIAGONAL specifies 12 values to use as initial estimates of communalities in principal axis factoring.
- The factor pattern matrix is rotated using varimax rotation.

CRITERIA Subcommand

CRITERIA controls extraction and rotation criteria.

- CRITERIA can be specified before any implicit or explicit request for an extraction or rotation.
- Only defaults specifically altered are changed.
- Any criterion that is altered remains in effect for *all* subsequent analysis blocks until it is explicitly overridden.

The following keywords on CRITERIA apply to extractions:

FACTORS(n)   *Number of factors extracted.* The default is the number of eigenvalues greater than MINEIGEN. When specified, FACTORS overrides MINEIGEN.

MINEIGEN(n)   *Minimum eigenvalue used to control the number of factors extracted.* The default is 1.

ECONVERGE(n)   *Convergence criterion for extraction.* The default is 0.001.

The following keywords on CRITERIA apply to rotations:

RCONVERGE(n)   *Convergence criterion for rotation.* The default is 0.0001.

KAISER   *Kaiser normalization in the rotation phase.* This is the default. The alternative is NOKAISER.

NOKAISER   *No Kaiser normalization.*

DELTA(n)   *Delta for direct oblimin rotation.* DELTA affects the ROTATION subcommand only when OBLIMIN rotation is requested. The default is 0. The maximum acceptable value is 0.8. If you specify a value greater than 0.8, SPSS/PC+ displays a warning and resets the value to the default.

The following keywords on CRITERIA apply to both extractions and rotations:

ITERATE(n)   *Maximum number of iterations for solutions in the extraction or rotation phases.* The default is 25.

DEFAULT   *Reestablish default values for all criteria.*

Example

```
FACTOR VARIABLES=V1 TO V12
  /CRITERIA=FACTORS(6)
  /EXTRACTION=PC
  /ROTATION=NOROTATE
  /CRITERIA=DEFAULT
  /EXTRACTION=ML
  /ROTATION=VARIMAX
  /PLOT=ROTATION(1 2)(1 3).
```

- This example initiates a single analysis block that analyzes all variables between and including *V1* and *V12* in the active file.
- Six factors are extracted in the first extraction. The extraction uses the default principal components method, and the factor pattern matrix is not rotated.
- The default criteria are reinstated for the second extraction, which uses the maximum-likelihood method. The second factor pattern matrix is rotated using the varimax rotation.
- PLOT requests plots of the variables in the factor space defined by the first and second factors and of variables in the factor space defined by the first and third factors.
- PLOT applies to both extractions, since there is only one analysis block.

EXTRACTION Subcommand

EXTRACTION specifies the factor extraction technique.

- Multiple EXTRACTION subcommands can be specified within an analysis block.
- If EXTRACTION is not specified or is included without specifications, principal components extraction is used.
- If you specify criteria for EXTRACTION, the CRITERIA subcommand must precede the EXTRACTION subcommand.
- When you specify EXTRACTION, you should always explicitly specify the ROTATION subcommand. If ROTATION is not specified, the factors are not rotated.

PC   *Principal components analysis* (Harman, 1967). This is the default. PC can also be requested with keyword PA1 or DEFAULT.

PAF   *Principal axis factoring*. PAF can also be requested with keyword PA2.

ALPHA   *Alpha factoring* (Kaiser & Caffry, 1965).

IMAGE   *Image factoring* (Kaiser, 1963).

ULS   *Unweighted least squares* (Harman & Jones, 1966).

GLS   *Generalized least squares.*

ML   *Maximum likelihood* (Jöreskog & Lawley, 1968).

Example

```
FACTOR VARIABLES=V1 TO V12
  /EXTRACTION=ULS
  /ROTATION=NOROTATE
  /ANALYSIS=V1 TO V6
  /EXTRACTION=ULS
  /ROTATION=NOROTATE
  /EXTRACTION=ML
  /ROTATION=NOROTATE.
```

- This example specifies two analysis blocks. In the first analysis block, variables *V1* through *V12* are analyzed using unweighted least-squares extraction. The factor pattern matrix is not rotated.
- In the second analysis block, variables *V1* through *V6* are analyzed first with an unweighted least-squares extraction and then with a maximum-likelihood extraction. No rotation is performed for either extraction.

ROTATION Subcommand

ROTATION specifies the factor rotation method. It can also be used to suppress the rotation phase entirely.

- You can specify multiple ROTATION subcommands after each extraction.
- Rotations are performed on the matrix resulting from the previous extraction.
- If you specify the ROTATION subcommand without specifications or omit both the EXTRACTION and ROTATION subcommands, varimax rotation is used.
- If you include an EXTRACTION subcommand but omit the ROTATION subcommand, factors are not rotated.
- Keyword NOROTATE on the ROTATION subcommand produces a plot of variables in unrotated factor space if the PLOT subcommand is also included in the analysis block.

VARIMAX   *Varimax rotation.* This is the default if ROTATION is entered without specifications or if EXTRACTION and ROTATION are both omitted. Varimax rotation can also be requested with keyword DEFAULT.

EQUAMAX   *Equamax rotation.*

QUARTIMAX   *Quartimax rotation.*

OBLIMIN   *Direct oblimin rotation.* This is a nonorthogonal rotation; thus, a factor correlation matrix will also be displayed. For this method, specify DELTA on the CRITERIA subcommand.

NOROTATE   *No rotation.*

Example

```
FACTOR VARIABLES=V1 TO V12
  /CRITERIA=DELTA(.5)
  /EXTRACTION=ULS
  /ROTATION
  /ROTATION=OBLIMIN.
```

- The first ROTATION subcommand specifies the default varimax rotation.
- The second ROTATION subcommand specifies an oblimin rotation based on the same extraction of factors. The delta value (0.5) is specified on the CRITERIA subcommand.

SAVE Subcommand

SAVE allows you to save factor scores from any rotated or unrotated extraction as new variables in the active file. You can use any of the three methods for computing the factor scores.

- SAVE must follow the ROTATION subcommand specifying the rotation for which factor scores are to be saved. If no ROTATION subcommand precedes SAVE, a varimax rotation is used and factor scores are saved for varimax-rotated factors.
- You can specify SAVE more than once in a rotation block. Thus, you can calculate and save factor scores using different methods for a single rotation.
- Each specification applies to the previous rotation.
- The new variables are added to the end of the active file.

Keywords to specify the method of computing factor scores are:

REG   *Regression method.* This is the default.

BART   *Bartlett method.*

AR   *Anderson-Rubin method.*

DEFAULT   *The same as REG.*

- After one of the above keywords, specify in parentheses the number of scores to save and a rootname to use in naming the variables.
- You can specify either an integer or the keyword ALL. The maximum number of scores you can specify is the number of factors in the solution.
- FACTOR forms variable names by appending sequential numbers to the rootname you specify. The rootname must begin with a letter and conform to the rules for SPSS variable names. It must be short enough so that the variable names formed will not exceed eight characters.
- FACTOR automatically generates variable labels for the new variables. Each label contains information about the method of computing the factor score, its sequential number, and the sequential number of the analysis.

Example

```
FACTOR VARIABLES=V1 TO V12
  /CRITERIA FACTORS(4)
  /ROTATION
  /SAVE REG (4,PCOMP)
  /CRITERIA DEFAULT
  /EXTRACTION PAF
  /ROTATION
  /SAVE DEF (ALL PAFAC).
```

- Since there is no EXTRACTION subcommand before the first ROTATION, the first extraction will be the default principal components.
- The first CRITERIA subcommand specifies that four principal components should be extracted.
- The first ROTATION subcommand requests the default varimax rotation for the principal components.
- The first SAVE subcommand calculates scores using the regression method. Four scores will be added to the file: *PCOMP1*, *PCOMP2*, *PCOMP3*, and *PCOMP4*.
- The next CRITERIA subcommand restores default criteria. Here it implies that subsequent extractions should extract all factors with eigenvalues greater than 1.
- The second EXTRACTION subcommand specifies principal axis factoring.
- The second ROTATION subcommand requests the default varimax rotation for PAF factors so that varimax-rotated factor scores are saved. If this subcommand had been omitted, the rotation phase would have been skipped, and scores for unrotated factors would be added to the file.
- The second SAVE subcommand calculates scores using the regression method (the default). The number of scores added to the file is the number extracted and their names will be *PAFAC1*, *PAFAC2*, and so on.

WRITE Subcommand

Use the WRITE subcommand to write a correlation or factor matrix to the results file.

- WRITE is an analysis block subcommand and can be specified within any analysis block.
- The variables in the analysis block are the only variables included in the matrix.
- When WRITE is included without keywords, FACTOR writes a correlation matrix.
- The matrix is written to the results file specified on the SET command (by default, *SPSS.PRC*).
- If FACTOR writes a correlation matrix, the matrix is indexed by the number and order of variables on the ANALYSIS subcommand immediately preceding WRITE. If no ANALYSIS subcommand precedes WRITE, the list on the VARIABLES subcommand is used.
- If FACTOR writes a factor matrix, each variable in the analysis defines a row, and each factor extracted defines a column.
- One factor matrix is written for each extraction in the analysis block.
- The factor matrix that is written is unrotated.
- Unless you edit the results file, only the first factor matrix written to the file can be read into a subsequent Factor procedure.

The following can be specified on WRITE:

CORRELATION   *Write a correlation matrix.* The correlation matrix can also be requested with keyword DEFAULT.

FACTOR   *Write an unrotated factor matrix for each EXTRACTION subcommand in the analysis block.*

Example

```
DATA LIST FREE FILE='GSS80.DAT'
 /ABANY,ABDEFECT,ABHLTH,ABNOMORE,ABPOOR,ABRAPE,ABSINGLE.
SET RESULTS='GSS80.MAT'.
FACTOR VAR=ABANY TO ABSINGLE
 /WRITE FACTOR.
```

- The DATA LIST command requests that data be read from the file *GSS80.DAT*. DATA LIST also specifies that the data will be read in freefield format and provides names for the variables.

- The SET command identifies *GSS80.MAT* as the results file.

- FACTOR analyzes all variables in the active file. The default principal components extraction and varimax rotation are performed.

- The WRITE subcommand writes out a factor matrix of the unrotated factors.

READ Subcommand

Use the READ subcommand to indicate that a correlation or factor matrix is to be read.

- READ is a global subcommand and can be specified only once on the FACTOR subcommand.

- The VARIABLES subcommand must be the first subcommand specified when you use READ.

- READ must be specified before the first analysis block.

- When READ is included without specifications, FACTOR assumes that it is reading a correlation matrix that is in the same format as the matrices FACTOR writes.

- When you specify READ on FACTOR, you must first specify a DATA LIST MATRIX command that points to the file containing the matrix materials and names the variables that will be read (see the example below).

- Only a single factor matrix can be read from a file, regardless of how many matrices were written (by multiple EXTRACTION subcommands) in the analysis block containing the WRITE command.

- The number and order of variables named on DATA LIST MATRIX must match the number and order of variables in the correlation or factor matrix.

- You can analyze a subset of variables when you read a correlation matrix but not when you read a factor matrix.

- Because FACTOR does not read the number of cases with matrix materials, specify an N command before FACTOR to obtain significance levels for extraction techniques using a chi-square test or when KMO is specified on PRINT.

The following can be specified on the READ subcommand:

CORRELATION   *Read a correlation matrix.* A correlation matrix can also be requested with keyword DEFAULT or by entering the READ subcommand with no specifications.

TRIANGLE   *Read a correlation matrix in lower-triangular form.* TRIANGLE can be specified only after the CORRELATION keyword.

FACTOR(n)   *Read a factor matrix.* The number of factors (columns) in the matrix is *n*.

Example

```
DATA LIST MATRIX FREE
 /ABANY,ABDEFECT,ABHLTH,ABNOMORE,ABPOOR,ABRAPE,ABSINGLE.
BEGIN DATA
   .6747329   .2183443
   .6522527   .1644450
   .3511271   .8334249
 -.0181689   .8180816
   .6998996 -.0986098
   .6363841 -.1623558
   .7479211 -.4813617
END DATA.
FACTOR VAR=ABANY TO ABSINGLE
 /READ FAC (2)
 /ROTATION=EQUAMAX
 /ROTATION=QUARTIMAX.
```

- This example reads a factor matrix computed on seven variables. Two factors were extracted when the matrix was computed.
- The DATA LIST MATRIX command is required in order to read matrix input. Here the matrix is inline.
- The matrix is analyzed using equamax and quartimax rotations.

Annotated Example

For a complete example with output, see the Annotated Examples following the Syntax Reference section of this manual.

QUICK CLUSTER

```
QUICK CLUSTER {varlist}
              {ALL    }

 [/MISSING=[{LISTWISE**}] [INCLUDE]]
            {PAIRWISE  }
            {DEFAULT   }

 [/INITIAL=(value list)]

 [/CRITERIA=[CLUSTER({2** })][NOINITIAL][MXITER({10**})] [CONVERGE({0.02**})]]
                     {n   }                          {n   }              {n    }

 [/METHOD=[{KMEANS[(NOUPDATE)]**}]
           {KMEANS(UPDATE)      }
           {CLASSIFY            }

 [/PRINT=[INITIAL**] [CLUSTER] [ID(varname)] [DISTANCE] [ANOVA] [NONE]]

 [/SAVE=[CLUSTER[(varname)]] [DISTANCE[(varname)]]]
```

**Default if subcommand or keyword is omitted.

Example:

```
QUICK CLUSTER V1 TO V4
  /CRITERIA=CLUSTER(4)
  /SAVE=CLUSTER(GROUP).
```

Overview

When the desired number of clusters is known, QUICK CLUSTER groups cases efficiently into clusters. It is not as flexible as CLUSTER, but it uses considerably less processing time and memory, especially when the number of cases is large.

Options

Algorithm Specifications. You can specify the number of clusters to form with the CRITERIA subcommand. You can also use CRITERIA to control initial cluster selection and the criteria for iterating the clustering algorithm. With the METHOD subcommand, you can specify how to update cluster centers, and you can request classification only.

Initial Cluster Centers. By default, QUICK CLUSTER chooses the initial cluster centers. Alternatively, you can provide initial centers on the INITIAL subcommand.

Optional Output. With the PRINT subcommand, you can display the cluster membership of each case and the distance of each case from its cluster center. You can also display the distances between the final cluster centers and a univariate analysis of variance between clusters for each clustering variable.

Saving Results. With the WRITE subcommand, you can write the final cluster centers to the results file specified on the SET command (the default is *SPSS.PRC*). In addition, you can save the cluster membership of each case and the distance from each case to its classification cluster center as new variables in the active file using the SAVE subcommand.

Basic Specification

The basic specification is a list of variables. By default, QUICK CLUSTER produces two clusters. The two cases that are farthest apart based on the values of the clustering variables are selected as initial cluster centers and the rest of the cases are assigned to the nearer center. The new cluster centers are calculated as the means of all cases in each cluster, and if neither the minimum change nor the maximum iteration criterion is met, all cases are assigned to the new cluster centers again. When one of the criteria is met, iteration stops, the final cluster centers are updated, and the distance of each case is computed.

Subcommand Order

- The variable list must be specified first.
- Subcommands can be named in any order.

Operations

The procedure generally involves four steps:

- First, initial cluster centers are selected, either by choosing one case for each cluster requested or by using the specified values.
- Second, each case is assigned to the nearest cluster center and the mean of each cluster is calculated to obtain the new cluster centers.
- Third, the maximum change between the new cluster centers and the initial cluster centers is computed. If the maximum change is not less than the maximum change value and the maximum iteration number is not reached, the second step is repeated and the cluster centers are updated. The process stops when either the maximum change or maximum iteration criterion is met. The resulting clustering centers are used as classification centers in the last step.
- In the last step, all cases are assigned to the nearest classification center. The final cluster centers are updated and the distance for each case is computed.

When the number of cases is large, directly clustering all cases may be impractical. As an alternative, you can cluster a sample of cases and then use the cluster solution for the sample to classify the entire group. This can be done in two phases:

- The first phase obtains a cluster solution for the sample. This involves all four steps of the QUICK CLUSTER algorithm.
- The second phase requires only one pass through the data. First, enter the obtained final cluster centers on the INITIAL subcommand, to be used as the initial cluster centers for the second analysis. Keyword CLASSIFY is specified on the METHOD subcommand to skip the second and third steps of the clustering algorithm, and cases are classified using the initial cluster centers. When all cases are assigned, the cluster centers are updated and the distance of each case is computed. This phase can be repeated until final cluster centers are stable.

Example

```
QUICK CLUSTER V1 TO V4
  /CRITERIA=CLUSTERS(4)
  /SAVE=CLUSTER(GROUP).
```

- This example clusters cases based on their values for all variables between and including *V1* and *V4* in the active file.
- Four clusters, rather than the default two, will be formed.
- Initial cluster centers are chosen by finding four widely spaced cases. This is the default.
- The cluster membership of each case is saved in variable *GROUP* in the active file. Variable *GROUP* has integer values from 1 to 4, indicating the cluster to which each case belongs.

Variable List

The variable list identifies the clustering variables.

- The variable list is required and must be the first specification on QUICK CLUSTER.
- You can use keyword ALL to refer to all user-defined variables in the active file.
- QUICK CLUSTER uses squared Euclidean distances, which equally weight all clustering variables. If the variables are measured in units that are not comparable, the procedure will give more weight to variables with large variances. Therefore, you should standardize variables measured on different scales using the Descriptives procedure before clustering.

CRITERIA Subcommand

CRITERIA specifies the number of clusters to form, and it controls options for the clustering algorithm. You can use any or all of the keywords below.

CLUSTER(n)   *Number of clusters.* QUICK CLUSTER assigns cases to *n* clusters. The default is 2.

NOINITIAL   *No initial cluster center selection.* By default, initial cluster centers are formed by choosing one case (with valid data for the clustering variables) for each cluster requested. The initial selection requires a pass through the data to ensure that the centers are well separated from one another. If NOINITIAL is specified, QUICK CLUSTER selects the first *n* cases without missing values as initial cluster centers.

MXITER(n)   *Maximum number of iterations for updating cluster centers.* The default is 10. Iteration stops when maximum number of iterations has been reached. MXITER is ignored when METHOD=CLASSIFY.

CONVERGE(n)   *Convergence criterion controlling maximum change in cluster centers.* The default value for *n* is 0.02. The maximum change value equals the convergence value (*n*) times the minimum distance between initial centers. Iteration stops when the largest change of any cluster center is less than or equal to the maximum change value. CONVERGE is ignored when METHOD=CLASSIFY.

The NOINITIAL option followed by the remaining steps of the default QUICK CLUSTER algo-rithm makes QUICK CLUSTER equivalent to MacQueen's *n*-means clustering method.

METHOD Subcommand

By default, QUICK CLUSTER recalculates cluster centers after assigning all the cases and re-peats the process until one of the criteria is met. You can use the METHOD subcommand to recalculate cluster centers after each case is assigned or to suppress recalculation until after classification is complete.

KMEANS (NOUPDATE) *Recalculate cluster centers after all cases are assigned for each iter-ation.* This is the default.

KMEANS(UPDATE) *Recalculate a cluster center each time a case is assigned.* QUICK CLUSTER calculates the mean of cases currently in the cluster and uses this new cluster center in subsequent case assignment.

CLASSIFY *Do not recalculate cluster centers.* QUICK CLUSTER uses the initial cluster centers for classification and computes the final cluster centers as the means of all the cases assigned to the same cluster. When key-word CLASSIFY is specified, the CONVERGE or MXITER specification on CRITERIA is ignored.

INITIAL Subcommand

INITIAL specifies the initial cluster centers. One value for each clustering variable must be included for each cluster requested. Values are specified in parentheses cluster by cluster.

Example

```
QUICK CLUSTER  A B C D
  /CRITERIA = CLUSTER(3)
  /INITIAL = (13 24  1  8
               7 12  5  9
              10 18 17 16).
```

- This example specifies four clustering variables and requests three clusters. Thus, 12 val-ues are supplied on INITIAL.

- The initial center of the first cluster has a value of 13 for variable *A*, 24 for variable *B*, 1 for *C*, and 8 for *D*.

PRINT Subcommand

QUICK CLUSTER always displays the centers used to classify cases (initial cluster centers), the mean values of the cases in each cluster (final cluster centers), and the number of cases in each cluster. Use PRINT to request other types of output. If PRINT is not specified or is specified without keywords, the default is INITIAL.

INITIAL   *Initial cluster centers.* When SPLIT FILES is in effect, the initial cluster center for each split file is displayed. This is the default.

CLUSTER   *Cluster membership for each case.* Each case displays an identifying number or value, the number of the cluster to which it was assigned, and its distance from the center of that cluster. This output is extensive when the number of cases is large.

ID(varname)   *Case identification.* The value of the specified variable is used to identify cases in output. If ID is not specified, the number of each case is used as an identifier. This number may not be sequential if cases have been selected.

DISTANCE   *Pairwise distances between all final cluster centers.* This output can consume a great deal of processing time when the number of clusters requested is large.

ANOVA   *Descriptive univariate* F *tests for the clustering variables.* Since cases are systematically assigned to clusters to maximize differences on the clustering variables, these tests are descriptive only and should not be used to test the null hypothesis that there are no differences between clusters. Statistics after clustering are also available through the Discriminant procedure or MANOVA (MANOVA is available in the SPSS/PC+ Advanced Statistics option).

NONE   *No additional output.* Only the default output is displayed. NONE overrides any other specifications on PRINT.

Example

```
QUICK CLUSTER A B C D E
  /CRITERIA=CLUSTERS(6)
  /PRINT=CLUSTER ID(CASEID) DISTANCE.
```

- Six clusters are formed on the basis of the five variables *A*, *B*, *C*, *D*, and *E*.
- For each case in the file, cluster membership and distance from cluster center are displayed. Cases are identified by the values of the variable *CASEID*.
- Distances between all cluster centers are printed.

WRITE Subcommand

WRITE saves the final cluster centers in the results file specified on the SET command (the default is *SPSS.PRC*). You can later use these final cluster centers as initial cluster centers for a different sample of cases that use the same variables. You can also cluster the final cluster centers themselves to obtain clusters of clusters. WRITE has no further specification.

Example

```
SET RESULTS='CLUS.DAT'.

QUICK CLUSTER A B C D
  /CRITERIA = CLUSTER(3)
  /WRITE.
```

- QUICK CLUSTER writes the final cluster centers to file *CLUS.DAT*.

SAVE Subcommand

Use SAVE to save results of cluster analysis as new variables in the active file.

- You can specify a variable name in parentheses following either keyword. If no variable name is specified, QUICK CLUSTER forms unique variable names by appending an underscore and a sequential number to the rootname *QCL*. The number increments with each new variable saved.
- QUICK CLUSTER displays a message listing each new variable with a description in parentheses.

CLUSTER(varname)   *The cluster number of each case.* The value of the new variable is set to an integer from 1 to the number of clusters.

DISTANCE(varname)   *The distance of each case from its classification cluster center.*

Example

```
QUICK CLUSTER A B C D
  /CRITERIA=CLUSTERS(6)
  /SAVE=CLUSTER DISTANCE.
```

- Six clusters of cases are formed on the basis of variables *A*, *B*, *C*, and *D*.
- A new variable *QCL_1* is created and set to an integer between 1 and 6 to indicate cluster membership for each case.
- Another new variable *QCL_2* is created and set to the Euclidean distance between a case and the center of the cluster to which it is assigned.
- QUICK CLUSTER lists the two variables saved into the active files: *QCL_1* (cluster membership) and *QCL_2* (distance).

MISSING Subcommand

MISSING controls the treatment of cases with missing values.

LISTWISE   *Delete cases with missing values listwise.* A case with a missing value for any of the clustering variables is deleted from the analysis and will not be assigned to a cluster. This is the default.

PAIRWISE   *Assign each case to the nearest cluster on the basis of the clustering variables for which the case has nonmissing values.* Only cases with missing values for *all* clustering variables are deleted.

DEFAULT   *Same as LISTWISE.*

INCLUDE   *Treat user-missing values as valid.*

LISTWISE, PAIRWISE, and DEFAULT are alternatives. However, each can be used with INCLUDE.

Annotated Example

For a complete example with output, see the Annotated Examples following the Syntax Reference section of this manual.

RELIABILITY

```
RELIABILITY VARIABLES={varlist}
                      {ALL    }

 [/SCALE(scalename)=varlist [/SCALE...]]

 [/MODEL={ALPHA**        }] [/VARIABLES...]
         {SPLIT[(n)]     }
         {GUTTMAN        }
         {PARALLEL       }
         {STRICTPARALLEL }

 [/STATISTICS=[DESCRIPTIVE]   [SCALE]      [{ANOVA          }] [ALL]]
              [COVARIANCES]   [TUKEY]       {ANOVA FRIEDMAN }
              [CORRELATIONS]  [HOTELLING]   {ANOVA COCHRAN  }

 [/SUMMARY=[MEANS] [VARIANCE] [COV] [CORR] [TOTAL] [ALL]]


 [/METHOD=COVARIANCE]

 [/FORMAT={LABELS** }]
          {NOLABELS }

 [/MISSING={EXCLUDE** }]
           {INCLUDE   }
```

**Default if subcommand or keyword is omitted.

Example:

```
RELIABILITY  VARIABLES=SCORE1 TO SCORE10
  /SCALE (OVERALL) = ALL
  /MODEL = ALPHA
  /SUMMARY = MEANS TOTAL.
```

Overview

RELIABILITY estimates reliability statistics for the components of multiple-item additive scales. It uses any one of five models for reliability analysis and offers a variety of statistical displays. RELIABILITY can also be used to perform a repeated measures analysis of variance, a two-way factorial analysis of variance with one observation per cell, Tukey's test for additivity, Hotelling's T^2 test for equality of means in repeated measures designs, and Friedman's two-way analysis of variance on ranks. For more complex repeated measures designs, use the MANOVA procedure (available in the SPSS/PC+ Advanced Statistics option).

Options

Model Type. You can specify any one of five models on the MODEL subcommand.

Statistical Display. Statistics available on the STATISTICS subcommand include descriptive statistics, correlation and covariance matrices, a repeated measures analysis-of-variance table, Hotelling's T^2, Tukey's test for additivity, Friedman's chi-square for the analysis of ranked data, and Cochran's Q.

Computational Method. By using the METHOD subcommand, you can force RELIABILITY to use the covariance method, even when you are not requesting any output that requires it.

Basic Specification

The basic specification is the VARIABLES subcommand and a variable list. By default, RELI-ABILITY displays the number of cases, number of items, and Cronbach's alpha (α) . Whenever possible, it uses an algorithm that does not require the calculation of the covariance matrix.

Subcommand Order

- Subcommand VARIABLES must be specified first.
- The remaining subcommands can be named in any order.

Operations

- STATISTICS and SUMMARY are cumulative. If you enter them more than once, all request-ed statistics are produced for each scale.
- If you request output that is not available for your model or for your data, RELIABILITY ignores the request.
- RELIABILITY uses an economical algorithm whenever possible but calculates a covariance matrix when necessary (see the METHOD subcommand on p. 205).

Limitations

- Maximum 10 VARIABLES subcommands.
- Maximum 50 SCALE subcommands.
- Maximum 200 variables on one SCALE subcommand.

Example

```
RELIABILITY  VARIABLES=SCORE1 TO SCORE10
  /SCALE (OVERALL) = ALL
  /SCALE (ODD) = SCORE1 SCORE3 SCORE5 SCORE7 SCORE9
  /SUMMARY = MEANS TOTAL.
```

- This example analyzes two additive scales.
- One scale (labeled *OVERALL* in the output) includes all 10 items. Another (labeled *ODD*) includes every other item.

- Summary statistics are displayed for each scale, showing item means and the relationship of each item to the total scale.

Example

```
RELIABILITY  VARIABLES=SCORE1 TO SCORE10.
```

- This example analyzes one scale (labeled *ALL* in the display output) that includes all 10 items.
- Because there is no SUMMARY subcommand, no summary statistics are displayed.

VARIABLES Subcommand

VARIABLES specifies the variables to be used in the analysis. Only numeric variables can be used.

- Subcommand VARIABLES is required and must be specified first.
- You can use keyword ALL to refer to all user-defined variables in the active file.
- You can specify VARIABLES more than once on a single RELIABILITY command. A reliability analysis is performed on each set of variables.

SCALE Subcommand

SCALE defines a scale for analysis, providing a label for the scale and specifying its component variables. If SCALE is omitted, all variables named on the VARIABLES subcommand are used, and the label for the scale is *ALL*.

- The label is specified in parentheses after SCALE. It can have a maximum of eight characters and can use only the letters A to Z and the numerals 0 to 9.
- RELIABILITY does not add any new variables to the active file. The label is used only to identify the output. If the analysis is satisfactory, use COMPUTE to create a new variable containing the sum of the component items.
- Variables named on SCALE must have been named on the previous VARIABLES subcommand. Use keyword ALL to refer to all variables named on the preceding VARIABLES subcommand.
- To analyze different groups of component variables, specify SCALE more than once following a VARIABLES subcommand.

Example

```
RELIABILITY VARIABLES = ITEM1 TO ITEM20
  /SCALE (A) = ITEM1 TO ITEM10
  /SCALE (B) = ITEM1 ITEM3 ITEM5 ITEM16 TO ITEM20
  /SCALE (C) = ALL.
```

- This command analyzes three different scales: scale A has 10 items, scale B has 8 items, and scale C has 20 items.

MODEL Subcommand

MODEL specifies the type of reliability analysis for the scale named on the preceding SCALE subcommand.

ALPHA   *Cronbach's* α. Standardized item α is displayed. This is the default.

SPLIT (n)   *Split-half coefficients.* You can specify a number in parentheses to indicate how many items should be in the second half. For example, MODEL SPLIT (6) uses the last six variables for the second half and all others for the first. By default, each half has an equal number of items, with the odd item, if any, going to the first half.

GUTTMAN   *Guttman's lower bounds for true reliability.*

PARALLEL   *Maximum-likelihood reliability estimate under parallel assumptions.* This model assumes that items have the same variance but not necessarily the same mean.

STRICTPARALLEL   *Maximum-likelihood reliability estimate under strictly parallel assumptions.* This model assumes that items have the same means, the same true score variances over a set of objects being measured, and the same error variance over replications.

STATISTICS Subcommand

STATISTICS displays optional statistics. There are no default statistics.

DESCRIPTIVES   *Item means and standard deviations.*

COVARIANCES   *Inter-item variance–covariance matrix.*

CORRELATIONS   *Inter-item correlation matrix.*

SCALE   *Scale means and scale variances.*

TUKEY   *Tukey's test for additivity.* This helps determine whether a transformation of the items is needed to reduce nonadditivity. The test displays an estimate of the power to which the items should be raised in order to be additive.

HOTELLING   *Hotelling's* T^2. This is a test for equality of means among the items.

ANOVA   *Repeated measures analysis-of-variance table.*

FRIEDMAN   *Friedman's chi-square and Kendall's coefficient of concordance.* These apply to ranked data. You must request ANOVA in addition to FRIEDMAN. Friedman's chi-square appears in place of the usual F test.

COCHRAN   *Cochran's* Q. This applies when all items are dichotomies. You must request ANOVA in addition to COCHRAN; the Q statistic appears in place of the usual F test.

ALL   *All applicable statistics.*

The STATISTICS subcommand is cumulative. If you enter it more than once, all requested statistics are produced for each scale.

SUMMARY Subcommand

SUMMARY displays summary statistics for each individual item in the scale. You can specify one or more of the following:

MEANS *Statistics for item means.* This displays the average, minimum, maximum, range, ratio of minimum to maximum, and variance of the item means.

VARIANCE *Statistics for item variances.* This displays the same statistics as for MEANS.

COVARIANCES *Statistics for inter-item covariances.* This displays the same statistics as for MEANS.

CORRELATIONS *Statistics for inter-item correlations.* This displays the same statistics as for MEANS.

TOTAL *Statistics comparing each individual item to the scale composed of the other items.* The output includes the scale mean, variance, and Cronbach's α without the item, as well as the correlation between the item and the scale if the item were deleted.

ALL *All applicable summary statistics.*

SUMMARY is cumulative. If you enter it more than once, all requested statistics are produced for each scale.

METHOD Subcommand

By default, RELIABILITY uses a computational method that does not require the calculation of a covariance matrix wherever possible. METHOD forces RELIABILITY to calculate the covariance matrix. Only a single specification applies to METHOD.

COVARIANCE *Calculate and use the covariance matrix, even if it is not needed.*

If METHOD is not specified, RELIABILITY computes the covariance matrix for all variables on each VARIABLES subcommand only if any of the following is true:

• You specify a model other than ALPHA or SPLIT.

• You request COVARIANCE, CORRELATIONS, FRIEDMAN, or HOTELLING on the STATISTICS subcommand.

• You request anything other than TOTAL on the SUMMARY subcommand.

FORMAT Subcommand

By default, RELIABILITY displays variable names and labels before an analysis. Use FORMAT to suppress this initial display.

LABELS   *Display names and labels before the analysis.* This is the default.

NOLABELS   *Do not display names and labels for all items before the analysis.*

MISSING Subcommand

By default, RELIABILITY deletes cases from analysis if they have a system- or user-missing value for any variable named on the current VARIABLES subcommand. Use MISSING to control the treatment of user-missing values.

EXCLUDE   *Exclude both user- and system-missing values.* This is the default.

INCLUDE   *Include user-missing values as valid.* Only system-missing values are excluded.

Annotated Example

For a complete example with output, see the Annotated Examples following the Syntax Reference section of this manual.

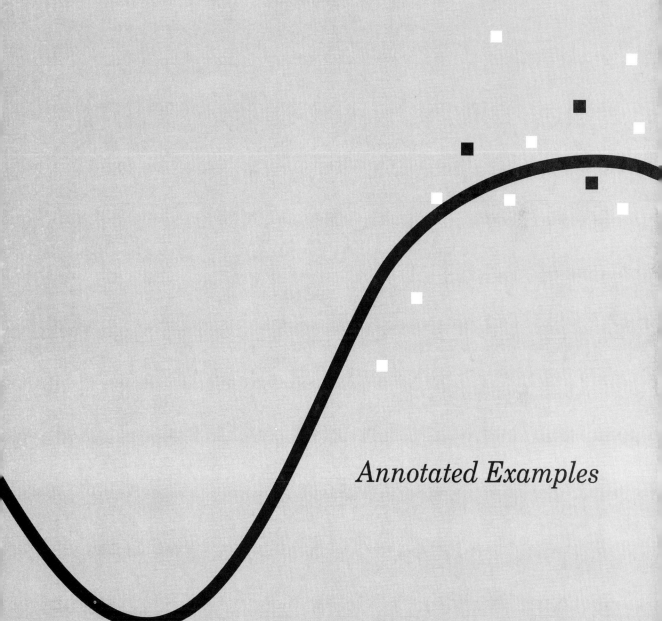

SPSS

Annotated Examples

CLUSTER

This example clusters the 25 most populous cities in the U.S. in 1980 using data from the 1982 *Information Please Almanac*. The variables are:

- *CITY*— the city in question.
- *CHURCHES*—number of churches.
- *PARKS*—number of parks. Some cities report only total acreage and have a missing-value code of 9999 for this variable.
- *PHONES*—number of telephones.
- *TVS*—number of television sets.
- *RADIOST*—number of radio stations.
- *TVST*—number of television stations.
- *POP80*—city population in 1980.
- *TAXRATE*—property tax rate in the city.

We use these variables to cluster cities into groups that are relatively homogeneous with respect to these variables. Cities differ on these variables simply as a function of their population. Therefore, we rescale the variables to number of parks, phones, etc., per person. The data are in an external file named *ACLUS.DAT*. The SPSS/PC+ commands are as follows:

```
DATA LIST FILE='ACLUS.DAT'/
   CITY 6-18(A) POP80 53-60
   CHURCHES 10-13 PARKS 14-17 PHONES 18-25 TVS 26-32
   RADIOST 33-35 TVST 36-38 TAXRATE 52-57(2)/.
MISSING VALUE PARKS (9999).
COMPUTE CHURCHES=CHURCHES/POP80.
COMPUTE PARKS=PARKS/POP80.
COMPUTE PHONES=PHONES/POP80.
COMPUTE TVS=TVS/POP80.
COMPUTE RADIOST=RADIOST/POP80.
COMPUTE TVST=TVST/POP80.
CLUSTER CHURCHES TO TAXRATE
  /METHOD=BAVERAGE
  /ID=CITY
  /PRINT=CLUSTER(3,5) DISTANCE SCHEDULE
  /PLOT=VICICLE HICICLE DENDROGRAM.
```

- DATA LIST names the file that contains the data and gives variable names and column locations. There are three records per case. No variables are read from the third record, so an extra slash is included to skip the unread record for each case.
- The MISSING VALUE command tells SPSS/PC+ to treat the value 9999 as a user-missing value for variable *PARKS*.

209

- The COMPUTE commands divide each measure by the population of the city in 1980. This yields the number of churches, phones, etc., per person.
- The CLUSTER variable specification names six variables using the TO convention.
- METHOD clusters cases by the method of average linkage between groups. It uses the default squared Euclidean distances over the six specified variables.
- The ID subcommand requests that the string variable *CITY* be used to label CLUSTER output.
- The cluster membership table is part of the default display (Figure 1).
- PRINT requests the computed distances between cases, the cluster to which each case belongs for the three-, four-, and five-cluster solutions, and the cluster agglomeration schedule (Figure 2).
- PLOT presents the cluster solution as a horizontal icicle plot (Figure 3), a vertical icicle plot (Figure 4), and a dendrogram (Figure 5).

The display is shown in Figure 1 through Figure 5. The exact appearance of the printed display depends on the characters available on your printer.

Figure 1   Cluster membership of cases

```
Data Information

        22 unweighted cases accepted.
         3 cases rejected because of missing value.

Squared Euclidean measure used.

1 Agglomeration method specified.

. . . . . . . . . . .

Cluster Membership of Cases using Average Linkage (Between Groups)

                             Number of Clusters

    Label           Case    5    4    3

    Baltimore          1     1    1    1
    Chicago            2     2    2    2
    Cleveland          3     1    1    1
    Columbus           4     3    3    3
    Dallas             5     4    3    3
    Denver             6     4    3    3
    Detroit            7     3    1    1
    Houston            8     4    3    3
    Indianapolis       9     5    4    2
    Jacksonville      10     4    3    3
    Los Angeles       11     4    3    3
    Memphis           12     3    1    1
    Nashville         13     1    1    1
    New Orleans       14     2    2    2
    New York          15     2    2    2
    Philadelphia      16     1    1    1
    Phoenix           17     4    3    3
    San Diego         18     3    1    1
    San Francisco     19     3    1    1
    San Jose          20     4    3    3
    Seattle           21     4    3    3
    Washington        22     4    3    3
```

Figure 2   Agglomeration schedule for clustering

```
Agglomeration Schedule using Average Linkage (Between Groups)

          Clusters Combined                    Stage Cluster 1st Appears   Next
    Stage Cluster 1  Cluster 2   Coefficient   Cluster 1    Cluster 2     Stage

       1       5        20         .213571          0            0           8
       2      17        22         .261159          0            0           6
       3       4        18         .292620          0            0          11
       4       8        21         .656814          0            0           8
       5       3        13        3.067434          0            0          14
       6      10        17        3.173483          0            2          16
       7       1        16        5.655861          0            0          14
       8       5         8        8.083636          1            4          12
       9       7        12       13.270878          0            0          11
      10      14        15       16.843193          0            0          13
      11       4         7       33.221970          3            9          15
      12       5        11       38.605606          8            0          17
      13       2        14       48.604111          0           10          19
      14       1         3       73.268425          7            5          18
      15       4        19       88.134598         11            0          18
      16       6        10       97.164703          0            6          17
      17       5         6      250.892288         12           16          20
      18       1         4      651.011230         14           15          20
      19       2         9     1026.891968         13            0          21
      20       1         5     1710.035156         18           17          21
      21       1         2     5559.288086         20           19           0
```

Figure 3   Horizontal icicle plot

Horizontal Icicle Plot Using Average Linkage (Between Groups)

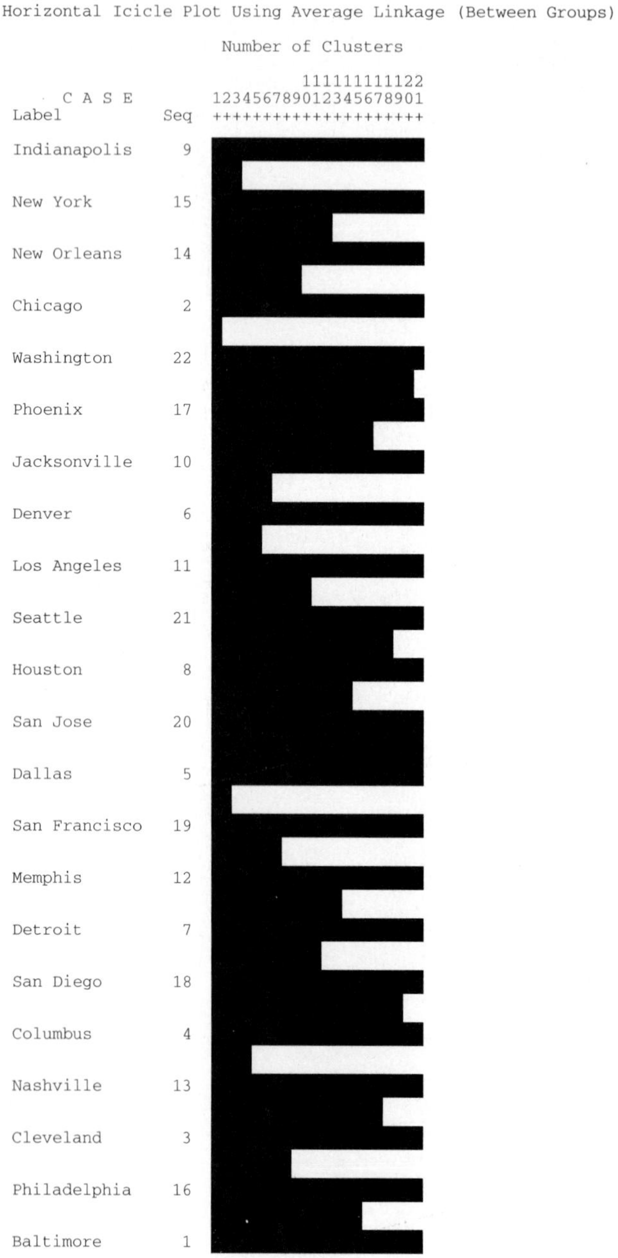

Figure 4 Vertical icicle plot

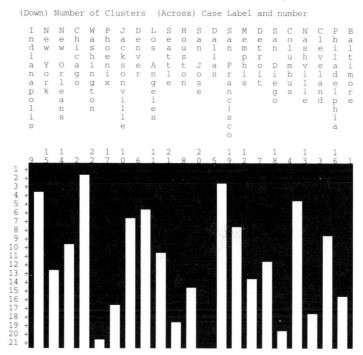

Figure 5 Dendrogram

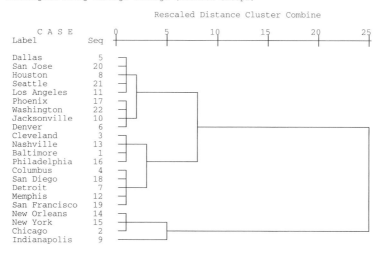

DSCRIMINANT

This example analyzes 1979 prices and earnings in 45 cities around the world, compiled by the Union Bank of Switzerland. The variables are:

- *FOOD*—the average net cost of 39 different food and beverage items in the city, expressed as a percentage above or below that of Zurich, where Zurich equals 100%.

- *SERVICE*—the average cost of 28 different goods and services in the city, expressed as a percentage above or below that of Zurich, where Zurich equals 100%.

- *BUS, MECHANIC, CONSTRUC, COOK, MANAGER, FSALES*—the average gross annual earnings of municipal bus drivers, automobile mechanics, construction workers, cooks, managers, and female sales workers, working from five to ten years in their respective occupations. Each variable is expressed as a percentage above or below that of Zurich, where Zurich equals 100%.

- *WORLD*—economic development status of the country in which the city is located. This variable is divided into three groups: economically advanced nations, such as the United States and most European nations; nations that are members of the Organization for Petroleum Exporting Countries (OPEC); and nations that are economically underdeveloped. The groups are labeled *1ST WORLD*, *PETRO WORLD*, and *3RD WORLD*, respectively.

There are two objectives to this analysis. First, we discriminate between cities in different categories by examining their wage and price structures. Second, we predict a city's economic class category from coefficients calculated using wages and prices as predictors. The data are in an external file named *ADSC.DAT*. The SPSS/PC+ commands are as follows:

```
DATA LIST FREE FILE='ADSC.DAT'
 /WORLD FOOD SERVICE BUS MECHANIC CONSTRUC
  COOK MANAGER FSALES.
MISSING VALUE ALL (0).
VALUE LABELS WORLD 1 '1ST WORLD'
                   2 'PETRO WORLD'
                   3 '3RD WORLD'.
DSCRIMINANT GROUPS=WORLD(1,3)
 /VARIABLES=FOOD SERVICE BUS MECHANIC
            CONSTRUC COOK MANAGER FSALES
 /PRIORS=SIZE
 /SAVE=CLASS=PRDCLAS SCORES=DISCSCR
 /STATISTICS=11 13 .
```

- The DATA LIST command names the file that contains the data and assigns variable names. The FREE keyword indicates that the data are in freefield format.

- The MISSING VALUE command assigns 0 as a user-missing value to all the variables.

- The VALUE LABELS command assigns descriptive labels to the values of variable *WORLD*.

- The DSCRIMINANT command requests a three-group discriminant analysis. The variable *WORLD* named on the GROUPS subcommand defines the groups.

- The variables *FOOD, SERVICE, BUS, MECHANIC, CONSTRUC, COOK, MANAGER,* and *FSALES*, named on the VARIABLES subcommand, are used as predictor variables during the analysis phase.

- The PRIORS subcommand tells SPSS/PC+ that during the classification phase, prior probabilities are equal to the known size of the groups (Figure 1).

- The SAVE subcommand saves three variables in the active file: the predicted group for each classified case (variable *PRDCLAS*) and the two discriminant scores (variables *DISCSCR1* and *DISCSCR2*). The saved variables are shown in Figure 2.

- The STATISTICS subcommand requests the display of the unstandardized discriminant functions (Figure 3) and the classification results table (Figure 4).

The display is shown in Figure 1 through Figure 4. The exact appearance of printed display depends on the characters available on your printer.

Figure 1   Prior probabilities

```
Prior Probabilities
    Group     Prior    Label
        1    0.58140   1ST WORLD
        2    0.13953   PETRO WORLD
        3    0.27907   3RD WORLD
    Total    1.00000
```

Figure 2   The saved variables

```
These new variables will be created:
   Name          Label
 --------    ----------------------------------------
PRDCLAS   --- PREDICTED GROUP FOR ANALYSIS     1
DISCSCR1  --- FUNCTION    1 FOR ANALYSIS       1
DISCSCR2  --- FUNCTION    2 FOR ANALYSIS       1
```

Figure 3   Discriminant coefficients

```
Unstandardized Canonical Discriminant Function Coefficients

                FUNC  1          FUNC  2
FOOD         -.7133619E-02     .6194062E-01
SERVICE       .8472984E-02    -.5365943E-01
BUS           .5255502E-01    -.2000084E-01
MECHANIC      .2805062E-01     .1326366E-01
CONSTRUC     -.4256104E-02    -.7536312E-02
COOK         -.1677760E-01     .2545888E-01
MANAGER      -.2570614E-01    -.2155895E-01
FSALES        .1637516E-01     .1486991E-01
(constant)   -1.852548        -.9620797
```

Figure 4   Classification results

```
Classification Results -

                     No. of   Predicted Group Membership
        Actual Group  Cases      1         2         3
    --------------------  ------  --------  --------  --------
    Group     1            25        24         1         0
    1ST WORLD                      96.0%      4.0%      0.0%

    Group     2             6         0         5         1
    PETRO WORLD                     0.0%     83.3%     16.7%

    Group     3            12         1         0        11
    3RD WORLD                       8.3%      0.0%     91.7%

Percent of "grouped" cases correctly classified:  93.02%

Classification Processing Summary
        45 Cases were processed.
         0 Cases were excluded for missing or out-of-range group codes.
         2 Cases had at least one missing discriminating variable.
        43 Cases were used for printed output.
        45 Cases were written into the active file.
```

FACTOR

This example uses six items from a 500-case sample from the 1980 General Social Survey. Respondents indicate whether they favor or oppose abortion in the following contexts:

- *ABHLTH*—if the woman's health is seriously endangered.
- *ABRAPE*—if the woman is pregnant as a result of rape.
- *ABDEFECT*—if there is a strong chance of a serious defect in the child.
- *ABPOOR*—if the woman has a low income and cannot afford more children.
- *ABSINGLE*—if the woman is not married and doesn't want the child.
- *ABNOMORE*—if the woman is married and wants no more children.

The data are in an external file named *AFACTOR.DAT*. The SPSS/PC+ commands are as follows:

```
DATA LIST FREE FILE='AFACTOR.DAT'/
   ABDEFECT ABNOMORE ABHLTH ABPOOR ABRAPE ABSINGLE.
RECODE  ABDEFECT TO ABSINGLE(1=1)(2=0)(ELSE=9).
MISSING VALUE ABDEFECT TO ABSINGLE (9).
VALUE LABELS  ABDEFECT TO ABSINGLE
   0 'NO' 1 'YES' 9 'MISSING'.
FACTOR  VARIABLES=ABDEFECT TO ABSINGLE
  /MISSING=MEANSUB
  /FORMAT=SORT BLANK(.3)
  /PLOT=ROTATION(1 2)
  /EXTRACTION=ULS
  /ROTATION=OBLIMIN.
```

- The DATA LIST command names the file that contains the data and assigns variable names. Keyword FREE indicates that the data are in freefield format.
- The RECODE and MISSING VALUE commands redefine the variables, and VALUE LABELS provides labels for the redefined responses.
- The VARIABLES subcommand on FACTOR names all the variables that are used in this Factor procedure.
- The MISSING subcommand forces mean substitution for missing data.
- The FORMAT subcommand displays the factor loadings in descending order of magnitude and suppresses the printing of factor loadings less than 0.3.
- The PLOT subcommand requests a plot of the variables in factor space, where 1 and 2 are the factor numbers to be plotted.
- The EXTRACTION subcommand specifies unweighted least squares as the method of extraction.
- The ROTATION subcommand specifies an oblimin rotation.

217

Portions of the output produced by this set of commands appear in Figure 1 through Figure 4. The exact appearance of printed output depends on the characters available on your printer.

- Figure 1 contains initial statistics, which are produced by default. **Initial statistics** are the initial communalities, eigenvalues of the correlation matrix, and percentage of variance explained.
- Figure 2 contains extraction statistics, which are produced by default. **Extraction statistics** are the communalities, eigenvalues, and unrotated factor loadings. Note the effect of SORT and BLANK specified on the FORMAT subcommand.
- Figure 3 contains rotation statistics, which are produced by default if the model is rotated. **Rotation statistics** are the rotated factor pattern and structure matrices (since this is an oblimin rotation) and the factor correlation matrix.
- Figure 4 contains a plot of the variables in rotated factor space. Although the rotation is oblimin, the axes are orthogonal.

Figure 1   Initial statistics

```
Initial Statistics:

Variable      Communality  *  Factor   Eigenvalue   Pct of Var   Cum Pct
                           *
ABDEFECT         .44988    *    1        3.38153        56.4        56.4
ABNOMORE         .66747    *    2        1.19287        19.9        76.2
ABHLTH           .35555    *    3         .50823         8.5        84.7
ABPOOR           .66600    *    4         .40867         6.8        91.5
ABRAPE           .39760    *    5         .28847         4.8        96.3
ABSINGLE         .60394    *    6         .22024         3.7       100.0
```

Figure 2   Extraction statistics

```
Factor Matrix:

                 FACTOR  1      FACTOR  2

ABPOOR            .81970       -.32158
ABNOMORE          .81704       -.34273
ABSINGLE          .78051
ABDEFECT          .65764        .46888
ABRAPE            .62257        .33014
ABHLTH            .53469        .44445


Final Statistics:

Variable      Communality  *  Factor   Eigenvalue   Pct of Var   Cum Pct
                           *
ABDEFECT         .65233    *    1        3.05462        50.9        50.9
ABNOMORE         .78502    *    2         .81821        13.6        64.5
ABHLTH           .48344    *
ABPOOR           .77532    *
ABRAPE           .49658    *
ABSINGLE         .68014    *
```

Figure 3   Rotation statistics

```
Pattern Matrix:

                 FACTOR   1     FACTOR   2

ABNOMORE           .90007
ABPOOR             .88136
ABSINGLE           .80050

ABDEFECT                          .80734
ABHLTH                            .72675
ABRAPE                            .63777


Structure Matrix:

                 FACTOR   1     FACTOR   2

ABNOMORE           .88574         .46583
ABPOOR             .88052         .48028
ABSINGLE           .82393         .48046

ABDEFECT           .44195         .80767
ABRAPE             .45976         .69852
ABHLTH             .33632         .69342


Factor Correlation Matrix:

                 FACTOR   1     FACTOR   2

FACTOR   1       1.00000
FACTOR   2        .54667        1.00000
```

Figure 4   Factor plot

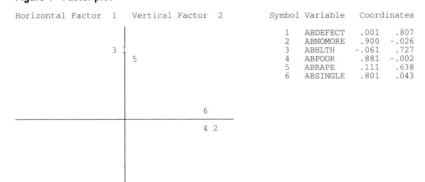

```
Horizontal Factor  1   Vertical Factor  2        Symbol Variable   Coordinates

                                                    1   ABDEFECT   .001    .807
                                                    2   ABNOMORE   .900   -.026
                     3                              3   ABHLTH    -.061    .727
                         5                          4   ABPOOR     .881   -.002
                                                    5   ABRAPE     .111    .638
                                                    6   ABSINGLE   .801    .043

                                 6
                                 4 2
```

QUICK CLUSTER

This example uses Fisher's classic data on irises to group the irises into clusters. The clusters are then compared with the actual botanical classification. The variables used are:

- *SEPLEN*—sepal length.
- *SEPWID*—sepal width.
- *PETLEN*—petal length.
- *PETWID*—petal width.
- *IRISTYPE*—type of iris.

The data are in an external file named *AQCLUST.DAT*. The SPSS/PC+ commands are as follows:

```
DATA LIST FILE='AQCLUST.DAT'/
   SEPLEN 1-2 SEPWID PETLEN PETWID 3-11 IRISTYPE 13.
VARIABLE LABELS   SEPLEN   'SEPAL LENGTH'
                  SEPWID   'SEPAL WIDTH'
                  PETLEN   'PETAL LENGTH'
                  PETWID   'PETAL WIDTH'
                  IRISTYPE 'TYPE OF IRIS'.
VALUE LABELS   IRISTYPE  1 'SETOSA'
                         2 'VERSICOLOR'
                         3 'VIRGINICA'.
QUICK CLUSTER  SEPLEN TO PETWID
  /CRITERIA=CLUSTERS(3)
  /PRINT=INITIAL ANOVA
  /SAVE=CLUSTER(CLUSTMEM).
VARIABLE LABELS CLUSTMEM 'CLUSTERS FROM DEFAULT METHOD'.
CROSSTABS TABLES=IRISTYPE BY CLUSTMEM
  /STATISTICS=CHISQ LAMBDA UC.
```

- The DATA LIST command names the file that contains the data and defines the five variables.
- The VARIABLE LABELS command assigns descriptive labels to the variables. The VALUE LABELS command assigns labels to the three values of variable *IRISTYPE*—three types of irises.
- The QUICK CLUSTER command bases clustering on the values of four variables: *SEPLEN, SEPWID, PETLEN*, and *PETWID*.
- The CRITERIA subcommand specifies three clusters.
- The PRINT subcommand requests the display of initial cluster centers and an analysis-of-variance table describing differences between clusters for each of the four clustering variables (Figure 1).
- The SAVE subcommand saves the cluster membership of each case in a new variable, *CLUSTMEM*, in the SPSS/PC+ system file.

220

- The VARIABLE LABELS command assigns a descriptive label to the new variable *CLUSTMEM*.
- The CROSSTABS command crosstabulates the cluster membership variable with variable *IRISTYPE*, which identifies the actual type of iris. The STATISTICS subcommand requests a chi-square test of significance plus two measures of the predictability of iris types from the cluster types (Figure 2). The CROSSTABS output shows that the clusters are strongly associated with the actual classifications.

The display is shown in Figure 1 and Figure 2. The exact appearance of printed display depends on the characters available on your printer.

Figure 1   QUICK CLUSTER output for the iris data

```
Initial Cluster Centers.

Cluster     SEPLEN       SEPWID       PETLEN       PETWID

   1       58.0000      40.0000      12.0000       2.0000
   2       77.0000      38.0000      67.0000      22.0000
   3       49.0000      25.0000      45.0000      17.0000

Convergence achieved due to no or small distance change.
The maximum distance by which any center has changed is .5783
Current iteration is   3

Minimum distance between initial centers is 38.2361

Iteration       Change in Cluster Centers
                    1        2        3
   1            1.01E+01  1.23E+01  1.14E+01
   2              .0000   1.75E+00  1.21E+00
   3              .0000   6.98E-01  4.73E-01


Final Cluster Centers.

Cluster     SEPLEN       SEPWID       PETLEN       PETWID

   1       50.0600      34.2800      14.6200       2.4600
   2       68.5000      30.7368      57.4211      20.7105
   3       59.0161      27.4839      43.9355      14.3387

Analysis of Variance.

Variable    Cluster MS   DF        Error MS      DF           F     Prob

SEPLEN      3688.7647     2          19.315    147.0    190.9794    .000
SEPWID       639.8805     2          10.550    147.0     60.6490    .000
PETLEN     21910.8775     2          17.760    147.0   1233.6898    .000
PETWID      3886.4352     2           6.014    147.0    646.1839    .000


Number of Cases in each Cluster.

Cluster    unweighted cases    weighted cases

   1               50.0               50.0
   2               38.0               38.0
   3               62.0               62.0

Missing              0
Valid cases      150.0              150.0
```

Figure 2   Comparing clusters to the actual botanical classifications

```
IRISTYPE   TYPE OF IRIS   by   CLUSTMEM   CLUSTERS FROM DEFAULT METHOD

                   CLUSTMEM                Page 1 of 1
            Count

                                                   Row
                        1        2        3    Total
     IRISTYPE    ─────────────────────────────
                   1   50                          50
       SETOSA                                    33.3

                   2            2       48         50
     VERSICOLOR                                  33.3

                   3           36       14         50
     VIRGINICA                                   33.3

            Column    50       38       62        150
            Total   33.3     25.3     41.3      100.0
```

```
     Chi-Square              Value          DF        Significance
----------------------     ----------      ----      ------------

Pearson                    223.59933        4           .00000
Likelihood Ratio           247.67733        4           .00000
Mantel-Haenszel test for    54.96254        1           .00000
    linear association

Minimum Expected Frequency -   12.667
```

```
                                                        Approximate
     Statistic              Value      ASE1     T-value  Significance
--------------------     ---------   --------   -------  ------------


Lambda :
    symmetric             .82979      .04099   16.11075
    with IRISTYPE dependent .84000    .03666   13.81699
    with CLUSTMEM dependent .81818    .04845    8.90043
Goodman & Kruskal Tau :
    with IRISTYPE dependent .74533    .04371              .00000 *2
    with CLUSTMEM dependent .75530    .03977              .00000 *2
Uncertainty Coefficient :
    symmetric             .75818      .03777   19.48129   .00000 *3
    with IRISTYPE dependent .75149    .03857   19.48129   .00000 *3
    with CLUSTMEM dependent .76499    .03774   19.48129   .00000 *3


*2 Based on chi-square approximation
*3 Likelihood ratio chi-square probability
```

RELIABILITY

The following example demonstrates the use of RELIABILITY to analyze an attitude scale of confidence in institutions in the United States. The data come from a 500-case sample of the 1980 General Social Survey. Respondents were asked how much confidence they had in the people running the following: banks and financial institutions, major companies, organized religion, education, the executive branch of the federal government, organized labor, the press, medicine, television, the United States Supreme Court, the scientific community, Congress, and the military. The SPSS/PC+ commands are as follows:

```
GET FILE='ARELY.DAT'.
RELIABILITY VARIABLES=CONFINAN TO CONARMY
  /SCALE (CONSCALE)=ALL
  /MODEL=SPLIT
  /SUMMARY=TOTAL
  /STATISTICS=ANOVA TUKEY HOTELLING.
```

- The GET command makes the data from file *ARELY.DAT* available for analysis.
- The RELIABILITY command analyzes the scale formed from the 13 confidence variables *CONFINAN* to *CONARMY.*
- The SCALE subcommand supplies a name (CONSCALE) for the scale.
- The MODEL subcommand specifies a split-half analysis.
- The SUMMARY subcommand produces item-total statistics.
- The STATISTICS subcommand produces the analysis-of-variance table, the Tukey test for additivity, and Hotelling's T^2.

Portions of the output produced by these commands appear in Figure 1 through Figure 4.

- Figure 1 contains the item-total statistics produced by the SUMMARY subcommand.
- Figure 2 contains the analysis-of-variance table. The *F* statistic for variation between measures is significant, indicating that the items have significantly different means. *F* for nonadditivity is not significant, so we can accept the hypothesis that the items are additive.
- Figure 3 contains Tukey's test for nonadditivity and Hotelling's T^2. Tukey's estimated power for the transformation is close to 1, which again indicates that the items are additive. Hotelling's T^2 is significant, which indicates that we can reject the hypothesis that the items have equal means in the population.
- Figure 4 contains the split-half reliability coefficients.

Figure 1   Item-total statistics

```
     # OF CASES =                 415.0

ITEM-TOTAL STATISTICS
```

	SCALE MEAN IF ITEM DELETED	SCALE VARIANCE IF ITEM DELETED	CORRECTED ITEM-TOTAL CORRELATION	SQUARED MULTIPLE CORRELATION	ALPHA IF ITEM DELETED
CONFINAN	22.8361	17.8958	.4550	.2989	.7831
CONBUS	22.8410	18.6317	.3556	.2424	.7918
CONCLERG	22.8554	18.3172	.3693	.1671	.7912
CONEDUC	22.8458	18.0679	.4652	.2321	.7823
CONFED	22.4578	18.0459	.4692	.2961	.7820
CONLABOR	22.5181	18.4242	.3763	.2102	.7902
CONPRESS	22.7108	18.8147	.3215	.2220	.7947
CONMEDIC	23.1036	18.0158	.4962	.2740	.7798
CONTV	22.5518	18.5909	.3670	.1938	.7908
CONJUDGE	22.7446	17.5771	.5061	.3125	.7783
CONSCI	23.1036	18.6632	.3910	.2185	.7887
CONLEGIS	22.4145	18.0790	.5277	.3481	.7779
CONARMY	22.7952	17.7381	.4930	.2903	.7796

Figure 2   ANOVA table

```
                      ANALYSIS OF VARIANCE
```

SOURCE OF VARIATION	SUM OF SQ.	DF	MEAN SQUARE	F	PROB.
BETWEEN PEOPLE	669.7412	414	1.6177		
WITHIN PEOPLE	1858.9231	4980	.3733		
BETWEEN MEASURES	240.9631	12	20.0803	61.657	.000
RESIDUAL	1617.9600	4968	.3257		
NONADDITIVITY	.0041	1	.0041	.013	.911
BALANCE	1617.9559	4967	.3257		
TOTAL	2528.6643	5394	.4688		

```
   GRAND MEAN =          1.8960
```

Figure 3   Tukey's and Hotelling's tests

```
TUKEY ESTIMATE OF POWER TO WHICH OBSERVATIONS
MUST BE RAISED TO ACHIEVE ADDITIVITY        =          .9778

HOTELLINGS T-SQUARED =   694.5944    F =   56.3449    PROB. =  .0000
     DEGREES OF FREEDOM:           NUMERATOR =   12   DENOMINATOR    403
```

Figure 4   Split-half reliability estimates

```
RELIABILITY COEFFICIENTS    13 ITEMS

CORRELATION BETWEEN FORMS =        .6583

EQUAL LENGTH SPEARMAN-BROWN =      .7940

GUTTMAN SPLIT-HALF =               .7923

UNEQUAL-LENGTH SPEARMAN-BROWN =    .7948

ALPHA FOR PART 1 =        .6446    ALPHA FOR PART 2 =        .6955

     7 ITEMS IN PART 1             6 ITEMS IN PART 2
```

Bibliography

Anderberg, M. R. 1973. *Cluster analysis for applications*. New York: Academic Press.

Andrews, D. F., R. Gnanadesikan, and J. L. Warner. 1973. Methods for assessing multivariate normality. In: *Multivariate Analysis III*, P. R. Krishnaiah, ed. New York: Academic Press.

Cattell, R. B. 1966. The meaning and strategic use of factor analysis. In: *Handbook of Multivariate Experimental Psychology*, R. B. Cattell, ed. Chicago: Rand McNally.

Churchill, G. A., Jr. 1979. *Marketing research: Methodological foundations*. Hinsdale, Ill.: Dryden Press.

Consumer Reports. 1983. Beer. *Consumer Reports*, July, 342–348.

Everitt, B. S. 1980. *Cluster analysis*. 2nd ed. London: Heineman Educational Books Ltd.

Gilbert, E. S. 1968. On discrimination using qualitative variables. *Journal of the American Statistical Association*, 63: 1399–1412.

Goldstein, M., and W. R. Dillon. 1978. *Discrete discriminant analysis*. New York: John Wiley and Sons.

Green, B. F. 1979. The two kinds of linear discriminant functions and their relationship. *Journal of Educational Statistics*, 4:3, 247–263.

Hand, D. J. 1981. *Discrimination and classification*. New York: John Wiley and Sons.

Harman, H. H. 1967. *Modern factor analysis*. 2nd ed. Chicago: University of Chicago Press.

Harman, H. H., and W. H. Jones. 1966. Factor analysis by minimizing residuals (Minres). *Psychometrika*, 31: 351–368.

Jonassen, C. T., and S. H. Peres. 1960. *Interrelationships of dimensions of community systems*. Columbus: Ohio State University Press.

Jöreskog, K. G., and D. N. Lawley. 1968. New methods in maximum likelihood factor analysis. *British Journal of Mathematical and Statistical Psychology*, 21: 85–96.

Kaiser, H. F. 1963. Image analysis. In: *Problems in Measuring Change*, C. W. Harris, ed. Madison: University of Wisconsin Press.

Kaiser, H. F. 1970. A second-generation Little Jiffy. *Psychometrika*, 35: 401–415.

Kaiser, H. F. 1974. An index of factorial simplicity. *Psychometrika*, 39: 31–36.

Kaiser, H. F., and J. Caffry. 1965. Alpha factor analysis. *Psychometrika*, 30: 1–14.

Kim, J. O., and C. W. Mueller. 1978. *Introduction to factor analysis*. Beverly Hills, Calif.: Sage Publications.

Kshirsager, A. M., and E. Arseven. 1975. A note on the equivalency of two discrimination procedures. *The American Statistician*, 29: 38–39.

Lachenbruch, P. A. 1975. *Discriminant analysis*. New York: Hafner Press.

Lord, F. M., and M. R. Novick. 1968. *Statistical theories of mental test scores*. Reading, Mass.: Addison-Wesley.

Milligan, G. W. 1980. An examination of the effect of six types of error perturbation on fifteen clustering algorithms. *Psychometrika*, 45: 325–342.

Moore, D. H. 1973. Evaluation of five discrimination procedures for binary variables. *Journal of the American Statistical Association*, 68: 399.

Morrison, D. F. 1967. *Multivariate statistical methods*. New York: McGraw-Hill.

Nunnally, J. 1978. *Psychometric theory*. 2nd ed. New York: McGraw-Hill.

Romesburg, H. C. 1984. *Cluster analysis for researchers*. Belmont, Calif.: Lifetime Learning Publications.

Sneath, P. H. A., and R. R. Sokal. 1973. *Numerical taxonomy*. San Francisco: W. H. Freeman and Co.

Stoetzel, J. 1960. A factor analysis of liquor preference of French consumers. *Journal of Advertising Research*, 1:1, 7–11.

Tatsuoka, M. M. 1971. *Multivariate analysis*. New York: John Wiley and Sons.

Tucker, L. R. 1971. Relations of factor score estimates to their use. *Psychometrika*, 36: 427–436.

Tucker, R. F., R. F. Koopman, and R. L. Linn. 1969. Evaluation of factor analytic research procedures by means of simulated correlation matrices. *Psychometrika*, 34: 421–459.

Van Vliet, P. K. J., and J. M. Gupta. 1973. THAM v. sodium bicarbonate in idiopathic respiratory distress syndrome. *Archives of Disease in Childhood*, 48: 249–255.

Wahl, P. W. and R. A. Kronmal. 1977. Discriminant functions when covariances are unequal and sample sizes are moderate. *Biometrics*, 33: 479–484.

Young, F. W., and R. M. Hamer, 1987. *Multidimensional scaling: History, theory, and application*. Hillsdale, N.J.: Lawrence Erlbaum Associates.

Index